ALSO BY SERGIO LUZZATTO

The Body of Il Duce:
Mussolini's Corpse and the Fortunes of Italy

Padre Pio: Miracles and Politics in a Secular Age

PRIMO LEVI'S
RESISTANCE

PRIMO LEVI'S RESISTANCE

Rebels and Collaborators
in Occupied Italy

Sergio Luzzatto

Translated by Frederika Randall

METROPOLITAN BOOKS

HENRY HOLT AND COMPANY

NEW YORK

Metropolitan Books
Henry Holt and Company, LLC
Publishers since 1866
175 Fifth Avenue
New York, New York 10010

Originally published in Italy in 2013 under the title Partigia *by Mondadori, Milan.*
Revisions to this English-language edition have been made with the approval of the author.

Library of Congress Cataloging-in-Publication data

Luzzatto, Sergio, 1963–
    Primo Levi's resistance : rebels and collaborators in occupied Italy / Sergio Luzzatto ;
translated by Frederika Randall.
        pages cm
    ISBN 978-0-8050-9955-3 (hardback) — ISBN 978-0-8050-9956-0 (e-book)
    1. Levi, Primo.   2. Jews—Italy—Biography.   3. Holocaust, Jewish (1939–1945)—
Italy—Biography.   4. World War, 1939–1945—Underground movements—Italy.
5. Italy—Biography.   I. Title.
    PQ4872.E8Z7254 2016
    853'.914—dc23

                                                                              2015018568

First U.S. Edition 2016
Designed by Meryl Sussman Levavi
Map by Jeffrey L. Ward

Printed in the United States of America

1   3   5   7   9   10   8   6   4   2

Contents

SWITZERLAND

Plateau Rosa

Valtournenche

Monte Rosa

Lake Maggiore

Meina

Area of detail

Dora River

Aosta

Brusson

Saint-Vincent

Verrès

ITALY

Aosta Valley

VALLE D'AOSTA

Cogne

Biella

FRANCE

Prascorsano

Canavese Plain

Ivrea

Dora River

Vercelli

Chivasso

Po River

Cerrina

Casale Monferrato

Turin

PIEDMONT

Po River

Asti

Alessandria

Santa Libera

0 Miles   20

0 Kilometers   20

Cuneo

LIGURIA

© 2015 Jeffrey L. Ward

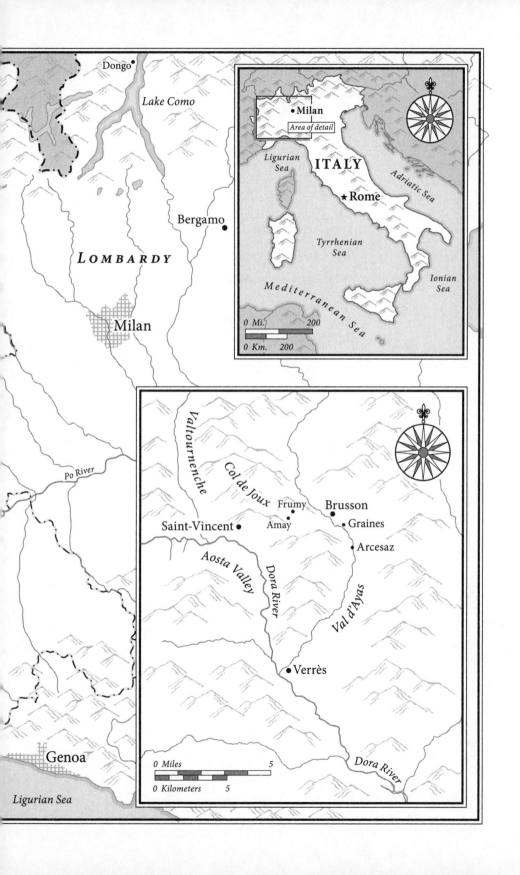

Prefatory Note to
the English Edition

ON JULY 25, 1943, MUSSOLINI WAS SUDDENLY AND BLOODLESSLY ousted during a meeting of the Grand Council of Fascism, his own governing body. The war was generally unpopular in Italy by that point, and it was also going badly. After a bloody campaign in Russia and defeat at El Alamein in North Africa, Italy's army was ill supplied, exhausted, and had suffered many losses. Two weeks before, the Allies had landed in Sicily, driving the Germans north.

Il Duce was spirited away, and after some peregrinations ended up on the remote heights of the Gran Sasso plateau in Abruzzo, at a place that could only be reached by air or cable car. King Victor Emmanuel III appointed Marshal Pietro Badoglio as head of government to replace Mussolini. On September 8, Badoglio surrendered to the Allies. Italy was no longer Hitler's ally.

Badoglio announced the armistice by saying that "all acts of hostility against Anglo-American forces on the part of Italian forces everywhere must immediately cease." Given these stark counterorders from one day to the next, Italian soldiers—some 350,000 were stationed in

France, Greece, Yugoslavia, and Albania—suddenly had to provide for their own defense, deployed as they often were alongside the Germans. The soldiers of the Wehrmacht had been their allies until the day before, but now the Italians were suddenly exposed to reprisals or deportation to Germany. Some would join the resistance in the Balkans. The rest had to find their way home by their own means. Meanwhile Allied prisoners of war in Italy were abruptly, if briefly, free to leave their prison camps.

The very day of the armistice, September 8, the Germans began invading northern Italy. Two days later, in central Italy, they had taken Rome. The king and Badoglio boarded a ship at Pescara, on the Adriatic, and sailed to Brindisi in the south, a safe area controlled by the Allies. There, in the Southern Kingdom under the Allied wing, Badoglio declared war on Germany and fought along with the Allies. He would remain prime minister of the armistice government until 1944.

Meanwhile, on September 12, the Germans made a daring air raid on Mussolini's place of confinement on the Gran Sasso plateau and carried him off. Il Duce became leader of the Italian Social Republic, an only nominally independent state based in the German-occupied portion of Italy. Mussolini's headquarters during 1943–45 were at Salò, a town on Lake Garda; thus the second Fascist regime is often called the Republic of Salò.

When the Italian Social Republic was proclaimed on September 23, 1943, Italians in the north and center of the country not only faced a foreign invader—the Germans—but also had to choose whether to side with the Republic of Salò or fight for a free Italy against what was officially their own government. There was the patriotic "war of liberation," a battle to oust the foreign invader and disarm its local pawn. But there was as well another aspect to the struggle. That second strain would become known as Italy's "civil war," an all-out conflict in which Italians of the Resistance fought to wrest the country not just from its immediate occupiers but from the Italians who for twenty years had embodied Fascist rule.

The war of liberation and the civil war often coincided in the same battles. But the partisans were fighting two enemies, not one. The conflict was all the more sharp and cruel because one side was made up of army regulars and the other of largely untrained guerrilla rebels, however well-organized militarily they would become by the end of the war.

The civil war demanded that Italians make a choice. And even today, many Italians have not forgotten who took which side. There was nothing automatic about any one person's allegiance; after all, Italy had been an Axis partner until September 8. The moment of decision for many young Italians at home came when the Republic of Salò issued conscription orders in November 1943, backed up by harsh punishments. To join the Salò army, or run away to the hills? That was the question in the autumn and winter of 1943. And these became the months of what Primo Levi would call "inventing the Resistance."

As the war in Italy continued through 1944 (the German forces in the south and center of the country slowly pushed northwards by the Allies), the Anglo-Americans began to supply weapons, first to the Italian Army of the South, then to Italian partisans in the north. They distrusted the native Resistance, however, and especially feared the powerful Communist forces in it. The partisans' battles against the Germans and Salò demanded particular courage because the Allies were reluctant to arm them too much. This would be a point of pride for some Italians after the war—the belief that they had largely defeated the enemy themselves. The Italian Resistance was probably the largest such movement in Western Europe during World War II, with perhaps as many as 340,000 partisans, of whom about 45,000 died and 20,000 were injured.

Liberation came on April 25, 1945, when Resistance forces took the cities of Milan and Turin. Three days later, Mussolini was shot near Lake Como while trying to escape to Switzerland.

*   *   *

MUCH of the action in this book takes place in and around Valle d'Aosta, an area of northwest Italy bordering Switzerland and France. In 1943, when Primo Levi began his Resistance, Valle d'Aosta was a province of Piedmont. (After World War II it would be separated from Piedmont to become one of Italy's twenty official regions, roughly equivalent to American states.) The largely mountainous Valle d'Aosta is named after the Aosta Valley, which runs east–west through the territory. The principal city, which sits in the valley, is also named Aosta.

Branching off from the central east–west Aosta Valley are several side valleys heading north, including the Val d'Ayas and the Valtournenche. On the ridge between those two side valleys lies the Col de Joux mountain pass, part of an ancient salt and wine track that connected Aosta to Switzerland via a series of mountain crossings. The village of Amay, where Levi went after the German invasion began, is right under the Col de Joux. And the rest of the landscape that will demand our attention is remarkably compact as well. Heading west (and steeply down) from the Col de Joux, it is only a few kilometers as the crow flies to the small town of Saint-Vincent, located at the junction of the Aosta Valley and the Valtournenche. Heading east over the Col de Joux pass, the same distance brings you to the Val d'Ayas, including the town of Brusson, the medieval castle of Graines, and the village of Arcesaz. Just down the mountain from Arcesaz is the town of Verrès, at the junction of Val d'Ayas and the Aosta Valley.

While the Resistance forces tended to have their bases in the mountains, the Nazi-Fascists were concentrated on the plain, in cities such as Aosta and Turin. Their forces dominated much of the Piedmont region south of the Valle d'Aosta—including the city of Ivrea in the Canavese plain, at the foot of the Valle d'Aosta mountains, and the city of Casale Monferrato, some ninety kilometers from the Col de Joux.

—FREDERIKA RANDALL

PRIMO LEVI'S RESISTANCE

Prologue

THE MEMORY IS VIVID, ETCHED IN MY MIND. I WAS TEN, MAYBE eleven years old, and my mother was reading to my brothers and me from a collection of letters written by Italian partisans who had been condemned to death. It was evening, we were sitting on the bed, and she was reading from those last letters, often quite brief and terrible, of the men and women who had liberated Italy at the cost of their lives. The source must have been the Einaudi edition I have before me now, *Letters of Italian Partisans Condemned to Death*, published in 1952,[1] one of those books with their orange bindings that our shelves were full of. I remember that my mother, before reading us the letters themselves, consulted the biographical notes about each partisan. These notes had been laid out like epitaphs on the page, as if they were engraved on tombstones: elegies inscribed on a paper monument to the fallen.

Now that my children are as old as I was then, I wouldn't find it easy to explain to them why that moment—a mother reading aloud not some classic Italian poetry or one of Jack London's stories, but letters by doomed partisans—was in no way strange or morbid. I wouldn't find it easy, but

I ought to try; it matters that my children understand. When I was their age, in the mid-1970s, the Resistance still seemed close to us, decisive. It marked a beginning, and it signified an identity. My own parents, overwhelmed, frightened, displaced, threatened, had known the struggle firsthand during their own childhood. They were ten and twelve in September 1943, when Italy surrendered to the Allies and German troops seized control of Italy's northern half, and a bit older in April 1945, when the war finally ended. When they spoke to us of World War II and of the racial persecution my father had known as a Jew, when they sought to pass on their anti-Fascist legacy, it was a way to make us feel the privilege of having come into the world in another season, the mercy of having been born beyond all that.

It matters, I think today, that I too find a way to transmit that immaterial legacy to my children: some sense of the hard, cruel history they indirectly come from, via the youthful trials of their grandparents, and above all via the fundamental trials of those young people who fought against fascism to make Italy free. A packet wrapped in red gift paper from the Feltrinelli bookstore sits on my desk today; inside is a more recent edition of the *Letters of Italian Partisans*.[2] This is a present that sooner or later, knowing it risks raised eyebrows and a cool reception, I'll put under the Christmas tree. I hope (I'm confident) that one day my children will read the letters of Italy's anti-Fascist martyrs. I hope (without being very confident) that my children's children will one day read them too.

And yet I don't believe that my obsession with the Resistance began back in the 1970s, with that striking scene of a mother reading aloud to a ten-year-old from the letters of the condemned. Quite honestly, I don't even think of it as an obsession. It's long been a powerful curiosity, not all that unusual, really, for someone who has chosen to become a historian. It is only in recent years that my curiosity has turned to passion, driven by the newfound popularity of crudely revisionist antipartisan books about the Italian civil war of 1943–45.[3] As the twenty-first century began, I found myself asking how this version of our past could be so popular: what it meant not in intellectual terms but as a signal that anti-Fascism was faltering in Italy.[4] Teaching at a university has made me alert to other signals, as I meet students ever more neutral, for whom the values of anti-Fascism are almost as alien as the fraudulent truths of Fascism.

It was this that made me want to take on—as a son, a father, a citizen, and a teacher—the turning point in modern Italian history that was our dramatic civil war. But perhaps my intention might not have turned into the practical work of researching and writing a book had my obsessive notion that the Resistance was the founding act of a free Italy not been joined by another obsession of mine. Obsession? Again, it was a kind of vivid intellectual curiosity, plus a kind of civil worship and literary veneration, regarding the figure of Primo Levi. In Italy's twentieth century, to my mind, he is the epitome of civilized intelligence and dignified memory. I would never have tried to write this book had I not felt summoned to take stock of two subjects at once that were of intense concern to me: the Resistance and Primo Levi.

My memory of reading Levi for the first time is also vivid. It was the summer of 1977, not long after my mother had introduced us to the letters of the condemned partisans. A tyrannical teacher had assigned a long list of required reading, from Thomas Mann's *Buddenbrooks* to Ignazio Silone's *Fontamara*, to my classmates and me for the vacation months between the first and second year of secondary school. Primo Levi's unforgettable *If This Is a Man* was also on the list; so, as a dutiful student, I picked it up, emerging from the encounter as changed as an adolescent can be by the reading of a book. In subsequent years Levi's books were my companions, both those published before 1977, from *The Truce* to *The Periodic Table*, and those that were published during the decade that remained of his life: *If Not Now, When?*, the poems of *At an Uncertain Hour*, and finally *The Drowned and the Saved*. That last I bought and read just after it came off the presses in the spring of 1986—when the figure of Levi, dramatic as his life had been, did not yet wear the vestments of tragedy.

I know exactly where I was when word of his death reached me, in the late morning of one April day in 1987: in front of the Gare de Lyon in Paris, a twenty-four-year-old doctoral student who had just climbed down from the overnight train. I remember the shock and the chagrin, the awful sensation that the void would always be impossible to fill. Primo Levi was no more. Now we would have to get by without him, we would have to go without a compass through the post-Auschwitz landscape. And those of us—the historians—who had decided to live our lives in dialogue with the dead would have to make our way through the twentieth-century Inferno without that guide, that Virgil, to rely on.

* * *

MUCH later—one winter night four or five years ago—I reread *The Periodic Table*. It is Primo Levi's most extended autobiographical work, the one in which the chemist from Turin said the most and reflected the most about himself. Published in 1975, the same year Levi retired from his industrial job, the book was quickly recognized for its literary qualities. Now, on rereading, I became aware of something I had not paid much attention to before. There was a season in Levi's life for which his testimony, his cultural reflections, his memory, his historical references were scarce. This was his brief and unfortunate season as a partisan, or something like a partisan. Three months in the mountains of the Valle d'Aosta in northwest Italy as a twenty-four-year-old, linked to a little band that had come together at the Col de Joux—a mountain pass high above the town of Saint-Vincent—in the autumn of 1943.

Of the 238 pages of the first edition of *The Periodic Table*, the Resistance takes up not more than four, in the chapter called "Gold." Levi devotes just two pages to his move into the hills, the weeks of waiting (waiting, more than action), the capture of some of the Col de Joux band, and his own arrest—on December 13, 1943—along with several of his companions. Two more pages dispose of his transport down the valley, the interrogations in the local jail, and Levi's decision to admit that he was a Jew, thus consigning himself to be deported to some unknown destination rather than tried as a partisan by the special military tribunal of the Republic of Salò. Only at the end of the chapter does the narrative relax its breakneck pace, when Levi describes a gold smuggler he met in prison (an incident that offers him the chapter's title, following the Mendeleevian logic of his memoir, which links the name of an element to each different stage of his life).

After I had read these pages with the attention they deserve, I wondered about Levi's scant account of his Resistance experience. That his time as a partisan had been brief, not even the entire three months of autumn, was not enough to explain it. Beyond the small number of pages, what was striking was how severe his judgment was. "Gold" supplies an anything but gilded picture of the Resistance as seen from Col de Joux. "We were cold and hungry, we were the worst-armed partisans in Piedmont, and probably also the worst-prepared," wrote Levi in *The Periodic Table*.[5] Nor was he more indulgent in a half page he'd inserted into a new edition of *If This Is a Man* in 1958. "We needed capable men, and we were swamped by people with no preparation, people in good faith and in bad, who came up from the plain seeking an organization that didn't exist," he wrote. That the Fascists would discover the band on December 13, he said, was logical and even "consistent with justice."[6]

"Consistent with justice," the attack of the Fascist militia on the Col de Joux band? In Primo Levi's lexicon, *justice* is no random word.[7] I wondered what could account for this iconoclastic version of the dawn of the Resistance, so little in accord with anti-Fascist mythology about the heroic first partisans up in the hills. And what could be hidden behind those painful lines about the mental state of those rebels who were arrested in the mountains?

> An ugly secret weighed on us, in every one of our minds: the same secret that had exposed us to capture, and just a few days before had extinguished all our will to resist, even to live. Conscience had compelled us to carry out a sentence, and we had carried it out, but we had come away devastated, empty, wanting everything to finish

and to be finished ourselves; but also wanting to be together, talk, help each other exorcise that still so recent memory. Now we were finished, and we knew it; we were in the trap, each one in his own trap, and there was no way out but down.[8]

Thus the secret of the Col de Joux is told, in the first-person plural. Along with some companions in his band, Levi had agreed on and carried out a fatal sentence. No further details are provided. Nothing is said in "Gold" about why that sentence was decided or about who was the victim, or victims; all we are told is that partisan justice responded to the exacting demands of conscience. When it came to the Resistance, concision, something Levi the writer excelled at, was more like omission. Not entirely, though; not enough to silence all mention of how that event had affected the partisans of Col de Joux. Whatever happened had utterly destroyed the morale of Levi and his comrades.

"There was no way out but down," writes Levi in those lines, drawing a clear connection to the dominant imagery of *If This Is a Man*, in which deportation to Auschwitz is depicted as the descent to a Dantesque underworld ("a journey downward, toward the abyss"; "too late, too late, we are all going under"; "we have reached the bottom. Lower than this one cannot go"). And the fate of those partisans who have carried out the sentence—and are thus themselves condemned—likewise recalls the destiny of Dante's Ulysses, who has dared to sail past the Pillars of Hercules and goes down with his ship. That is the canto that Levi relates to Pikolo, his young friend at Auschwitz, reciting from memory the moment when a whirlwind drowns the vessel: "Three times it turned her round with all the waters; / and at the fourth it lifted up the stern, / so that our prow plunged deep, as pleased an Other . . ."[9]

Thus Levi, in *The Periodic Table*, pointed to that episode in his life as a partisan to explain his descent into the underworld of the camps. He needed a fair amount of intellectual, moral, and political courage to do so, for the middle 1970s marked the high point of what would later be called, rather unpleasantly, "Resistance holy writ." At no other moment in Italy's postwar history would the great deeds of the Resistance and the horrors of Salò be celebrated with such granitic certainty in public discourse. Among other things, it was a moment when fascism threatened to reemerge in Italy, with the Italian neo-Fascists carrying out terrorism under the approving gaze of segments of the army and secret services. There was never a time when democratic Italians were more convinced that in the civil war of 1943–45 all the qualities, all the virtues belonged to the side of the partisans, and all the wrongs and vices pertained to the Republic of Salò. Salò was the side of absolute evil, as depicted in Pier Paolo Pasolini's outraged and outrageous last film, *Salò, or the 120 Days of Sodom*.

In those years Primo Levi, by now an intellectual in the public eye (and although shy and reserved, a well-known supporter of the left), surely paid obligatory tribute to the Resistance. But in *The Periodic Table* he dared to sharply devalue the importance of his role as a partisan in the mountains. And he dared to hint at something almost unthinkable in the Italy of 1975, or in any case unmentionable in the reassuring parables of the anti-Fascist gospel: that in the civil war, it had fallen to partisans to condemn other partisans to death.

However sparing in its details, "Gold" was in fact potentially transparent to anyone who read it with attention and sensitivity. If, that is, there were readers in Italy thirty years on from the war ready to follow Levi on that hard terrain where his memoir ventured. On the eve of his capture on December 13, 1943, what had left Primo Levi and his companions devastated, empty, wanting everything to finish and to be finished themselves, was not that they had carried out a sentence against one or more *enemies*, be they Italians or Germans. From what can be read between the lines, it was that martial law had been applied *within* their group: by some rebels in the Col de Joux band against one or more rebels of the same band. This was in part why these partisans found themselves in a trap, each in his own trap. And this was the reason, perhaps the main reason, why the only way out was down.

* * *

I have been a historian for thirty years, but I have never done research on a case that challenged me, moved me, troubled me as much as this tale of the Resistance. Never before did the more or less conventional stages of study, digging into the archives, reading in the library, and meeting surviving participants or their descendants produce such intense and contrasting impressions in me, and an equally intense feeling of responsibility—and also of unease. On the one hand, it seemed essential to take up this message in a bottle from *The Periodic Table*, to investigate the story of the Col de Joux band in full, including the "ugly secret." On the other, perhaps I was insisting on a very minor episode in the overall experience of the Italian Resistance, not to mention in Primo Levi's personal existence.

In another century, a writer once scathingly condemned the critics of the French Revolution, who had the freedom to bemoan its bloodshed thanks to the very revolutionaries whose actions they deplored. They were, he wrote, like the impoverished clan of desert dwellers who chip at the bases of the pyramids of the pharaohs, subtracting from those giant monuments a handful of mortar and a few stones to build their huts.[10] I thought of his words, and wondered if I wasn't at risk of behaving like those parasites, chipping away at the pyramid of the Resistance and the pyramid of Primo Levi.

There was never a moment while I worked on this book when I didn't ask myself why. Why spend so much time on something that seemed to be no more than micro-history, so restricted, apparently, in its subject and its object, in time and space? It was a question I asked myself over and over, until finally I felt able to reply: I was doing it not out of obsession or to chip away at our memories of Primo Levi and the Resistance, but to add to our knowledge. The story of Levi's little partisan band promised to be more illuminating than I had thought at first.[11] Above all because of when it took place: the autumn of 1943, the founding moment of the Italian resistance that would reveal, for better or worse, its original ingredients.

To delve into how Levi's band came together, allied itself with other partisans nearby, caught the attention of pro-Salò officials, and fell prey to the roundup operation of December 13 could shed light on larger historical questions concerning Italy's civil war. Questions such as whether the earliest rebels were politically motivated or not, what relations they had with the local population, how permeable the rebel bands were to thieves and spies. And another question as well: What was the contribution to the Resistance of that particular species of Italian no longer fully Italian, the Jews of Primo Levi's generation, whom Italy in 1938 had denied the right and duty to bear arms? Would they once again affirm their loyalty to Italy, as their forebears had so forcefully done not long before, when Italian Jews played an important role in Italy's nineteenth-century liberation and unification?[12]

What at first had seemed an almost ridiculously small story, in both space and time, also promised to illustrate the choices facing the young men of a floundering nation after the armistice. What amalgam of reason and passion guided the earliest resisters to the Nazi-Fascist order? Lust for adventure, the spirit of anarchy, a need to belong, the fascination of an ideology, the temptation of material gain? My small story also offered insight into the problem—a huge one for inexperienced rebels—of whether violence was legitimate and morally justified. Classic questions for historians,[13] which however promised to take on new colors when observed in detail, through a zoom lens rather than a wide angle. One story from the Resistance to illuminate the Resistance as a whole.

Examining that brief autumn and winter of 1943 would also open a longer span of time, beyond Levi's arrest and even past the end of the war. I would not only need to follow the partisans of the region, who unlike Levi were able to carry on their fight for another sixteen months, and eventually managed to come down from the mountains to fight on the plain and finally liberate Turin. I would also need to follow—in their era of power and their time of disgrace—the servants of Salò responsible for the arrest of Primo Levi and his companions, many of whom went on trial in 1945–46. Their fates highlight many crucial issues of Italy's twentieth century: who the collaborators were in political and human terms; the role played by the Allies and their secret services; the consequences of the amnesty granted to most collaborators in 1946; the difficulty of impressing anti-Fascist values on the new Italian republic "born of the Resistance."

Seen close-up, the changing fortunes of armed individuals who opposed each other in those early days of the civil war and then after the war saw their roles reversed—the "bandits" of 1943 becoming the heroes of 1945, the men of order becoming war criminals—seen close-up, their story has the urgency of individual choices. It may seem a thin history, politically useless and morally futile, about men who hated other men. Yet ultimately, I believe, it's only such an intimate perspective that allows a history of the Resistance to speak to us today. It allows us to see that conflict as a clash between people battling not just out of hatred but because they have different conceptions of humanity, justice, and society. The historian, too, must grapple with these people, to avoid seeing them either as saints or as monsters, and to help renew (along with the best of them) our values and our memory.

* * *

DESPITE his central role as my inspiration, Primo Levi is at times merely a supporting actor in this story. This is not only because he was deported to Poland in February 1944 and did not return to Italy until October 1945, and so was absent during the mature phase of the Resistance as well as in the fierce, intoxicating weeks right after the war's conclusion. Levi also plays a supporting part because even in the autumn of 1943, before his capture, he had been a partisan so discreet as to seem inoffensive to the police of Salò. "We thought we were safe because we had not yet moved out of our refuge buried under three feet of snow":

that's how, in *The Periodic Table*, Levi describes the Hotel Ristoro in Amay, a village high on the mountain near Saint-Vincent and just under the Col de Joux, where he had gone to stay after the armistice and where he was taken prisoner.[14]

With Levi to one side of the stage, the center will often be occupied by other characters, many of them just as helpful as he is in unfolding the plot. Other Jews—men, women, the old, children—seeking a safe hiding place in the mountains, or a passage across the border to salvation in Switzerland. Other partisans, Jewish and not, sharing with Levi the strange, sometimes miserable days of this Resistance that was still politically and militarily immature, still seeking its significance. Officers and soldiers in their gray-green army uniforms who had to decide in the autumn of 1943 whether to stick by the German ally or fight for a new idea of the nation. Farmers caught between the Nazi-Fascist occupiers and the partisans pressuring locals for food and lodging. Men of Salò, part of one repressive apparatus or another, for whom those times afforded an occasion, first unexpected, then desperately serious, to become someone or to grab something. And then the mayors, the magistrates, the parish priests, the bureaucrats, the mountain hikers and skiers, less keen to take sides than simply to get through the day and go unnoticed.

With so much going on, the figure of Primo Levi risks being overshadowed. Yet it is thanks to Levi's presence that this Resistance tale is charged with meaning and purpose. For forty years after that autumn in Amay, Primo Levi wrestled—at first tacitly, then openly—with the young man he had been at the Hotel Ristoro and the partisans around him. On the eve of his deportation to Poland, his experience in the mountains gave Levi an accelerated course in the basics of that civil war he was not to fight. When he returned from Auschwitz to post-Liberation Italy, the contest between anti-Fascists and collaborators meant that Levi would consider himself a veteran of a partisan band, as well as a man saved from the gas chamber. His moral sense engaged him in a retrospective struggle that was never as evident and dramatic as his struggle to make sense of the Final Solution, but that is nevertheless worth recognizing and making sense of today. The chemist from Turin is the ethical reagent that brings this Resistance tale to life.

The strongest evidence of that conflict between Primo Levi and his younger self and comrades at the Col de Joux—evidence so obvious that no one had ever seen it—is to be found in Levi's 1982 novel, *If Not Now, When?* So I will try to demonstrate at the end of this book. Another piece of evidence is in a poem Levi wrote and published in 1981, "Partigia." A persistent undertone accompanying me on my research, that poem would end up offering me the Italian title for my book. According to a note provided by Levi himself, *partigia* was a colloquial term "widespread in Piedmont," meaning "partisans without many scruples, decisive, light-fingered, or quick to brawl."[15] Hotheads, roughnecks. And so it was that decades after he joined his fate with "*partigia* from every valley, / Tarzan, Hedgehog, Sparrowhawk, Thunderbolt, Ulysses," Levi himself, sixty-two years old, felt the need to address "those still here" and urge his "white-haired companions" to the hills again. "Stand up, old men: there's no discharge for us. / We must enlist again. Up in the hills." No matter how slow and wheezing, "stiff-kneed" and with "many winters in our backbones," they must keep watch "as we did then . . . so that with dawn, the enemy does not surprise us."[16]

At this point, near the end of the poem, the reader might expect to hear "the enemy" identified with the familiar target of the many comments Primo Levi published in the early 1980s: that two-headed beast composed of Resistance revisionists and Shoah-deniers, a monster threatening the return of fascism in Italy and in Europe.[17] When he calls on the partisans to mount the hills again, to struggle up those slopes and endure those uncomfortable nights in mountain huts ("The trail will be steep and hard, / The bed hard, too, and hard the bread"), when he considers actions without scruples, hands quick to rob or strike, he seems to speak of the obvious enemy, the Nazi-Fascist. Yet that is not the enemy mentioned in the final lines of "Partigia":

What enemy? Every man's his own foe,
Each one split by his own frontier,
Left hand enemy of the right.
Stand up, old enemies of yourselves,
This war of ours is never done.[18]

One cannot read that last verse without thinking of the moment in *The Truce* when Levi, having just left Auschwitz, hears words of warning from another of the saved: *guerra è sempre*, "war is always."[19] The poem, written almost forty years later, is equally eloquent and emphatic: the enemy is not outside, but inside the band of comrades—indeed, inside each one of them. "Every man's his own foe, / Each one split by his own frontier."

It would be reassuring to think that in war the enemy is always *outside*, and that once the enemy is defeated the problem of wrongdoing has been resolved. On close inspection, however, the Italian civil war (where it doesn't seem difficult, at least in retrospect, to distinguish the side of rights and humanity from the side of inhumanity and abuse) tells another story. It is a story of unquestionable good, the fight against Nazi-Fascism, intermixed with a story of profound wrong, a wrong no human being, not even the best, can say he is totally free of. Between black and white lie many shades of gray. At times this story is one of simple, sharp contrasts. More often, its truths are expressed in gradations.

1

——

Inventing the Resistance

Amay

Mario Pelizzari had seen them with his own eyes: Italian soldiers, perhaps those who had been serving in France, climbing the passes of the Val d'Ayas, "thinking of nothing but saving their own skins." He had seen them, in those dramatic days after the armistice of September 8, 1943—when their commanders gave them no orders at all except to cease fighting the Allies—scrambling over the snow fields of Testa Grigia or straight up the glaciers of Monte Rosa to cross the border and reach neutral Switzerland, "tossing their hand grenades down the ravines and smashing their guns." He had seen them run off and abandon Italy to the Germans. He had seen a piece of his country in utter disarray, and he'd made a vow to himself. If Italy was to be occupied by the Nazi-Fascists, he would try to do something useful, "so as not to become a laughing stock, one of the sheep," and to try to redeem that spectacle of men fleeing that had made his "heart bleed."[1]

Just a few weeks before, when Il Duce was ousted on July 25,

Pelizzari, a forty-year-old draftsman for the Olivetti company in the Piedmontese city of Ivrea, had been one of those at the factory most alert to the dangers, one of the readiest to roll up his sleeves. He cruised the streets of his town with a colleague, hammers and chisels in hand, to chip off the public buildings every carving they saw of the fasces, the ruling party's symbol.[2] Along with his boss, the engineer Riccardo Levi, director of the technical department at Olivetti, Pelizzari also tried to establish a factory committee that was, in effect, a primitive Resistance unit.[3] Under the name Alimiro he would one day be a legendary partisan of Ivrea.

In early September he moved to the Val d'Ayas, where Olivetti had a summer retreat for employees on the slopes of Monte Rosa. It was a picture-postcard spot, a dream in normal times. But now the German army was moving in to occupy Italy—even the little region of Valle d'Aosta, even the tiny Val d'Ayas. And German occupation, Pelizzari sensed, meant an immediate risk for Italian Jews: for Riccardo Levi, who had a wife and children, and for the many other Olivetti managers and employees of Jewish origin—perhaps no longer self-consciously Jewish, yet in one way or another forever Jews.

Not everyone was of Pelizzari's mind. After Mussolini's fall in July, and right up to the Italian surrender in September, some Italian Jews were naive enough to think that the worst was over; that the ghastly season that had begun with the anti-Semitic Racial Laws of 1938 had ended when Mussolini and the Fascist regime fell. "The Jewish situation seems to continue to improve," wrote the Turinese Jew Emanuele Artom, one of Primo Levi's circle, on September 3. Hadn't the post-Mussolini government of Pietro Badoglio repealed some of the anti-Jewish measures—the prohibitions on posting obituaries, or employing Aryan domestic servants, or staying in holiday resorts?[4] In August, Primo Levi himself had left for a vacation in the mountains without great worries about the future. Or at least that is how he would remember things forty years later.[5]

By the end of July, though, a battalion of German grenadiers was already posted at Aosta. And when the armistice was announced on September 8, things moved quickly. By the evening of September 10, the Wehrmacht controlled Turin, and the Germans needed just four days to occupy most of Piedmont—the city of Ivrea, the Canavese plain—as well as much of the Valle d'Aosta region, including the city of Aosta itself. Meanwhile Mussolini, on Hitler's orders, was freed from his prison by a parachute commando, and installed as the leader of the so-called Republic of Salò. In Aosta and its province, the Italian Fascists quickly reorganized themselves around the German command and the various Nazi police services. There were not so many, though: the 30,000 Fascists in Aosta before Mussolini fell had dwindled to just over 1,000.[6]

The anti-Fascists of Valle d'Aosta and Piedmont also moved quickly, if not very professionally. At night a group of Olivetti factory workers went out to steal weapons and munitions from the unguarded barracks of the carabinieri, the military police corps. They hid them in the house of one of the workers, and when two machine guns proved too big to carry up the stairs they were forklifted up to the balcony.[7] In Valle d'Aosta, the parish vicar helped move machine guns and munitions abandoned by Italian soldiers to a cavern under the cemetery.[8]

Primo Levi was close by. He had arrived in the Valle d'Aosta town of Saint-Vincent on the afternoon of September 9, and on the morning of the twelfth his mother, Ester—known as Rina—and his sister, Anna Maria, joined him. (His father, Cesare, had died the year before.) Initially the Levi family stayed with some relatives in their rented lodgings in Saint-Vincent, but five days later the three Levis moved again.[9] On foot or perhaps mule-back, they climbed what locals call "the hill" and moved into the Hotel Ristoro, the only hotel in Amay, a village high above Saint-Vincent just under the Col de Joux pass. On September 19, Primo Levi took the pass to reach Val d'Ayas. He was on his way to a trattoria to meet a dozen Jewish friends and acquaintances. The agenda: how to reach safety in Switzerland.[10]

There seemed to be two alternatives. You could proceed to Valtournenche and pin your hopes on the cable car to Plateau Rosa and then down to Zermatt in Switzerland. The risk was that this might put you immediately into the hands of the Germans, if they had already taken command of the cable car stations. Otherwise you could try crossing the Monte Rosa glacier before winter came, with all the evident mountain-climber's risks, as well as the risk the *passeurs*[11] might not be trustworthy. *Passeurs*: cross-border smugglers accustomed to carrying various sorts of illegal merchandise, to whom the war offered the additional opportunity to earn money transporting men and women whose lives were at risk.[12] To evade the guards of the border militia, the smugglers demanded between 5,000 and 15,000 lire per person (the equivalent of roughly $3,000 to $9,000 today).[13] But some of them could also abandon their clients in the high Alps and simply disappear. Such unappealing options perhaps explain why nothing was decided at that meeting.[14]

Levi then returned to Amay, where he would spend, almost without interruption, the three months before his capture by the Fascist militia. "There are many little villages scattered around a valley, and then there is . . . a minuscule settlement called Amay": so Levi recalled the place thirty years later in a conversation with a young friend of the family.[15] The lodgings at Amay's Hotel Ristoro were not luxurious, somewhere between a country inn and a mountain hut for hikers. But the managers were agreeable and the rooms had running water and were reasonably priced.[16] Up on the top floor under the roof, the Levi family could feel relatively at ease, as much as was possible in those difficult times.

I first saw the village of Amay on a sunny day in September 2011. I had been studying the Resistance at Col de Joux and Primo Levi's role in it for years, but I had not yet gone to see the main theater of action. For years, driving back and forth between Geneva and Turin, I had raised my eyes toward "the hill" where I knew Amay sat, and all those years I recognized, from down in the valley, the outlines of houses nestled in the green of vegetation or silhouetted against the white of the snow. Not even once, however, had I exited the motorway to climb the switchback road up that hill, arrive at the village half an hour away, and walk down its all but deserted alleyways. I had utterly forgotten the lesson of Richard

Cobb, historian of the French Revolution, who held that history must be pursued on foot and not just read, must be studied *in loco* and not only in archival folders and the pages of books. It mattered, because before I went to Amay, I had never got past the surface of Primo Levi's Resistance.

Until I saw the Hotel Ristoro, now transformed into a condominium; until I saw, right next to the former hotel, the tiny church and bell tower of Amay, a seventeenth-century chapel like one in a fairy tale; until I saw, above all, the stunning landscape that on a sunny day in autumn 1943 lay before the guests on the top floor of the Ristoro, I was unable to understand one of the basic facts of the Resistance experience: the geographical nature of partisan existence,[17] the direct connection between the rebel and the territory in which he found himself. Before I went to Amay, I was unable to understand how difficult, how almost impossible, it was to carry out resistance in a place like that.

For Amay is too luminous, too airy, too visible a place to fight a war, let alone a guerrilla insurgency. The village, once a popular stopping point on a long mountain route, remains enchanting even today, when it is something like a ghost town. Its three or four streets are empty, the chapel is closed up, the haylofts and wooden granaries are in ruins, but the sweeping panorama of mountains and plain that opens out from Amay toward the great Aosta Valley is remarkably picturesque. But because of its astonishingly aerial nature, Amay was the last place that a clever partisan would choose as a base to hide out. Certainly, this perch over the plain offered the rebels a chance to mark eventual enemy incursions in good time. The problem was that this visibility worked in the other direction, too, at least for anyone with a pair of binoculars. Although it was just a bit lower down the mountain, Amay was different from Frumy, a pasture with Alpine huts where most (a dozen men!) of the Col de Joux band settled in. Frumy was off the track of the road that led up the hill. The huts were invisible, except from even farther up the hill; they could not be seen at all from the valley. At Frumy, there was none of the giddy visibility of Amay.

In 1932, a journalist for the Turin daily *La Stampa* praised Saint-Vincent as an "Alpine Eldorado" and called Amay "a delicious village immersed in emerald green," a land of plenty close at hand. One May day in 1800, the (probably apocryphal) story goes, as Napoleon's army was crossing the Alps into Italy, the First Consul himself ascended the hill on a reconnaissance mission, stopped at the inn of Amay, and drank some "rosy Carema wine." The wine cup was dutifully preserved and proudly displayed to the guests of the Ristoro.[18]

The fall

The presence of Primo Levi's whole family in that improbable Eldorado says much about their situation in late September 1943. In German-occupied Italy, Jews simply believed they were safer in the mountains than in the city. Certainly the epic aura that clings to the first partisans does not characterize their circumstances, which we might rather call domestic.[19]

Like most of his Jewish friends, the twenty-four-year-old Levi had not gone up into the hills for any pressing military or intrinsically political purpose. He was not evading an army call-up, since adult males "of the Jewish race" had been banned from military service in 1938 and were even less welcome in the collaborationist Italy of Salò. He wasn't there to hide out and pursue guerrilla action, since he wouldn't have taken along his sister and fifty-year-old mother. Nor was he there in response to a great call to take up the anti-Fascist resistance, for there had been no such call in the days just after the eighth of September; the resistance scattered here and there did not immediately become the Resistance with a capital *R*. Certainly Primo Levi stood with the anti-Fascists, and he had taken sides at least a year before Mussolini fell. Pressed by his charismatic cousin, Ada Della Torre, he and his friends—half a dozen Turinese Jews working in Milan—had already approached the anti-Fascist Partito d'Azione and even carried out some clandestine activities.[20] But when Il Duce was ousted they were unable to translate that determination into concrete military or political action. The German occupation hit them more as endangered Jews than as rebels of the first hour.

Among Primo Levi's closest friends from those days in Milan were Vanda Maestro, a chemist, and Luciana Nissim, who had earned a medical degree. Both were now in the mountains: Nissim was staying with her parents in a village in the lower Val d'Ayas, while Maestro was lodged with her brother in another nearby village. Five months later, the three would share a railway car and deportation to Poland. Della Torre, meanwhile, had left Milan for a job at Olivetti, down on the plain in Ivrea, and so she too was not far away.

On October 10 Vanda Maestro sent to another friend from those Milanese days a letter that was strangely lighthearted, given the gravity of the moment. She told of some romantic novels she'd enjoyed, complained of the "disgusting" Italian-made cigarettes she had smoked, spoke of how she missed her friends, and "of my humble hope we'll be together at New Year's" if "this awful period passes."[21] Later that month Vanda and her brother Aldo made an attempt to cross the border into Switzerland. When they didn't succeed, Aldo returned to the plain while Vanda decided to go and stay with Luciana in Val d'Ayas. Eventually the two of them decided to leave the Nissim family and traveled first up to Brusson, then over the Col de Joux pass to meet Primo Levi at the Hotel Ristoro. It is difficult to be sure of the dates, but this was probably deep in the autumn, between the end of November and the beginning of December. "I don't recall exactly," Luciana would say half a century later; "I know that we two, dressed in ski pants, went up and settled in there."[22]

As Eugenio Gentili Tedeschi, another of Primo Levi's friends from the Milan circle, remembers it, in early December Vanda Maestro walked much of the way across Valle d'Aosta from east to west and climbed up to the village where Eugenio was staying, hoping to convince him to join the group of Jewish friends at the Col de Joux. Vanda was enthusiastic about the situation around Brusson. "She told me the civilian population there was very cooperative, and that even the mayor's wife was knitting woolen socks for the partisans to wear in winter."

Eugenio did not share Vanda's optimism at all. "I'm not coming, and you had better take care and change your routes right away, close up the place where you are staying, go somewhere else where no one knows you, and change your habits completely, for the risk is grave." No, she said, she didn't believe it. The two friends would never see one another again.[23]

There were other Turinese Jews in those mountains, people connected to Levi or to his friends, many of them related. Among them were Emilio and Guido Bachi, who will have a certain weight in our story. The Bachi brothers were some ten years older than Levi, and although they came from the same world as he did their experiences had been somewhat different. Born in 1907 and 1909, Emilio and Guido were old enough to recall celebrating, along with their elders, Italy's victory against Austria in the Great War.[24] They had grown up under Mussolini but had finished their university studies and completed their military service long before the racial laws of 1938 made Levi and his contemporaries pariahs in Fascist Italy—barred from serving in the Royal Army, the air force, and the navy, disdained as unworthy of any uniform and unfit for manly deeds.[25]

In family photographs Emilio Bachi looks vigorous, with blue eyes and blond hair, while Guido is less tall, dark eyed and dark haired. Their papers portray the Bachi family as a sort of low-key version of the Finzi-Continis, the prosperous, unwary protagonists of Giorgio Bassani's novel *The Garden of the Finzi-Continis* set among the Jews of 1930s Ferrara. The Bachi family, it must be said, was more political than the Finzi-Continis. Emilio and Guido's father, Donato, was a longtime Socialist who had worked with Camillo Olivetti, founder of the company of the same name, and after World War I they had started up an anti-Fascist review called *Tempi nuovi*.[26] Donato Bachi, for his part, was enough of an opponent of the regime to be sent into internal exile in 1940.[27] Beyond that, however, the Bachi story is very like the one Bassani told of Ferrara. It is a story of the fall of Italian Jews as they plunged, unwitting and stunned, from life abundant into nakedness and fear.

I have before me a copy of a photograph. "Bardonecchia, July 1935" is written on it, but it is not difficult to imagine it as an illustration for Bassani's novel, which revolves around the Finzi-Contini tennis court, symbol of their innocent myopia, their oblivious, foreseeable defeat in the match of life. During a pause in the game at Bardonecchia, a dozen young men and women have posed for the camera, tennis rackets in hand. Or, more likely, they have posed before the game, for no one's hair is out of place, no one is sweaty; all look impeccable in their tennis whites. One of them, playing a silly joke, hides behind the others with a hand up, two fingers extended, "making the horns." Elena Bachi, Emilio's sister-in-law, is on one side of the group. On the other, wearing a childish white cap, is Primo Levi, then sixteen years old. He is smiling and—so it appears—timidly waving.[28]

Elena Bachi would go on to marry Primo's cousin Roberto Levi, a union loveless from the beginning, fated to end in tragedy. But those events pertain to the story of the fall. Before she resigned herself to an arranged marriage, celebrated almost glumly in February 1943, in the grim era of racial discrimination, Elena had quite happily enjoyed her circumstances as a privileged young woman at a time when an Italian Jew could grow up with every advantage: education, sports, games of bridge, travel. One day in Rome in the autumn of 1933, Elena and her sister Luisella had even been introduced to Vittorio and Bruno Mussolini, Il Duce's sons, at a luncheon on the Via Camilluccia. Two years later, on May 1, 1936, they had celebrated the conquest of Addis Ababa—Italy's victory in the war with Ethiopia and the birth of the Fascist empire—along with the jeunesse dorée of Turin's Jewish community. In no hurry to settle down, Elena refused to make do with the several dull Jewish suitors the family turned up for her, and instead continued to flirt with various young model Fascists, tennis pros, ski buffs, and track and field champions.[29]

Bardonecchia, Sestrière, Courmayeur, Cervinia: so many pages of Elena Bachi's diary were dedicated to her holidays in mountain resorts before the summer of 1938. Elena, like Primo Levi, spent that summer in Cogne, a mountain town south of Aosta. In July there was the Hotel

Miramonti, the lawn, tennis matches, mountain hikes with the Gran Paradiso glacier as a backdrop. The newspapers, meanwhile, printed the "Manifesto of the Racial Scientists" and brought news of the Racial Laws. "We are all very worried," wrote Elena in her diary, "that we, too, may be forced to leave the country, as has happened to the German Jews."[30] On July 31, Primo Levi celebrated his nineteenth birthday.[31] He was at Cogne with his family, and many relatives and friends were nearby. His holiday followed his first year of university, which had been quite successful, but "beyond the walls of the Chemistry Institute," he would write in *The Periodic Table*, "it was nighttime in Europe."[32] Elena Bachi was aware of this too, in her own, exclamation-pointed way. "Very down because of the terrible anti-Semitic campaign of which I don't wish to speak, for I would have to write about it for a thousand hours on end. It is a dreadful thing, and on October 1 there will be further provisions. Certainly it means no more dances, no more parties and carefree fun! Who knows how all this will end!"[33]

Police Directive Number Five

For the hundred or so inhabitants of Amay, as for the 2,000 who lived in Saint-Vincent and the 90,000 in the entire province of Aosta, the fact that a few dozen Piedmontese Jews had sought refuge from the Nazi-Fascists in the mountains in September 1943 was far from their main concern.

The war had been raging for three years, the defeats of the Italian armed forces had spread panic; the losses in every household, the difficulties of every family were so great that even Mussolini's fall had not distracted the "miserable populace" of Valle d'Aosta from "everyone's nightmare," the "animal anxiety to procure food." Such was the impression of Émile Chanoux, the anti-Fascist notary who would be the most distinguished martyr of the Valle d'Aosta Resistance, and there is no reason to think he was mistaken.[34] As it happens, Chanoux's view of things finds an indirect (if politically opposite) confirmation in the report of Aosta prefect Cesare Augusto Carnazzi, who had been installed by the

Republic of Salò in October 1943. The population, he wrote, cared nothing for politics, or foreign affairs, or anything else beyond ravenous self-
interest. "The cornering of the market for milk products and their
hyperbolic prices is for them the most interesting aspect of the war." For
the people of Valle d'Aosta, world war and civil war came down to a
matter of milk, butter, and cheese.[35]

In those first months after the Germans moved in, the mortal danger
facing Italian Jews was perfectly evident, if administratively vague. In
late September, the Reich Security Main Office had ordered German
police in Nazi-occupied Rome to "expel eastward" all Jews who were
Italian citizens. The relative lethargy of the Republic of Salò moved the
Germans to carry out anti-Jewish actions on their own, for the Italian
police were not very efficient collaborators. The Nazis carried out their
first roundups and massacres between September and October around
the cities of Bolzano and Cuneo and on the Piedmontese shores of
Lake Maggiore. There was also the devastating operation in the Rome
Ghetto, where a thousand Jews—men, women, the elderly, children—
were arrested and deported to Auschwitz. But it was not until November 30 that the Interior Minister of the Social Republic issued Police
Directive Number Five, which decreed that all Jews within the territory
of Salò, whatever their nationality, be arrested and confined in internment camps awaiting deportation to the Lager.[36]

The population of Valle d'Aosta reacted ambivalently to the influx
of Jews and foreigners seeking a chance to cross the border into Switzerland, or merely to be less visible than they were in the city. On the one
hand, the locals considered these extra people a further problem, because
the Jewish refugees were extra mouths to feed and risked making already
scarce resources even more so. On the other, the people of Valle d'Aosta
also recognized that this was an unexpected economic opportunity, the
Jews being all the more willing to pay for their food and lodgings because
they were not tourists but people fighting for survival. The locals' sentiments were also ambivalent. The situation of the Jews spurred some to
sympathy and mercy. And yet wartime needs pushed others to extract

the most profit from the Jewish drama, so that some of the fees imposed for board and rent were little less than usurious.[37]

Contrary to what one might expect, the people of the small Valle d'Aosta town of Saint-Vincent had already become rather familiar with displaced Jews during the war. This had been an indirect result of the occupation of the Balkans by the Axis powers. During the second half of 1941, the roundup and murder of Jews in Serbia and Croatia by the Germans and their Croatian fascist ally, the Ustasha, had provoked thousands to flee to the zone of Italian occupation, in the reasonable expectation that the soldiers of Mussolini would treat them somewhat less barbarously than did those of Hitler. About 2,000 of these Jews were in fact deported from Dalmatia to Italy, and about 250 of these were assigned by the government to be interned in Aosta and its province. Of these, 101 were in turn sent to reside in "hotels or furnished rooms" in Saint-Vincent, where, in late 1941 and early 1942, they settled in.[38]

Considering that the total population of Saint-Vincent was only around 2,000 inhabitants, it is obvious that the sudden arrival (and prolonged presence) of such a large number of foreign Jews would have an impact. Most of those 101 foreigners would remain until February 1943, when the Interior Minister ordered that they be transferred to a civil internment camp in Calabria. Twenty-nine of them were exempted from leaving Saint-Vincent on account of their "advanced age" or their "grave" health conditions. All of these were, of course, to be kept "under tight surveillance" to prevent any "subversive propaganda."[39] Up until the eighth of September 1943, the prefect and police chief of Aosta were fairly lenient with the Yugoslav Jews in their territory. They had even resisted the Interior Minister's orders to send all of them south independent of their age or health conditions.

Cesare Augusto Carnazzi, the new prefect of Aosta under Salò, took a very different line. A zealous anti-Semite even before the Germans arrived, he had warned the previous prefect in a top-secret missive that "hundreds of Yugoslav and Croatian Jews along with their families" had "meticulously" staked out "rentals, cottages, and hotel rooms, that is, all the best lodgings that are usually reserved for Turinese families during the summer season." That was not all that the Balkan Jews were guilty of. "Being well furnished with cash," they were buying up various food items, "whether they had ration cards or not." And worse: "Among them some who can speak, even badly, a bit of Italian, find ways to make clever anti-Axis propaganda, suggesting they were forced to leave their country of origin because German officers had carried out atrocities."[40]

A lawyer by trade, Carnazzi was an energetic twenty-nine-year-old who knew the area well because he had been Fascist Party secretary of Aosta between May 1941 and July 1943. Nor did he lack military experience, for he had the stripes of an air force lieutenant and had volunteered for combat both in East Africa and in the Balkans.[41] When Carnazzi became prefect of Aosta at the end of October 1943, he was determined to be a Nazi-Fascist patriot.

As of November 19, 1943, some seventeen of the twenty-nine Yugoslav Jews who had not been transferred to Calabria were still interned at Saint-Vincent. "They have not moved beyond town limits even during and after the recent circumstances," wrote the deputy sergeant who'd been left to oversee the local carabinieri barracks, discreetly alluding to Mussolini's fall and the armistice.[42] Only a few days remained until November 30, when Police Directive Number Five would be issued by the Salò Interior Ministry: a blanket arrest warrant for all Jews in the Salò territory, including those last Yugoslav refugees at Saint-Vincent. And including those three Italian Levis who, two and a half months before, had found a hiding place nine hundred meters farther up, at the Hotel Ristoro of Amay.

We can try to imagine the life of Levi, his mother, and his sister in that little hotel, but there are few documentary traces to fill out the picture. One is Levi's signature as a witness to a marriage celebrated at the town hall of Saint-Vincent on October 23. The couple—both of the "Jewish race," as the mayor of Ivrea dutifully informed the prefect and police chief of Aosta, and as the marriage certificate also specified[43]— were Giorgio Fubini, an engineer at Olivetti, and Lia Segre, resident of

Turin. The bride was Levi's cousin, and the other witness was a longtime friend of his, the engineer Livio Norzi. The wedding banns had been published in the usual manner. And the signatures at the bottom of the marriage document were firm and clear: bride, groom, two witnesses. It was a wedding like any other, as Italian Jews struggled to maintain an impossible normality even while the Final Solution was materializing around them.

Indeed, although the guests at the Hotel Ristoro did not know it, the extermination machine had already overtaken and crushed a piece of the Levi family. On September 15, Primo Levi's paternal uncle Mario Levi, an eye doctor in Turin, and his son Roberto, Primo's cousin, were arrested by the Germans on a main street in the town of Orta, in the Lombardy lake district. Transferred to Meina on Lake Maggiore, Mario and Roberto Levi were murdered on September 23 along with several dozen Greek, Turkish, and Italian Jews whom the SS had captured in the town's most elegant hotel. The victims' bodies were then tossed into the lake, a stone tied to each of their necks.[44] Mario Levi's wife, Emma Coen, and Roberto's wife, Elena Bachi, were spared. The same Elena Bachi who just a few years before had chattered on in her diary about tennis with Primo Levi or skiing with Emilio and Guido Bachi: in short order she had become a reluctant bride, and then a young widow.

At Orta, for whatever reason, the SS had not treated the two women as desirable prey. But the Jews killed alongside Mario and Roberto at Meina included men and women both. And two weeks later, at the beginning of October, the SS officers who captured an entire family in Valle d'Aosta—father, mother, daughter, son—showed no leniency to the women. The Ovazza family had been the incarnation of those Turin Jews loyal to Fascism during the 1930s.[45] Arrested at the Hotel Lyskamm in Gressoney-Saint-Jean, where they were trying to secretly expatriate to Switzerland, they were quickly robbed of a small fortune, taken to Lake Maggiore, shot in the basement of a school, and incinerated in the school furnace.[46]

Neither of these early tragedies involving Jews from Turin, however, became widely known at first. News traveled haltingly in occupied Italy. Collaborationist newspapers, of course, wrote nothing of German atrocities. And the Jews themselves, refugees, hidden, and in disguise, were often unable to share information, even the most grievous.

Word of Police Directive Number Five, however, seems to have circulated with lightning speed to every corner of occupied Italy where one or more Jews had hidden themselves away hoping better times would come.[47] And that included the town of Saint-Vincent and the village of Amay. According to Anna Maria Levi, she and her mother left the Hotel Ristoro in Amay on December 1—the day after the directive was issued. Her brother opposed their decision to abandon the mountains and seek refuge in some small country town outside Turin, hoping to evade the Italian and German police. "Primo was not really in agreement," Anna Maria would recall in 2009. It seems she organized their departure in secret to avoid his protest.[48]

Primo Levi's dissent certainly reflects an elder child's uneasiness about not being able to look after his widowed mother and younger sister directly. But perhaps it also reflects a reluctance to be the only member of the family left in the mountains. So long as his mother and sister were there in the hotel, Levi was a Jew from the city who had evacuated with his family to an Alpine village to evade the Nazi-Fascist predators. But the day the two women left, what would he be? A Jewish refugee rather lamely hidden in rented rooms in Amay—or a partisan fighting for what was not yet called the Resistance, a rebel with the band that was forming just ten minutes up the mountain, in the shepherd huts of Frumy?

Beyond their numbers

After the armistice on September 8, young non-Jewish Italian men of combat age faced a stark set of choices: remain at home, sign up for military service with the Social Republic, or join the partisans in the hills or in the cities. Jews had a different decision to make. For them, enlisting with Salò was out of the question: the Social Republic only wanted to deport them. Nor could they merely stay at home; discovery meant a fatal transfer to the sealed train. Although non-Jews were also at risk if they stayed at home and failed to respond to the ever-more-threatening enlistment calls, in practice the German and Italian police had neither the political interest nor the means to hunt down and punish hundreds of thousands of service-dodgers.[49] For Jews, though, the effective options were two: hide, or become partisans.

The narrowness of that choice helps to explain why Italian Jews were so numerous in the Resistance, far beyond their proportion of the overall population. When it was all over, about a thousand were officially recognized as Resistance fighters (another thousand were recognized as "patriots"): remarkably many, considering that the entire Jewish population—men, women, and children—was no more than 35,000.[50] As Primo Levi did in Amay after the promulgation of Police Directive Number Five, many Jews who were fit to do so opted to take up arms.[51]

We can borrow more than one page here from Emanuele Artom's *Diaries of a Jewish Partisan*. The older brother of one of Primo Levi's classmates, the diminutive, bookish, and timid Emanuele had been the butt of jokes from adolescence. At the D'Azeglio *liceo* in the early 1930s, the name Artom signified a hopeless and unmanly nerd.[52] Yet ten years later, facing the German occupation, Artom left Turin for the valleys of Piedmont at the service of the anti-Fascist Partito d'Azione.[53] He overcame his condescension toward comrades wilder and less intellectual than he. He learned how to handle weapons.

On December 1, news of Police Directive Number Five threw Artom into dismay at the thought of his parents, who had remained on the Piedmontese plain. What would become of them; what would be the point of surviving them? "In that case," he wrote, "I will ask my commander to be sent on a mission in which I'll be killed."[54]

But Artom's engagement in the partisan struggle was to grow tougher and more urgent. The Nazi-Fascist "hunt for the Jews"[55] turned him into a man ready to fight to the end—not to sacrifice himself, but to kill. On

December 20 his band raided Cavour, a town where the Republic of Salò was enrolling soldiers ("slave trade," Artom called it, "in males born in '24 and '25"). It was his baptism by fire: "I understand now that I wasn't born to be a professor, but a gangster." The engagement was quickly over. "Gunfire from the truck, and when I jumped down, all I could see were disappearing trouser hems as the Fascists bolted out of the doors of the covered market."[56]

Fighting alongside Artom was Giorgio Segre, a young Jewish doctor, also from Turin, who had just gotten his degree. And later in that winter of 1943–44 one of Artom's comrades in arms would be yet another Jew from his hometown, Franco Momigliano. One of the founders of the Partito d'Azione in Piedmont, Momigliano was romantically involved with Luciana Nissim, and Segre with Vanda Maestro.[57] The world of Primo Levi's generation of Turinese Jews, the ones who took to the hills after the armistice, was small indeed.

Beyond those human ties were political ties linking the rebel bands of the Valle d'Aosta with the movement then springing up in the Waldensian* valleys west of Turin. Links were also being forged that fall between Valle d'Aosta and the plain, as anti-Fascists established contact with each other. The young Fiat manager Aurelio Peccei climbed the mountains several times between October and December 1943 on behalf of the Partito d'Azione.[58] Vincenzo Grasso, an engineer working in Turin, also seems to have played a role,[59] while attorney Camillo Reynaud[60] collected funds, made contact with clandestine organizations, and sent early rebels to the Col de Joux. He went with them, in fact, to the Frumy lodge, where Guido Bachi was then in charge, "around the twentieth of September."

That, at any rate, was how Bachi remembered it just after the war, in an October 1946 report to the Piedmontese regional committee certifying partisan credentials. The report lauded Peccei as the man respon-

---

* Translator's note: The Waldensians (Valdesi, Vaudois), a Christian sect founded in the twelfth century, became Protestants during the Reformation. Often at odds with the established order in overwhelmingly Catholic Italy, they had their stronghold in the valleys of Piedmont.

sible for linking up "the patriot unit of Amay" and the military command of the Piedmontese National Liberation Committee. And it praised another "valuable contributor" leading the group in Amay, "second lieutenant Aldo Piacenza."[61] Who, I discovered, was still alive.

As chance would have it

Maurizio, Aldo Piacenza's son, was encouraging. "My father's over ninety, he's hard of hearing, and his recent memory can be faulty sometimes. But his memory for the past is excellent, and you can certainly go see him if you like."

The house faced onto Piazza dei Gardini Lamarmora, one of the many beautiful squares in the center of Turin: elegant apartment buildings, the usual monument to a Risorgimento hero, plane trees all around. I had crossed that square innumerable times on my way to the library or to the archives since I began to research the story of the partisans. But I hadn't known I was walking right by an important historical personage, sitting there behind the windows. Aldo Piacenza was confined to a wheelchair but otherwise alive and well, his mental faculties as bright as the tip of his cigarette.

About to ring the bell, I made another discovery: in that same building also lived Primo Levi's close friend Bianca Guidetti Serra, a trusted anti-Fascist in the 1930s and a major progressive figure in postwar Italian politics.[62] Again—small world.

When I was taken in to see Piacenza in his studio overlooking the gardens outside, he had his back to the door. He was facing the window, with a blanket over his knees. Waiting for me, it seemed, and perhaps for something more. I was touched by the sight of him, in part because it made me think of the wheelchair used for so long by my mother; in part because the man before me was the very image of the stalwart old partisan. For a second I felt like a character from the period I had studied for my thesis many years before, like one of the French Republicans who during the 1820s and '30s—battling the enemies of the Revolution—would go to visit old Montagnards, the last Jacobin survivors of 1793, and collect their memories as a sign of gratitude. Seated there beside Aldo Piacenza, I was briefly a son who had recently lost the mother who once read him the last letters of partisans condemned to death—and a citizen infinitely grateful to an old man like Piacenza for having been a partisan in the hills in his youth, for having made Italy free. More than a few moments went by before I regained the more neutral guise of the historian.

"That we were up in the mountains was largely by chance; don't think there was some great revolutionary plan behind it; we had been kicked up there by the eighth of September." Piacenza's very first words put history back in its place and recalled me to the present. He had been orphaned as a child and raised by his aunt and uncle, who owned a butcher shop; he had arrived at Amay in September 1943, after abandoning his army uniform, hoping to stay out of German hands. A driver in his unit had given him the idea; the fellow was a native of Valle d'Aosta and knew the area, "he knew that above Saint-Vincent, well above, there was a village where we might be able to stay out of trouble." Especially because there was no road above Saint-Vincent up to Amay, just an Alpine path, a two-hour hike uphill.

When Piacenza arrived he had taken a room at the Hotel Ristoro. There he met Primo Levi. Or rather recognized him, for the two were almost the same age (Levi, twenty-four; Piacenza, twenty-two), and they had crossed paths in secondary school in Turin. Aldo had been a classmate of Primo's sister, Anna Maria,[63] and now they all were under the same roof, having fled from one danger or another, in that Alpine Eldorado without any gold. "Everything was chaotic, makeshift, dangerous," Piacenza went on, "and we found ourselves there almost entirely by chance."

If Levi had no military experience, Piacenza had had more than his share. In July 1941 he had volunteered for the Eastern Front with the Italian Expeditionary Corps and the following year his unit was absorbed into ARMIR, the Italian Army in Russia. He had thus fought the entire

Russian campaign, "from Iasi in Romania right to the bend of the Don." Not on the front line, though: "I was a driver; our job wasn't to fire, it was to drive." Certainly, Piacenza said, "I saw things, yes; but not everything, not being at the front." In Moldavia, Bessarabia, Ukraine, "what I saw was behind the lines." And there, Piacenza saw, or glimpsed, the effects of the Final Solution. "When we were withdrawing from Russia, I was struck, in a town I don't remember the name of, that there were no adults there, only children. It was a Jewish town, I should say. There were just children, children destined to die." As he tells me this I wonder whether he spoke about it to Primo Levi during their days together in Amay. I do know that twenty years ago, writing to an English biographer of Levi, Ian Thomson, Piacenza told him how in October 1941, with the Italian Expeditionary Corps at the Dnipropetrovsk bridgehead, they met a long column of Jews escorted by the Germans. "The machine gun fire went on for three days."[64] Today scholars say that at least 12,000 Jews were eliminated in the Dnipropetrovsk massacre, shot in the back of the head and thrown into mass graves.[65]

In October 1943, when the combined efforts of Aurelio Peccei, Camillo Reynaud, and others linking Turin and Valle d'Aosta brought a dozen rebels to the area, Aldo Piacenza's military experience earned him a role as one of the leaders of the band, a group that would enlarge only slightly in subsequent weeks. "The most I had under me were fifteen men," Piacenza tells me. Outside the window, dusk is settling on the gardens, and his handsome old-man's face is wreathed in cigarette smoke. Just above Amay was "a wide plain used for pasture," he says, the plain of Frumy with its "shepherds' huts and lodges," and "it was there that I installed my men." Piacenza speaks as if he had been their undisputed leader, but archival material suggests that the real chief— insofar as such titles make any sense in reference to the earliest days of the Resistance, when hierarchies were still to be worked out—was Guido Bachi. Or at least that Bachi was the political leader, with Piacenza at his side as military leader.[66]

Both of the Bachi brothers had the necessary qualifications to lead the Col de Joux band. They were more mature than Piacenza or Levi, a dozen years older. And though they had not fought on any front in World War II, they had real military experience. Before being "permanently discharged" as a result of the anti-Jewish laws of 1938,[67] Emilio had been a reserve officer in the Alpine artillery, while Guido was a reserve officer in the Automotive Corps; both held the rank of lieutenant.[68] After his military service, Guido had worked with his father, Donato, in the insurance business and then with a cousin in the paper industry. His passion was music. He had a diploma in piano and had been prominent in the university music society while studying economics; after the Racial Laws he taught music at the Jewish School of Turin.[69]

Emilio Bachi, his older brother, was an attorney who had refused to enroll in the Fascist Party in 1932. Two years later Emilio had approached the Turinese branch of the anti-Fascist movement Giustizia e Libertà, but he did not take the step into outright conspiracy. In 1939 he left Italy for France, where with a distant cousin he tried to set up a plastics works in Brittany. In the summer of 1940 he had experienced firsthand the fall of France under Hitler's blitzkrieg. He would never forget it.[70]

How much of this human history Aldo Piacenza knew in the autumn of 1943 when, just back from the Russian campaign, he joined the Bachi brothers in organizing the Col de Joux band, I have no idea. The old partisan, speaking to me in 2011, seemed in no way keen to exaggerate his role in the Resistance or to minimize that of the brothers Bachi. Instead, Piacenza seemed to want to convince me that neither he nor the others had accomplished anything politically or militarily significant in those autumn months. "We hadn't done anything much because we were still in the process of recruiting; all I had done was put the band together," he told me. A statement that reminds me, in its mixture of modesty and pride, of something Primo Levi said in an interview in 1975 about *The Periodic Table*. "Really, we knew nothing. We had to invent the Resistance."[71]

"Primo Levi, pretty much like me, did nothing . . . at least at the beginning," Piacenza insisted. After those first few weeks they had undertaken a few actions, but hadn't accomplished much. They tried to recruit several people, procure some weapons. "The main thing I remember was that Primo and I had heard of a guy in a far-off town who had weapons and was willing to give them to us." One night the two young men set out for that town of Chambave, moving only along Alpine paths in order to minimize the chance of unfortunate encounters. "When we got there, we found out that this miserable fellow had only one gun, or maybe he only wanted to give us one. And so back we went—it was still night—and we spent the night inside the door of a church. It was damned cold!"

As a grown man, almost an old man, Primo Levi wrote that human memory was "a marvelous but fallacious instrument."[72] This comes to mind as I watch Piacenza's face light up recalling that fruitless night-time expedition of '43; I'm unable to avoid comparing what he tells me tonight with what he told Carole Angier for her 2002 biography of Levi. In that account Piacenza also spoke of how word had reached Amay of arms to be had at Chambave, and of the night he and Levi spent on mountain paths. But in that other version they had found as many weapons as they could want: hand grenades, rifles, pistols—in short, manna from heaven! They loaded them on their backs and returned to Col de Joux. Piacenza was thrilled, and Levi too was happy. And yet ("and this was typical," Piacenza told Angier), Levi was also unhappy. Bringing all those munitions back to the base had made him regret that men must take up arms against other men.[73]

As Piacenza finishes his tale yet another version of it occurs to me, this one Primo Levi's, from a radio conversation of 1983. This time the two young men are directed toward the town of Nus, not Chambave. And the weapons they find are neither a great arsenal nor a single gun; the spoils are even slighter than what Piacenza has told me today. "We set out, on foot obviously, by night, and we covered all those kilometers between Col de Joux and Nus, and then from Nus up to the barn, and we emptied out the barn (and that was a grueling job) in the midst of the snow, and we found a wooden cartridge clip, the kind you use in military drill. One. And because we were civilized people we replaced all the hay before we went back down the valley."[74]

As I gather up my notes and bid Aldo Piacenza farewell, trying to find a way to convey all my gratitude, I know I cannot take his words as the true story of true partisans. His memory is human, as memory is.

The war of Monferrato

History is written by the victors: the saying is a cliché, but it is not wrong. In the case of the Resistance, the more or less official reports on the actions of the partisan brigades, compiled after the Liberation by those brigades themselves, must undoubtedly be accepted with some reservations. The Resistance generated an enormous number of heroes and produced a broadly mythological story about their degree of political awareness and military preparation. But to criticize a myth is not to deny a reality: after September 8, 1943, there really were partisans in the hills. Were they no more than a few, poorly trained and poorly armed? All the more reason to credit them.

Just after the war, Guido Bachi wrote of his efforts to establish a partisan band at the Col de Joux, and like Piacenza he described serious problems recruiting enough members and gathering enough weapons. "During the month of October, the band remained small, about ten in number," he wrote. "We already had some weapons," but it continued to be difficult "to attract young people from the city and from the remains of the Royal Army." In those weeks, Bachi got word that "another band composed of folk from Casale Monferrato was shaping up a few kilometers away," at the Val d'Ayas hamlet of Arcesaz, near Brusson. And so Emilio Bachi was sent to "investigate how serious and effective they were." The group from Casale Monferrato, a small industrial city in the Monferrato district of Piedmont, amounted to some thirty partisans. Were they to join forces, the bands at Col de Joux and Arcesaz could be far more effective in battling the Nazi-Fascists.[75]

As Bachi told it in 1946, the rebels from Casale Monferrato had their command post "in a boardinghouse–tobacco shop" in the center of Arcesaz, and most of the band was positioned up on the mountains over the town.[76] Other documents confirm this, including the police records provided to the authorities of Salò after the capture of the rebels. The boardinghouse in question was an Arcesaz inn called the Croce Bianca, then as now located on the main road running through the valley.[77] Most of the band was lodged 250 meters higher up, away from the road, near the striking medieval castle of Graines. The castle still towers over Val d'Ayas.[78]

It seems the rebels of Casale Monferrato chose these hills because one of them, Francesco Rossi, lived with a woman who was a native of Arcesaz, and they owned a house nearby.[79] In any case, the Rossi brothers Francesco and Italo, thirty-one and twenty-nine years old respectively, along with their brother Bruno (seventeen) and father Oreste (fifty-five) were instrumental in transferring the nucleus of Casale Monferrato's Resistance some one hundred kilometers northeast to Valle d'Aosta. During the following twenty months the working-class Rossi family would pay a high price in blood for the cause and earn themselves a place in history.[80] Until the end of October, though, the Casale resistance was hardly detectable.[81]

But in the region of Piedmont, as elsewhere, things changed after the first military call-up ordered by the Republic of Salò, dated November 4 and made public a few days later. This was the first of the Graziani Draft Orders (named after Salò Minister of Defense Rodolfo Graziani), and after the draft order the situation hardened. The confusion and uncertainty that had followed the armistice, the collapse of the Italian state, and the arrival of German occupiers now gave way to a tight collaboration between Salò and the German forces. That led to a bitter struggle between die-hard Fascists and early partisans. The war of liberation from the Germans had begun, however tentatively, on September 8, but the civil war pitting Italian against Italian only really got its start at this point, two months later.[82]

When the draft order was issued, the ranks of the Fascists at Casale

Monferrato were at their lowest ebb. No more than 300 held party cards, as opposed to the 3,550 who had been members before Mussolini was ousted on July 25 that year.[83] Luciano Imerico, local commander of the Volunteer Militia for National Security, himself admitted that the militia, once the pride of the regime's military institutions, had no more than eight officers and twenty-two officials of lesser rank at its disposal.[84] But as the Social Republic regrouped its forces, the call to close ranks, back the Germans, and pitilessly pursue the traitors to the Italian nation sounded loud and clear. Draft dodgers—those young men born in 1923–25 who in huge numbers had failed to answer the November 4 call-up—had to be hunted down. The prefects of Salò were zealous in devising punishments, such as arresting the parents of draftees who didn't show up.[85] Soon Commander Imerico had dozens, then hundreds of young men coming forward to serve in the Republican Army or in the Republican National Guard, as the volunteer militia had been renamed.[86]

The threats from Salò, however, also turned some evaders into active resisters. In the district of Monferrato it was almost a given that young men reluctant to enlist under the Salò flag would rapidly move to the ranks of the partisans. It was fruitless for one of the prefects to denounce "a thorough and secret propaganda campaign" in the province, which supposedly was leading young men to desert by "inviting them instead to join groups of rebels"—a campaign, he said, backed by persons "possessing large sums of money" and promising "rich rewards."[87] The draft evaders were not selling their souls. Instead, the war in occupied Italy had already begun to evolve into a civil war.

On November 30, 1943, Ferdinando Morandi, an officer of the Republican National Guard stationed outside Casale, wrote to Imerico reporting a scene he had witnessed one night. The description, however modest, clearly foretold the coming war of Italian against Italian, never fiercer than when the adversaries were neighbors who knew and recognized one another, the enemy next door. On the night between November 25 and 26, Morandi wrote, "eleven subversive typewritten messages" were affixed to "the doors and walls of Republican Fascists" in Borgo San Martino. The suspected perpetrators? "Around 1 a.m. a red Fiat Topolino cruised slowly around the streets of the town for half an hour," and "the automobile was recognized as that of the Allara hauling firm of Casale Monferrato." Morandi had good reason to think that those in the car had put up the signs.[88]

A red Fiat Topolino cruising around a small town designating enemies one by one; a man of order—Nazi-Fascist order—who knows the firm that owns the car: we see here, in miniature, the great split that was beginning to divide Italians. The anti-Fascists of Casale hadn't limited themselves to that incident, in fact. Young people linked in one way or another to the Allara brothers, owners of the hauling company, had already begun to move back and forth between Casale on the plain and Arcesaz in the mountains, transporting rebels, food, and weapons. They were bringing young men avoiding conscription, as well as Allied prisoners of war (Englishmen, Australians, New Zealanders) who had fled from Italian camps after the eighth of September and did not want to be recaptured by Salò or Nazi forces. They brought provisions for the partisans in Val d'Ayas. They carried weapons, as many as they could, from the garrisons of the old Royal Army or the Republic of Salò.

Thanks to Imerico's investigative zeal we can reconstruct some of these comings and goings, at least as they were reported to police by Federico Barbesino, a draft evader (class of 1925) who took part in two or three expeditions before quarreling with the others, turning himself in to the Republican National Guard, and providing them with the names of his former rebel colleagues. The group had been meeting at a café near Piazza Castello, invited by one Giuseppe Carrera, a machinist. (Barbesino had met him at the machine shop where both had worked.) Sometimes Carrera would offer money—"a good day's pay"—to young men who were not only willing to ignore the draft call but ready to enroll in anti-Fascist activities. Barbesino said he had been offered a stack of thousand-lire notes to serve as driver of a small truck from Casale to an unnamed mountain village.[89]

In wartime, trucks had largely replaced automobiles for transporting people.[90] Carrera was nineteen years old, a draft evader himself (class of 1924) whose home on Via Mantova had become something like a head-quarters for the early resisters of Casale.[91] It was there that he had taken Barbesino "during the first ten days of November" to introduce him to the head of the expedition to the mountains, Italo Rossi. A few days later they met at the café and, "after spending a few hours together," went to the garage of the Allara brothers to load a Fiat-SPA 38 truck with food-stuffs, military overcoats and jackets, and arms and munitions, including a Tommy gun, three assault rifles, and a case of hand grenades. Thanks to a pass shown by Rossi at the guard post on the Po River, the men were able to cross and head toward the city of Ivrea, although it was now long past nightfall and the area was under curfew.[92]

About halfway there a priest signaled his presence by crossing the road as the truck approached, and after speaking to Rossi brought out five former English prisoners who jumped aboard. Just outside Ivrea, in front of a sawmill, the group met up with some fellow Casale natives. Barbesino recognized a couple of young men of Carrera's age, "who told us they had come to Ivrea to attack the carabinieri barracks but had put off the action because the sentry detail that they were in league with had not appeared." This second group of Casale rebels also had a truck, and they too were transporting English prisoners. By the time the two vehicles handed off the prisoners to a construction worker who was hid-ing runaways at his farmhouse, it was morning. Barbesino also informed police of another construction worker and two millers nearby who would supply the rebels with cash and 100 kilos of flour.[93]

Ivrea was not just any place on the road from Monferrato to the Valle d'Aosta. It was also home to the factory owned by Camillo Olivetti, who, according to Barbesino, had already donated "between 10,000 and 20,000 lire to the cause." These were hard times for Olivetti, however, a Jew hounded by the Germans, seventy-five years old and in poor health. Trained as an engineer and fluent in several languages, he was an unusual entrepreneur by any standards. Born in 1868, he had visited the United States in 1893 to meet Thomas Edison and learn about electric-powered industrial production. Back in Italy he founded a company in his native Ivrea and during World War I made high-quality aeronautic parts. In the 1920s, joined by his son Adriano, he started producing type-writers. A Socialist, Camillo ran factory schools for his workers, developed a strong research division for science and technology, and published reviews devoted to social and political questions until those were silenced by the regime. He would die in December 1943 and be buried in the Jewish cemetery of Biella, mourned by workers who rode their bicycles from Ivrea to his funeral, defying the pouring rain, the switchbacked mountain road, and the Wehrmacht.[94] Whether what the informer Barbesino told the authorities was true—that during the last months of his life, hiding from the Germans in the hills of Biella, Olivetti was still able to help the partisans with a generous donation—we have no way of knowing.

The men of Casale (so Barbesino's statement continues) then took off from Ivrea toward Arcesaz, where they arrived around 5 p.m. The Fiat went there directly, while the other truck, now carrying Italo Rossi and Carrera, stopped to rob the old Fascist headquarters before leaving Ivrea. But the haul was unspectacular: one typewriter, one calculating machine, one bicycle, "some fencing weapons," and one box of munitions. The following morning Carrera and Rossi drove the new recruits up to Graines, "the training camp for rebel forces." That afternoon Barbesino took the bus down the mountain and a train back to Casale.[95]

There is something poetic—or so it seems to me today, if I shed for a moment my role as historian—in small, epic deeds like those of the partisans of Casale in November of 1943. It was the dawn of the Resistance: when the partisans' activities were already dangerous and yet not grave and solemn but seemingly heedless and unself-conscious. Truly, as Primo Levi wrote, a Resistance still to be invented. A year later, Francesco Rossi, now head of a partisan division with the Socialists' Matteotti Brigade, would send a report to the Turin command describing the performance of the Arcesaz group in those early days in glowing terms: they were said to have accomplished some thirty-nine military actions and lost just one man, against some twenty dead "between Republicans and

Germans."[96] The truth seems to have been somewhat different: less a tale of invincible partisans and vanquished foes than a few risky adventures aboard a red Topolino or a Fiat-SPA 38.

Hunters of Jews

Commander Luciano Imerico was not merely a hunter of draft evaders, he was also a hunter of Jews. In Casale Monferrato, a handful of elderly men and women, many ailing, were all that remained of a flourishing nineteenth-century Jewish community that was rapidly shrinking: from 300 members in the 1920s, to 123 when the Racial Laws were imposed in 1938, to 79 in 1940, and no more than 30 by September 8, 1943.[97] Shopkeepers, housewives, retired teachers—such were the "well-known scoundrels" against whom the local Salò newspapers had mounted a brutal campaign[98] and whom the Republic of Salò's most eager functionaries could pursue following Police Directive Number Five. Not that the last Jews of Casale were hard to flush out. Those who remained in town, who hadn't even tried to hide elsewhere or flee to Switzerland, were of course the least combative and the weakest; they were already the "drowned" of Casale.[99]

Artom, Carmi, Fiz, Foà, Jaffe, Jarach, Levi, Morello, Raccah, Salmoni, Segre, Sonnino, Treves: the surnames of the nineteen Jews who would be arrested in Casale between February and April 1944—surnames we've already seen among some of the partisans in the mountains of Valle d'Aosta—go deep into Italy's history. These were families promised a future as Italians by the reformers of the Risorgimento, by the Italian state at unity in 1861, and by Fascism itself, and then consigned to their destiny as Jews by Salò and the Final Solution.[100] It was a fate Imerico did all he could to hasten, using the combined forces of the Republican National Guard and other Salò and German forces to draw the last Jews of Casale into a trap so that none could escape deportation.[101] And not only that; Imerico profited from his position as an agent for the insurance company Assicurazioni Generali to lay his hands on the property of the deported.[102]

On his return from Auschwitz, perhaps as early as 1946, Primo Levi wrote a first draft of "Argon," the ironic memoir of his Sephardic forebears in Piedmont that later would become the first chapter of *The Periodic Table*.[103] It was a work of Levi's imagination, not a factual account of his genealogical origins. Some of his "ancestors" were borrowed from close friends, and he made them into characters à la Calvino: nonexistent knights, cloven viscounts, barons in trees.[104] We would be wrong to read "Argon" literally and believe that relatives like great-grandfather "Nonô" Leônin and great-uncle Barbaricô really did come from Casale Monferrato. And yet Levi's pages are as good a place as any to begin to learn about Casale's tiny Jewish microcosm in the late nineteenth century and how the twentieth century destroyed it. "The little that I know about my forebears reminds me of these gases," writes Levi: like argon they were noble, inert, and rare. "It can hardly be by chance that all the deeds attributed to them, though quite various, have in common a touch of the static, an attitude of dignified abstention, a voluntary (or accepted) relegation to the margins of the great river of life."[105]

More combative than the last Jews of Casale during the autumn and winter of 1943 were those Italian and foreign Jews in Valle d'Aosta, near the Swiss frontier that promised salvation. But Switzerland would be a mirage for many who dreamed of crossing over.[106] As autumn gave way to winter, the Alpine passes grew ever more difficult to negotiate. And in the city of Aosta, Prefect Cesare Augusto Carnazzi was determined to show no mercy.

As in every city under the Salò regime, the prefecture of Aosta was responsible for all kinds of matters, military and political as well as social and economic. It had to cope with the fact that the Fascist Party of Salò enjoyed far less popular support than the one-time National Fascist Party, and it had to deal with the chaos that resulted when various repressive forces—the Guard, the Border Militia, the Italian SS—competed with one another instead of fighting united against the subversives. It also had to deal with perennially scant food supplies, a tottering transportation system, industries and tradesmen's shops that lacked supplies, and all the other problems that made daily life under Salò even more precarious than it had been during the final years of the Fascist regime.[107] You might even say there was something horrifically impressive about men like Carnazzi, raised in Il Duce's Italy, who remained steadfastly loyal to the cause even after the Germans arrived, when the agenda suddenly became an all-out war against the rebels and a merciless manhunt in search of Jews.

"Our dead await the supreme test of our courage Stop": Carnazzi, telegraphing the local authorities in Aosta province to urge maximum zeal in conscripting young men born in 1923–25, sounded even more Nibelungian than the Germans.[108] The reprisals for draft evasion that he ordered were harsh, but no harsher than those ordered by other Salò prefects in November and December 1943: the parents of evaders were to lose their business permits and ration cards, and they could be arrested themselves in place of the missing young men.[109] Carnazzi, however, seems to have been stricter in applying these penalties than other prefects. At the end of December, Mussolini himself urged Carnazzi to be less assiduous, suggesting that he "release, a few at a time and discreetly, the parents of draft evaders."[110] For the prefect of Aosta the reprisals were not merely to be threatened, they were concrete punishments.

Carnazzi was equally enthusiastic in pursuing Jews. Immediately after he was named prefect, he went to work ferreting out those Jews who had suddenly disappeared after September 8. To the authorities of Ivrea, he wrote seeking word on various Jewish employees at Olivetti. What had become of the engineer Riccardo Levi and his family, for example? They were not in Macerata, in Le Marche, where they had notified the authorities they intended to move. So where were they?[111]

Carnazzi was never able to solve that particular mystery. Today, we know that Riccardo Levi first took refuge in Issime, a mountain village in Valle d'Aosta, then hid his family at Torrazzo in the hills of Piedmont and went down to Turin himself to join the Resistance with the Partito d'Azione forces.[112] His experience was almost happy compared to that of other Jews who hid in the same valley. The Ovazza family, as we've already seen, was arrested at Hotel Lyskamm and murdered at Lake Maggiore. Remo Jona, a lawyer from Turin, also took refuge at Issime, where he had spent his holidays with his wife and children from the mid-1930s; it seemed natural to hide away there, where he considered he had quite a few friends.[113] The entire Jona family, however, was arrested by Italian police on December 7, 1943.[114] They were sent to the Aosta prison, then to the transit camp at Fossoli, then deported to Poland on the same train as Primo Levi, Luciana Nissim, and Vanda Maestro. Like Levi, Remo Jona would be among the "saved." But his wife, Ilka Vitale, and their two sons, twelve-year-old Ruggero and seven-year-old Raimondo, would not be. They were gassed at Auschwitz on February 26, 1944, the day of their arrival.

2

Part Partisan, Part Bandit

The spy

In a memorable passage from *If This Is a Man*, Primo Levi recites a verse from Dante's *Divine Comedy* to the Frenchman Pikolo. But just before that he shows us a brief flash of a figure walking past. "Frenkl the spy passes by. We quicken our pace, you never know; he does evil for evil's sake."[1] No more is said of Frenkl. The portrait of the camp spy is succinct: he is malevolent for no other purpose than malevolence itself. There is nothing to *understand* about the spy; merely pointing at him conveys everything.

Elsewhere in Levi's writings we find few indications of his thoughts on the moral and historical figure of the spy.[2] It's also unclear whether Levi thinks Frenkl was the only kind of spy that existed in the camp. Nevertheless, it's notable that this definition of the spy—someone who does evil for evil's sake—turns up again in *The Periodic Table* when Levi writes of Edilio Cagni, devoting an entire page to him among the four dedicated to the Resistance. "Cagni was the spy who had gotten us captured: a complete spy, in every ounce of his flesh, a spy by nature and tendency more than by Fascist conviction or for monetary gain; a spy who hurts, out of a kind of sporty sadism, as the hunter shoots free game."[3]

Cagni is a man we will come to know well for his crucial, his notorious role in the story of the partisans of Col de Joux. Thanks to the documents preserved in the archives, we will come to know far more about him than Primo Levi ever did, so much that it will be difficult to keep him within the bounds of the classical villain of the story. Yet after we have finally examined him at length, we will see that Cagni does correspond to the figure so vividly sketched by Levi: not a super-Fascist blinded by ideology or an opportunist motivated by personal gain, but a pure and disinterested hunter of human prey. A type of twentieth-century evil as portrayed by Kafka: evil unmoored from any moral or political calculus.[4]

The figure of the informer/spy has rarely been thoroughly explored in Resistance memory or by historians. Whether the informer was a local who denounced partisans to the Nazi-Fascist authorities or an outsider who infiltrated a group of partisans to destroy them, both memoirists and historians have been less interested in studying than in simply condemning the spy.[5] The communities where partisans operated have in turn been portrayed as almost entirely supportive of the rebels, marvelously cohesive in sharing their anti-Fascist beliefs and passions, and vulnerable only when evil—the diabolical action of a single corrupt element—intervened. It is a portrait too good to be true, especially when describing the first eight or nine months of the Italian Resistance, from autumn 1943 to spring 1944.

Those were difficult months indeed, when partisan bands were forever at risk of being denounced by villagers who struggled to accept the tangible and intangible costs of the partisan presence in their valleys: the animals and food supplies requisitioned, the casual way the young women of the villages were treated, the lack of respect for the priests, the pressures on young locals to join the rebels. The early rebel bands were also in danger of being infiltrated by agents of Salò, who took advantage of their still-loose military structure and political disorganization. Among the streams of drifter soldiers and draft-evading students and conscripts, it was often difficult to distinguish a double-dealing adventurer from one who was genuinely anti-Fascist.

Edilio Cagni was twenty-six years old in the fall of 1943. He boasted a degree in architecture and was a clever speaker, but his more immediate credentials in those first days of the civil war in Valle d'Aosta were military. He had trained for the army in 1940, served as a second lieutenant in Italy and France, and withdrew to Valle d'Aosta with the Italian troops from the latter post just after the armistice. He fled to avoid being captured by the Germans, then offered his services to the Social Republic via the Aosta Prefecture.[6] In *The Periodic Table* Levi would describe the spy who infiltrated the Casale partisans of Arcesaz as "about thirty, pallid and flabby-skinned."[7] Guido Bachi too remembered Cagni as pale, and of medium height. Although his "expression was guarded," he was "the sort of person who inspired trust."[8]

During those days after September 8, Cagni had made friends with two other drifters somewhat younger than he; they too were determined to seek their fortunes in the risky, equivocal world of collaborationism. Alberto Bianchi, twenty-three, from Florence, had also fled the army. He had lost his father in childhood (as had Cagni) and was penniless, clever, and unscrupulous.[9] Domenico De Ceglie was twenty-two, a Roman, also fatherless, and a deserter.[10] Half a century later Guido Bachi would recall De Ceglie as a fair-haired young man with delicate features and nice manners.[11] This apparently motley trio were destined to play a significant role as collaborators. Between the end of 1943 and the beginning of 1944, under the respective pseudonyms of Renato Redi, lieutenant, and Carlo Cerri and Mario Meoli, second lieutenants, the three would effectively act as secret police agents answering to Prefect Carnazzi.

The peculiar circumstances under which the Social Republic was born, following the dramatic collapse of the Fascist regime and the German occupation, meant that its repressive apparatus was a shady underground where the lines between the official forces of order and a broad variety of paramilitary, public, semipublic, and private police forces were never clearly drawn. All operated together and sometimes competed with one another.[12] Such circumstances help to explain how that trio headed by Cagni rose so rapidly inside the Valle d'Aosta secret police. According to a witness speaking after the Liberation, Cagni had earned his stripes as an informer early, when "after the eighth of September he traveled up and down the local valleys looking for groups of army deserters to report to Salò authorities."[13] Another postwar accuser said Cagni had tried to ensnare Lino Binel, one of the clandestine leaders of the early Valle d'Aosta Resistance. Pretending to be an officer loyal to Badoglio, Cagni had proposed to Binel they acquire weapons for the rebels.[14] Although Binel did not fall for the trap, his prudence did not save him from being arrested for smuggling arms in November that year, or from spending a month and a half in the Aosta jail.[15]

With such experience as an agent provocateur under his belt, Cagni was most likely feeling confident on the evening of December 5, 1943, when—along with Alberto Bianchi and with the blessing of Carnazzi—he prepared to climb the Val d'Ayas to infiltrate the Casale partisan band.

Arcesaz

When Cagni and Bianchi arrived in the town of Verrès, down the mountain from Arcesaz, on that December night, they were disposed to find trouble.[16] The next morning they walked the streets seeking information "on the whereabouts of the various rebel command posts" in the Val d'Ayas, rebels whose "presence in loco," Bianchi wrote in a subsequent report to the prefecture, was "notorious." In the Caffè dello Sport, the woman at the espresso machine asked the two if they wanted to join the partisans. She even introduced them to two other customers, who offered to take them the very next day to where the rebels of Casale Monferrato were lodged. Cagni said yes right away, while Bianchi found an excuse, for their plan was that he should return to Aosta that evening to report to Carnazzi. Then he would secretly return with the third spy, De Ceglie, who would offer some "Bolshevizing" propaganda material as proof of his rebel good faith.

The plan worked perfectly. Cagni climbed the Val d'Ayas on foot, escorted by "some elements" of the Casale band, arriving at the Croce Bianca inn in Arcesaz—where the Casale band had its headquarters— by lunchtime on December 7. Bianchi and De Ceglie appeared two days later in a tiny Fiat supplied by the prefect's office, with another "rebel element" aboard to serve as their guide. Thus the Casale partisans, utterly in the dark, joined forces with the enemy.[17]

In his report, Cagni described some of the assorted rebels at the Croce Bianca. Right away he picked out Giuseppe Sogno, draft evader (class of '24), as a "dangerous element." "The junior officer named Berto something" we too meet here for the first time; we shall hear more of him. The same man who would receive me nearly seventy years later at his home in Turin, Second Lieutenant Piacenza, was there, along with a fellow "with a shoulder wound from a musket" and a "rather badly" wounded Englishman. There was Carlo Eugenio Carretto, an elderly Communist printer who in Casale had been what passed for the founder of something like a National Liberation Committee. There were also two women: the wife of the injured man, and another rebel's wife from Casale.[18]

This nascent Resistance was a strange one, or in any case it was different from the Resistance of legend. It was a movement made up of comfortable meetings in town—at the Ristoro in Amay, the Caffè dello Sport in Verrès, the Croce Bianca in Arcesaz—rather than spartan gatherings in some mountain hut. A Resistance casually mixing men and women, young and old, soldiers and civilians, Italians and foreigners, anti-Fascists and opportunists, outright draft evaders and the merely reluctant. Among the Casale group, the Rossi brothers' political and military determination was certainly solid: they had brought the band together and had used Francesco Rossi's house to store their arms and munitions. But what about Giuseppe Barbesino, a fifty-year-old railway worker from a nearby town who was trying to wrest command from

Rossi? Was he less committed to the cause? According to a report signed by Bianchi, Barbesino appeared to be "the typical fake, a big talker, slick, no scruples."[19]

It would be absurd, of course, to rely unquestioningly on the opinions of spies like Cagni, Bianchi, and De Ceglie. Yet it would also be a mistake to ignore the ways in which a figure like Giuseppe Barbesino is at odds with Resistance legend. A veteran of World War I with the rank of carabinieri sergeant, he had fought with the dissident veterans against Mussolini's nascent Fascist party just after the war. When Il Duce came to power, Barbesino sold wine and cheese, then opened a bordello, later shut down by the authorities. Married with two children, he was expelled from the carabinieri, and his survival grew increasingly makeshift. On his police record were charges of threatening behavior, battery, attempted illegal expatriation, and bankruptcy. In February 1935, this future partisan petitioned to join the Fascist Party, volunteering to fight in East Africa as Mussolini prepared to go to war in Ethiopia. He was rejected for service on the basis of his "moral and political record."[20] For a man like Barbesino (and he was not alone), the Resistance was an unexpected chance for redemption, perhaps a last chance at life's roulette.

Even for men and women of Casale whose political motivations were much clearer than Barbesino's, the Resistance brought them up against a world very different from everyday life. Here, hierarchy meant *assuming* authority, rather than obeying, as under Mussolini. Resources were to be used sparingly, without seeking profit. The use of force was now legitimate, but it had to be distinguished from arbitrary use. Besides the risk inherent in being an "outlaw," there were all these new conditions to adjust to. Is it any surprise then that Cagni detected "a certain nervousness" among the partisans at Arcesaz, as soon as he set foot in the Croce Bianca?

Beyond conflicting personal ambitions, the members disagreed about how autonomous the Arcesaz group should be from the political forces (and covert financiers) down on the plain. In those first months, formations up in the mountains guided by one charismatic leader or another were often recalcitrant when "city folk," such as the Piedmontese National Liberation Committee, ordered them to follow the political and military strategy that had been worked out among Italy's main parties.[21] Partisan chiefs like the Rossi brothers were not inclined to take orders from some anti-Fascist emissary who'd come up on the bus from Casale or Turin.

Thus the Casale band was ready to implode even before meeting any pressure from outside. Cagni was bright enough to sense that and cunning enough to encourage it. Subtract the swaggering tone of the agent provocateur informing his superior, and his final report to Carnazzi offers a faithful portrait of an early resistance both courageous and naïve, energetic and fanciful. He describes the scene at the Croce Bianca the day he arrived in Arcesaz, December 7: "Armed with what information I'd been able to gain . . . I began, in the presence of all, to harshly criticize the way the camp was organized, and its leaders, knowing those leaders were present. I made it clear that I intended to abandon the group, who were more a bunch of buffoons than rebels, in my opinion." Those present, he wrote, "were captivated by my words." And so he continued his critique "until the rebels decided that I should be commander of the Graines camp," where the band slept near the medieval castle.[22]

Cagni was not just boasting. Other sources, including those from the partisan side,[23] confirm that within a few hours of his arrival in Arcesaz the informer had been handed military control of the Graines camp— or, as he wrote, "some 70 men 20 Englishmen 5 automatic rifles 6 Beretta machine guns some 30 rifles numerous pistols and bombs three vehicles food stocks and clothing." Only Francesco Rossi, the elder brother, really fought Cagni's ascendency. "That same day there was a spirited and decisive discussion," at which "of course Rossi" was present. "Reluctantly he yielded the command of the camp to me, although not before threatening to kill me (something he vowed more than once). We arranged that I would go to his house to take charge of the weapons and clothing stored there. I went that day to Graines where the rebels were based and was introduced to them as their new commander."[24]

No roof, no rules

The Casale group was lodged in the elementary school in Graines,[25] a fact that in itself suggests how problematic the presence of a partisan band in a small Alpine community could be. The town had a total of two hundred residents, and the rebels, between Italians and foreigners, numbered nearly a hundred. Coexistence wasn't easy, especially since schools were open that autumn, and the children of Graines, up to grade three, were attending classes.[26] Evidently the rebels relied on the locals for assistance; the Graines elementary school teacher, for example, somehow failed to inform the authorities of the Social Republic that dozens of men with weapons were camped out on the second and third floors of the school building. Others were not so obliging.

"This may be hard to believe, but it wasn't only the Germans who were trouble; it was certain individuals who would force us to give them food, clothing, woolen socks, and other things," recalled the Amay native Alice Coronel. To listen to her, in the autumn of 1943 the partisans, those freedom fighters, were browbeating the local inhabitants in every way, demanding their butter, stealing their salt. "I can't forget and I can't forgive them!"[27] Nor were things much more peaceful on the other side of the mountain ridge. According to Claudio Manganoni, a Communist militant and leader of a band active in the Val d'Ayas in 1944, the partisans often used "coercive means" to force themselves on the people of local villages, who were "almost entirely antipartisan."[28] In those Alpine valleys, another partisan recalled, the locals were deaf to politics and reasoned as poor people, with an instinctive, desperate avarice.[29] The rebels reasoned as tough guys: if you don't give me what I need, I'll be forced to take it.[30] In a time of scarce resources, it was reasonable for locals to see the outsiders as unwelcome mouths to feed, and under the regime of fear that came with the German occupation it would have been strange indeed if they did not perceive the partisans as a source of hardship and danger.

But even before they dealt with the mountain dwellers of Valle d'Aosta, the partisans of Casale had to deal with their own people on the plain. There were a hundred kilometers of roads between their home-town and the villages of the Val d'Ayas, and in occupied Italy that first autumn this meant supply and logistical problems that left traces. From what we know of the rebels' travels back and forth in November and December, their behavior evolved rapidly. In early November, they traveled to Arcesaz as if they were friends on an adventurous outing: there was that helpful priest who asked them to take the ex-POWs, the millers and masons who gave them cash. A few weeks later, those trips were markedly different.

The Salò manhunt for draft evaders had changed the political climate in the district of Monferrato that December, and hardened the opposition. "No heads will remain attached to necks": a leaflet distributed on the night of December 8 threatened to murder the entire Nazi-Fascist establishment, and singled out Luciano Imerico, the commander of the Republican National Guard, as the head villain among "those brutes dressed as guards" who were going to pay with their lives.[31] Deeds were even more expressive. By mid-November the Allara brothers and their hauling company, under cover of orders to pick up and deliver goods in Valle d'Aosta—supplies for the Cogne steel works, manure for farms around Vercelli—were loading their trucks with weapons and munitions for the Arcesaz band.[32] The railway station diner had become the main collection point for rebels on their way to Val d'Ayas.[33] And those rebels would let nothing stand in their way.

The confessions that Commander Imerico subsequently obtained from a couple of participants on those trips allow us to follow their tracks in detail and see how their casual early outings evolved into more organized raids. The Allara brothers' vehicles were soon insufficient to transport both war materials and draft evaders up to the mountains, and the rebels had to procure other vehicles and automobiles in summary fashion. For the most part just eighteen or nineteen years old, they were not only immature in terms of age but also inexperienced as fighters: their path from civilian to partisan life had included no intermediate step of military preparation.[34] Young men armed from one day to the next, with no barracks, no sergeants, no captains to obey, they were exhilarated by their new way of life, by the inebriating sense that they had no roof over their heads and no rules limiting their freedom.

On the evening of December 5, 1943, four such young men left a town in Monferrato, headed for Arcesaz via Casale. Two were draft evaders: Giuseppe Villata, nineteen, and Fulvio Oppezzo (he called himself Furio), who was eighteen. Along with them was Eligio Costelli, a delivery boy and at twenty-three the most experienced of the group. The fourth, recorded as "il Torinese," is still unidentified today; he may have been Luciano Zabaldano from Turin, who was just over seventeen. The four forced a hauling company owner to take them to a religious sanctuary at Serralunga di Crea. There, "waving their weapons," they forced the proprietor of a hired-car lot to take them to Casale, where they arrived around 10 p.m.[35]

That was but the first step. The following day the four met Giuseppe Carrera, the draft evader whose home on Via Mantova in Casale had for months now been a center of operations in the battle against the Nazi-Fascists. They would depart for Arcesaz that evening, Carrera told them, and procure a van from a man who owned a laundry on Via del Carmine. Around 7 p.m., the group (now including Federico Barbesino, who would confess all to Imerico when arrested) knocked on the man's door, but he said the van's engine was malfunctioning. So the young men, along with some others, perhaps eleven in all, decided to take the first truck they could find. They spotted one parked on a nearby street in front of a garage and, their faces disguised by scarves, hijacked it, threatening the driver with weapons drawn (some of the rebels had submachine guns). Just then another truck arrived to park in the garage; the rebels decided to grab that too. "Having immobilized the drivers, they demanded oil and two sets of blankets." By now it was 8:30 in the evening.[36]

What happened next says much about the nascent resistance of Casale, whether more picaresque or gangsteresque it is hard to say. As the masked men were about to depart, the driver of the second truck "wished them a good trip" and said, "Boys, take care, and let's hope nothing bad ever happens to you." It seems the hijacking was more like a forcible loan in the rebels' minds. The Salò police even recorded that "the perpetrators, as they were leaving, told the driver that if all went well he could recover his vehicle in two or three days . . . near his domicile." Now they were finally in motion, Barbesino at the wheel. Carrera "insisted they speed," although the truck was "old and defective." On the way it overturned, but no one was hurt. Now experienced hijackers, the partisans seized a Fiat van and a small car, and drove them to Val d'Ayas. They arrived in Arcesaz on the afternoon of December 7, at the same time that Edilio Cagni was taking charge of the Graines camp.

The historian Roberto Battaglia, in a fine memoir of his partisan days, described "the urge to be an outlaw" as one of the factors driving the early Resistance. There was "an early, and necessary, spirit of 'anarchy'"—a spirit politically motivated for those rebels who were best educated or most thoughtful, while for others it was a vague yearning for a new kind of freedom or greater justice.[37] Battaglia's observation remains useful and can help us understand more about the young men of Casale going back and forth between Monferrato and Val d'Ayas, teenagers who had abruptly turned their backs on the Fascist upbringing that all (or nearly all) of them had received and had chosen to be outlaws even before they were partisans. Bandits, in short: that was what the Germans and Salò officials called them.

Some may have considered themselves Communists—including apparently Giuseppe Carrera and Giuseppe Sogno, who had been influenced by a charismatic veteran Communist named Mario Acquaviva, an apostate of the official Italian Communist Party and leader of the local Internationalist Communist forces.[38] But often the youth of Monferrato who went up to Val d'Ayas seem to have been motivated more by that anarchic spirit, and of course by the desire to escape punishment for evading the Salò draft. "We need your truck urgently; we have very little time because we have to get to Valle d'Aosta before 5 a.m. tomorrow or we'll all be shot": according to police records, that's what one armed rebel said to the laundry owner that night of December 6, before they learned that his truck was out of commission.[39]

That spirit certainly motivated Fulvio Oppezzo, the eighteen-year-old who styled himself "Furio." His long wild night began on December 5, during the first ride to Serralunga di Crea, and continued the following evening. Nothing about Fulvio/Furio suggested a destiny as an anti-Fascist. His grandfather, Marcello Oppezzo, was known in the 1930s as a loyal Fascist, first commissary and then *podestà* (the appointed mayor) of Cerrina Monferrato, a town with some 2,000 inhabitants.[40] Fulvio's father, Ugo Oppezzo, was a low-ranking officer in the blackshirts, who served as president of the local branch of the Opera Nazionale Dopolavoro, the Fascist leisure organization, before he went to fight in the war in Ethiopia.[41] Fulvio himself, in addition to the Fascist air he breathed at home, had all the preparation to become a right-thinking young man: he was schooled by the Somascan Fathers at the Collegio Trevisio in Casale and then by the Military Academy in Milan.[42]

Had any of his teachers seen him in dark of night, machine gun in hand, menace those Monferrato drivers, they would have been hard-pressed to make out the delicate features behind his bandanna. Just a few months ago, this same young man had inscribed "Fulvio to his dearest mother" on a photo of himself in a second lieutenant's uniform. Fulvio-become-Furio was as surprising a figure as the other young men who shocked a school principal in Casale, astonishing him with their abrupt and unforeseen metamorphosis: "The young people had changed: it seemed they no longer felt anything for the Nation or Il Duce."[43]

It was the virulent Salò press campaign against the draft evaders of 1923–25, not to mention the authorities' harsh repressive measures, that drove young men like Oppezzo into hiding or into the arms of the rebels. In an article entitled "Cowards," a Casale paper described a group of women crowding the hallway of a carabinieri barracks: the mothers of draft evaders waiting to be taken to prison. The newspaper denounced their sons as "spoiled brats" who were interested only in film stars and sports champions, numbskulls under their greasy manes. These were the boys who would let their mothers go to jail in order to escape conscription. "Anything is possible for an eighteen-year-old," the paper fulminated—"errors, wildness, even revolt, but not this supreme cowardice: to allow one's own mother to be taken hostage, or worse, to pay for a pointless, phony liberty."[44]

The tightening noose

Some Fascists in Casale Monferrato, of course, also accused the Jews—those last few Jews in town—of encouraging draft evasion. In a report sent to the Salò authorities, one informer attributed the vehicle thefts in Casale to young Italians greedy for "easy income" from "Jews cursed by God" who pressed them into "endless treason against the Nation." The most ferociously anti-Semitic among them argued that it was time to begin "immediately concentrating all Jews" in places where they could be kept under strictest surveillance and rendered harmless.[45]

In his own way, Prefect Carnazzi subscribed to this view. In a memo dated December 12, he underlined a connection between various antipatriotic activities and a company that was particularly important to the local economy, that of "the Jew Camillo Olivetti." True, Olivetti himself had just died, but the company remained dangerous, Carnazzi wrote, because it was successful and locally accepted. "Despite the excellent Aryan camouflage, it lives and prospers (and does it prosper!) in a milieu and using methods that are decidedly Jewish." "A great deal of Olivetti money" had been spent secretly expatriating Jewish refugees to Switzerland, and the company gave financial support to army deserters and rebels. Even worse, he wrote, there was a direct link between that capitalist enterprise of Ivrea and the most insidious political movement in the Valle d'Aosta, because "the fulcrum and center-point of Communism in this province can be said with absolute certainty to be found in Olivetti."[46]

Carnazzi's invective reflected more than his personal anti-Semitism and anti-Communism. Although the history of Olivetti during the twenty months of German occupation is still largely to be written, we already know that a young Internationalist Communist could knock at Olivetti's doors and then boast of receiving donations of 10,000 or 20,000 lire. And we have also glimpsed more intimate links between Olivetti and the Valle d'Aosta resistance: the partisan Alimiro (the Olivetti draftsman Mario Pelizzari) watching from the hills in the days of the armistice, or the engineer Riccardo Levi, first a refugee in Valle d'Aosta, returning to the underground in Turin after hiding his wife and children in the mountains.

Carnazzi was not wrong to see hunting for Jews and hunting for partisans as two sides of a coin. On December 7—the same day that Edilio Cagni infiltrated the Casale band—the head of the Salò Fascist Party in Aosta reported to Carnazzi that "a group of so-called patriots" was lodged near Arcesaz, both at the Col de Joux and at Amay. He was referring to the men under Guido Bachi's command sheltered in the Frumy huts and those at Amay's Hotel Ristoro. According to local reports, those bandits ("all are armed") were financed by various "Israelites" from Ivrea.[47] Was that not enough to make further investigations necessary? Two days later, when Lieutenant Redi, alias Edilio Cagni, welcomed to Arcesaz his two spy accomplices, he took the first chance that arose to send "second lieutenant Meoli"—De Ceglie—to infiltrate the Amay group on the other side of the Col de Joux pass.[48]

The noose was now tightening around both partisan groups: the large band from Casale at Arcesaz, and the tiny one from Turin at Amay that included Guido and Emilio Bachi, Aldo Piacenza, Primo Levi, and a few others. For the police the first group, the large band that was "daily" reinforced with "new elements" and was beginning to take control of the valley, was obviously the priority. On December 9, the commander of the Aosta State Forestry Militia warned Carnazzi that rebels were by now openly threatening forest rangers, who were unable to respond because there were no Salò police or army forces anywhere in the Val d'Ayas.[49] The forestry commander was unaware that Carnazzi had already deployed his three infiltrators and was preparing to take action.

Meanwhile the Casale band and the little group from Turin had begun to cooperate, following the day when Emilio Bachi had trekked over the pass to measure how serious and well-organized the group at Arcesaz was. Between the end of November and early December their contacts had become "cordial and quite frequent," Guido Bachi would later recall. They "exchanged members in major actions, and shared weapons and the supervision of elements . . . distrusted by their companions."[50] The fact that Cagni, upon arriving at the Croce Bianca in Arcesaz on December 7, found at least two members of the Amay band there— Piacenza and the junior officer named Berto—serves as confirmation of the intensifying contact. Another confirmation: on the evening of December 8, two members of the Casale group—Fulvio Oppezzo and Luciano Zabaldano—were in the company of the Amay band.[51]

If documents supplied after the Liberation are correct, Oppezzo and Zabaldano had reached the Val d'Ayas just after the eighth of September. Oppezzo was supposed to have been active in the Casale band from September 10, while Zabaldano was supposed to have joined on September 20.[52] Such retrospective sources—in this case the official rolls of partisan activists compiled after the war—often stretched the truth. It is possible that in fact Oppezzo and Zabaldano only arrived in the Val d'Ayas for the first time on December 7, still intoxicated by their brazen night of banditry. Significantly, while numerous Arcesaz partisans, including Carrera, Sogno, and Barbesino, appear in police records as early as November, Oppezzo and Zabaldano do not show up before December 6, suggesting they first reached the province of Valle d'Aosta around that date.

Oppezzo would reappear as a villain in Salò police records in the following months. In January 1944, Commander Imerico labeled him a "fugitive" in an account of subversive actions that had been carried out by the rebels in the autumn of '43.[53] In February 1944, *La Stampa* identified Oppezzo as one of two thieves who had stolen 150,000 lire from a farmer near Casale, but reassured readers that both thieves "have been arrested by the Republican Guard."[54] A week later the paper corrected itself: not only had the suspicions regarding the two not been confirmed, but "they were never arrested."[55]

It would have been difficult indeed for Fulvio Oppezzo to have robbed anyone that February day, for he had been shot dead, along with Luciano Zabaldano, in the early morning of December 9, 1943. The two were the very first victims of the Resistance in Valle d'Aosta. But they did not die under attack from German or Salò forces. They lost their lives to their own companions near the huts of Frumy.

The Soviet method

We have come to the "ugly secret," the one that Primo Levi guarded within himself for more than thirty years, only revealing it, unasked, in 1975 in a few spare pages of his most autobiographical book. "Conscience had compelled us to carry out a sentence, and we had carried it out, but we had come away devastated, empty, wanting everything to finish and to be finished ourselves."[56]

Pronouns are crucial in Levi's writing. There is the plural *you*, which may be quite specific, or broadly general, as in the Biblical-sounding verse that prefaces *If This Is a Man*: "You who live safe / In your warm houses, / You who find, returning in the evening, / Hot food and friendly faces . . ."[57] There is the all-important *we*, important not only for how it designates inclusion or exclusion but also for how it oscillates, resonates, or conflicts with the *I*. There is the *we* of the Lager survivor that Levi adopted for a lifetime, as in the text entitled "To the Visitor," with its wonderful, many-faceted use of the first person plural, written by Levi in 1978 for the Italian pavilion at Auschwitz.[58] And there is the significant *we* used by Levi on those rare occasions when he wrote as a veteran (and a survivor) of the Resistance.

When it comes to the ugly secret, *we* suggests that on the thirtieth anniversary of Liberation, Levi wanted to assume, publicly, his share of a collective responsibility. Whatever had happened somewhere between the inn at Amay and the huts of Frumy in those twenty-four hours between December 8 and 9, 1943—whatever decision-making process had led to a death sentence for Oppezzo and Zabaldano, immediately put into effect—Levi used *we* to signify: I, too, pronounced that sentence; I, too, carried it out. Although more than thirty years had passed, Levi knew that a public confession of such a secret might raise questions not only about himself but about the other partisans of Amay. About people such as Guido Bachi, to whom Levi sent a copy of *The Periodic Table* with a note of dedication: "With friendship and the hope you can condone my reference to a scrap of our past."[59]

It is now the turn of professional historians to reconstruct, as far as possible, the scrap Levi was courageous enough to mention in 1975, and about which he wrote no more than those few lines in his memoir. What led the partisans to apply an unwritten martial law to eighteen-year-old Fulvio Oppezzo and seventeen-year-old Luciano Zabaldano? Who physically carried out the sentence? What exactly took place in the preceding days and hours? How did it happen that the Amay band—which before December 9 had never undertaken any important Resistance actions, and which would be easily broken up and defeated four days later—came to shed the blood of two of their companions?

That Italian partisans sometimes eliminated members of their own ranks, for various reasons and for causes more or less serious, has long been a taboo subject among historians, although it was featured in fiction about the Resistance as far back as the 1950s. But most partisan formations had no way to hold prisoners. They did not have the material or institutional structures that would let them punish by detention rather than by execution. Enemy prisoners, Salò or German military men captured by the partisans, actually had better chances of surviving, because they could be exchanged for partisans held by the other side. But for a member of a partisan band considered guilty of unpardonable crimes, a death sentence was often the sole practicable solution, if only to prevent the wayward comrade—if pardoned—from betraying the band to its enemies.[60] The literature of the Resistance contains a number of such harsh and dramatic accounts of partisans shot by their own side. Beppe

Fenoglio's story "Old Blister" is one such unforgettable tale; another is Saverio Tutino's "Morti Male."[61]

From the little the archives contain about the deaths of Oppezzo and Zabaldano, there does not appear to have been any preparatory phase, such as a trial. Nor does it seem they were told they'd been sentenced to die, or solemnly escorted to their place of execution. The two were not forced to sit "on a stool beside the wall" as was Old Blister in Fenoglio's story, "facing a row of innocent, angry partisans" accusing him of theft. They were not marched away from the huts at Frumy "with the hobbled pace of men following a funeral," dogs barking and chains rattling. They were not taken to a clearing where the partisans lined up double file, "like people waiting to watch a game of bocce"; nor were they given time to hope that this was all a sham, a mock execution arranged to frighten them.[62] Instead, Oppezzo and Zabaldano were shot by what once was called "the Soviet method"—suddenly and without warning. ("This is the most humane method," thought Emanuele Artom at Val Infernetto, writing in his diary, as it happened, on the same day. "It avoids the anguish of knowing that the end is inevitable, and never mind that the condemned man is unable to prepare himself and express his last wishes."[63])

Nearly everything I have been able to learn about the circumstances in which Oppezzo and Zabaldano died is contained in the interrogation report of Aldo Piacenza from January 11, 1944, a month after the event. He and others were questioned by the Salò police after the partisans from Casale and Turin were captured on December 13. Edilio Cagni himself led the investigation with the assistance of Alberto Bianchi and Domenico De Ceglie. In other words, the very same spies who had entrapped Piacenza, Guido Bachi, Primo Levi, and others not only captured them but added insult to injury by also conducting the interrogations. These circumstances alone are enough to tell us that the report of Piacenza's questioning must be used cautiously. There were many reasons why a captured partisan might not want to tell the truth, or want to tell only partial truths.

Still, here is what Piacenza told the police had happened to the "two elements," who are not named but are certainly Oppezzo and Zabaldano. "On Thursday the 9th I went to Amay early in the morning and Berto told me how the two young men had behaved the night before, the way they acted and some things they said: 'we want to be like the guys at Arcesaz'; 'we want to get the stuff we need on our own by force'; 'if you don't let us do what we want we'll shoot you'; 'even if you try to detain us we'll escape and denounce you.' As a result, Berto was forced to eliminate them. He told me he disarmed them and made them leave the hut, and when they were about 100m to 150m away he shot and killed them with a blast of Beretta machine gun fire. He also told me he recovered some documents and personal effects from the bodies which he intends to send to the families."[64]

The details of Piacenza's account to the Salò police sound anything but plausible. For example, it's hard to imagine that the decision to eliminate the two "elements" could have been made by the man called Berto entirely on his own initiative, without consulting Piacenza himself or Guido Bachi—the band's military leader and its political leader, respectively. It seems much more likely that it was made collectively, if not by means of a trial—which was how partisan justice would begin to function later, in 1944[65]—then at least jointly by the most respected members of the group, once again Piacenza, the two Bachi brothers, and perhaps Primo Levi. That the decision was collective seems to be confirmed (morally—certainly not legally) by Levi's use of that weighty "we" in *The Periodic Table*.

And who was "Berto," the man who supposedly carried out the sentence? It could have been Emilio Bachi, who was in effect third in charge at the Col de Joux band thanks to his age, political maturity, and military experience, and who later in the Resistance would take on the nom de guerre of "Bertolani."[66] Or it could have been Emilio's brother, Guido. Or it might perhaps have been Aldo Piacenza himself, after his own capture attributing the executions to a real partisan named Berto because he knew the latter had escaped.

Graves at Frumy

Whoever it was, that morning of December 9, who shot Oppezzo and Zabaldano Soviet-style in the snow outside the huts of Frumy, I do not think this story's heart of darkness lies there. And certainly I, as historian of these partisans, have no desire to be some small-time Conrad on the trail of a Kurtz in Valle d'Aosta. Seventy years after the death of two young men left Primo Levi and his companions "wanting everything to finish and to be finished ourselves," the last thing that matters to me is to posit some judicial finding about who pulled the trigger.

What does matter is to make sense of the severity of a punishment that the partisans of Col de Joux can only have arrived at after searching their consciences, but which the historical sources at our disposal suggest was out of proportion to whatever crimes had been committed. It would be too much to say the two were killed for trivial reasons, assuming anything Aldo Piacenza told the Salò police was true. Those threats to shoot other members, escape, and denounce the group were probably enough to justify draconian measures. Nothing in the archives, however, proves that Oppezzo and Zabaldano ever actually did anything worse than the Casale band did routinely during their raids between the plain and the Val d'Ayas.

Let us listen again to Piacenza responding to questions about the deaths of the two young men. Whether Oppezzo and Zabaldano had arrived at Frumy for the first time the day before they died or had been in the area for a while, it does seem to be true that they came up from the plain on the evening of December 8, "boasting of Communist beliefs, and, it seemed, determined to act thoughtlessly." Piacenza went on: "They told me of some of their adventures. They said they had 8 kg of flour that they intended to donate to the group at Frumy, and that they had managed to get some cash from people in Saint-Vincent."[67]

On December 8, Oppezzo and Zabaldano thus told Piacenza (was Primo Levi present?) of their exploits on the plain. Then they left the Hotel Ristoro for what they didn't know would be the last night of their lives, and climbed up the valley to Frumy to meet their destiny the following morning. Piacenza, for his part, traveled to the other side of the Col de Joux pass, toward Brusson. Going to the chalet where Guido Bachi was lodged, he told him "about this thing"—that is, about the nasty developments involving Oppezzo and Zabaldano. "I ate with him and spent the night there." Early the next morning Piacenza returned to Amay, where he met Berto, who told him what had happened at Frumy: the high-handedness of the two young men, their threats to prey on the villagers, their threats against the others in the group—to shoot, to escape, to denounce. Berto recounted how the two had been disarmed, either by force or by guile. Then the exit from the hut, those 100, 150 meters, the spray of bullets from the Beretta.[68]

Decades later, Primo Levi's sister, Anna Maria, added a small speck of memory to this scrap of history. It was indirect memory, perhaps something told her by Primo, for Anna Maria was not at Amay on December 9; she and her mother had left for the plain a few days earlier. Asked how Vanda Maestro and Luciana Nissim, the two young Jewish women who were together with Levi at the Ristoro, had felt about the execution of the partisans, Anna Maria said that "Luciana and Vanda had been made to leave" temporarily.[69] This too, perhaps, is evidence that the deaths were not decided on the spot by Berto, that even the Soviet method demanded some organization, some coordination of people and movements between the Frumy huts and the hotel at Amay.

In the late autumn of 1943, one of the denizens of the Hotel Ristoro was a nineteen-year-old carpenter and Salò draft evader, a young man always welcome there because he was the nephew of the managers, Eleuterio Page and Maria Varisellaz. He was Yves Francisco, born in France, son of anti-Fascist emigrants from Verrès. He had climbed to Amay not only to escape conscription but because he loved to ski through the woods and clearings up there. One afternoon in December 2010, I knocked on his door in a tidy building in the new section of Verrès to hear what he, too—now a surprisingly youthful and vigorous eighty-six-year-old—had to say. I knew Francisco had been arrested in the police raid on December 13, along with Primo Levi and his two women friends. My intention was to interview him about that raid and other matters, particularly the deaths of Oppezzo and Zabaldano. At that point in my research I was quite obsessed by the "ugly secret," and it seemed to me indispensable to resolve the mystery, the way the police resolve some criminal enigma.

An ex-student of mine, Erika Diemoz, a native of the area, had helped me make the appointment, calling Francisco to announce that a professor of history at the University of Turin would be coming to see him. Erika and I went to meet Francisco together. She, too, was a student of history, and she was curious to meet him; we also thought that the presence of someone local might put this former partisan more at ease. And in fact, after he invited us into his kitchen and introduced us to another elderly gentleman, also an ex-partisan from nearby, Francisco was eager to talk. Not only about Amay in December 1943, but about Valtournenche in 1944, his summer in Cogne, Switzerland in 1945, France when he was a boy . . .

I took three pages of notes in tiny script. The days are short in December, and when Francisco accompanied us to the door, it was pitch-dark outside.

But Francisco's memory—and his was excellent—provided no answers to my questions about the circumstances under which Oppezzo and Zabaldano were shot. (Nor could he shed any light on the mysterious Berto.) Did the two young men extort money? Yes, they had hit up someone in Saint-Vincent, but he could not remember the details. Had everyone at Amay, including Primo Levi, agreed that the two should be sentenced to death? Here I must quote my notes: "YF feels unable either to affirm or deny that PL was involved in the decision to execute the two young men for disciplinary reasons." Had they been executed according to the Soviet method? Yes, most likely they were shot in the back. Had they been buried up there on Col de Joux? My notes: "He says he recalls that two graves were dug near Frumy, and that their relatives went to recover their remains."

A reliable memory did not assist Aldo Piacenza either when we met at his home in Turin in November 2011. He spoke of "a couple of members of a nearby band" who had "become morally derailed and began to be gangsters, they were holding people up . . . this is probably why they sent them away, they sent them up to us, and this may be how the Fascists came to find us, to arrest us." While Piacenza thus followed Primo Levi's logic in *The Periodic Table*—the notion that the two undisciplined young men from the Arcesaz group were tightly connected to the arrest of the Amay band—he did not mention the missing link: the execution of the two that took place between those acts of extortion on the plain and the police raid of December 13. And who was Berto? Piacenza, in 2011, recalled nothing, but he did not rule out the possibility that the name had been invented to confuse the police of Salò.

It was pointless, I concluded, to seek to know more from the last survivors of the band. Pointless to scour their memories in hopes of confessions that they could not or did not wish to make. Decades after the events, was it not their right to declare "I don't remember"? And memory, after all—is it not a marvelous but flawed instrument? Thanks to the kindness of Emilio Bachi's daughter in Turin, I was able to read an autobiographical sketch that her father had circulated in the family in the 1980s, when the ex-partisan was at the end of his career as an attorney of civil law. But as for what happened at Frumy I found only a single line, both telling and elliptical: "Up on Colle [the Col de Joux pass] the boys spent their time shooting or going out to raid supplies from the farmers."[70]

Primo Levi's memory was also selective. In an interview from 1973, the chemist-writer told a young friend, high school student Marco Pennacini, how the band that settled at the castle of Graines ("I don't know whether you have ever seen it . . . there are the ruins of a castle there") in autumn 1943 was far more enterprising than the one grouped around "the miniscule town of Amay." The people at Graines "had weapons, trucks, and everything; they were part partisan, part bandit." In this account, Levi considered the rebels of Casale directly responsible for the raid on his own group. "They provoked a huge manhunt in the entire valley, and of course we were captured too. [The militia] came from both sides. But they [the Casale rebels] escaped; they didn't get caught."[71] Levi said nothing about the secret he would soon record in *The Periodic Table*, or anything about any connection between the death sentence that left the Amay partisans feeling devastated and their capture four days later.

In a 1981 interview Levi spoke even more sharply about the Casale rebels in the Val d'Ayas, and even less accurately. "Near Brusson there was the band led by Piero, and they were a disgrace to the Resistance, a bunch of bandits who were in the movement for personal gain; they had assaulted the Ivrea militia barracks in November '43 and got away with a lot of equipment. The Fascists organized a raid to get them, and they had three hundred men combing the valley, and they found us."[72] Piero Urati, a Veneto-born rebel known in the Piedmontese Resistance by the nom de guerre Piero Piero, was indeed an ambiguous figure, a rough-neck whose behavior was on the edge of criminal. And it is true that as of spring 1944 he was linked to the Casale rebels, who regrouped to the east in the upper Canavese after Arcesaz fell.[73] But during that previous autumn Urati was a prisoner of the Germans in Turin, and therefore could not have been leading the group Levi refers to.[74]

In short, even in the case of a man like Primo Levi, a man who made a chemist's precision the model of his life and thought,[75] memory does not necessarily yield the materials of history. The last word about the irreparable punishment meted out to Oppezzo and Zabaldano for having confused adventure with banditry, and banditry with the parti-san fight—that last word cannot be based on autobiographies, or inter-views, or the confidences of ex-partisans of Amay. Nor may the historian elect himself as judge of the actors in his story, even when his recon-struction and interpretation of events lead him to think their reactions were out of proportion to the crime.

Still, a few words uttered by Yves Francisco—those "two graves dug near Frumy"—lead us to imagine a last scene, that of the burials. And here the historian can turn again to the literature of the Resistance. Not to accounts of the ceremonies connected with partisans felled by the enemy, the scrupulous efforts the rebels made to give their companions killed by the Nazi-Fascists a proper service, but to the stories (rarer, of course) of partisans killed by their own side, condemned to death by their companions yet still held worthy of a decent burial. As the witnesses of Amay are silent, the historian may perhaps be permitted to cite one of the most acute literary portraits of partisans settling scores among themselves: the killing of the hawk Babeuf in Italo Calvino's *The Path to the Spiders' Nests*. Babeuf, mascot and member of the band, the feathered rebel struck down by his own master in a moment of crisis, is buried by Pin, the child rebel.

Perhaps, while they were digging those two graves for Fulvio Oppezzo, eighteen, and Luciano Zabaldano, seventeen, in the December snow of Frumy, the partisans—we don't know who, or how many, but there can't have been many if Primo Levi said they were only eleven in all[76]—perhaps they gazed down at the great landscape of Valle d'Aosta beneath them. And maybe they were thinking something like what Pin was thinking as he buried Babeuf.

> He feels an impulse to fling the hawk into the great empty space above the valley and see its wings open, then watch it rise in flight, circle above his head, and fly off toward a distant peak. And then he would follow it as they do in fairy stories, walking over mountains and plains until he reached an enchanted land where all the inhabitants were good. But instead Pin now puts the hawk down into the grave and rakes earth over it with the handle of the spade.[77]

3

A Snowy Dawn

Dancing with wolves

AND SO THERE WERE TWO NOTABLE SNOWY DAWNS ON THE COL de Joux, one just a few days after the other. There was the one on December 9, when two boys guilty of thievery were made to leave a hut in Frumy and walk a hundred meters to be gunned down Soviet-style, a dawn that remained little known. And then there was the "spectral snowy dawn" of December 13 that would become a part of Italian literature when Primo Levi published the second edition of *If This Is a Man*, adding a page at the outset that swiftly described the morning of his arrest.[1]

Between one dawn and the other, the fates of the Col de Joux band were sealed. The executions stifled the will of Levi and his friends "to resist, even to live." That's how the "ugly secret" was reconstructed by Levi in 1975, and that scrap of the past was cast before a now democratic Italy concerned with quite other matters, other threats. Yet Levi's sense of a tight connection between the two events does not correspond to the documentation available. The archives contain nothing to suggest there was a direct link between the execution of the two young men and the collapse four days later of a morally destitute band of partisans. It looks, instead, as if things would have taken much the same course even had the band not decided they must punish those two wayward "elements."

Alberto Bianchi and Domenico De Ceglie, the two spies who had infiltrated the Casale band along with Edilio Cagni, arrived in Arcesaz on the afternoon of December 9. The following day, De Ceglie, in the guise of Second Lieutenant Mario Meoli, went over the Col de Joux pass to join Guido Bachi and Aldo Piacenza at the head of the Amay band. Cagni, in his role as commander of the rebels' Graines camp, had ordered "Meoli" to go to Amay, thereby completing the infiltration of the local partisan groups. But Bachi himself had also requested Meoli to come to Amay that morning, because he was concerned about discipline at Frumy and thought the second lieutenant could help.[2] Thus, on the afternoon of Friday, December 10, De Ceglie climbed the Col de Joux pass and then came down a few turns of the road to the Ristoro in Amay. There, Piacenza introduced him to five people: "Miss Nissim (Jewish), Miss Maestro (Jewish), Mr. Levi (Jewish), Mr. Scavarda, and another Jew who turned out to be Bachi's cousin."[3]

The cousin was probably the young doctor Paolo Todros, who had sought refuge from racial persecution in Valle d'Aosta. We know the three others pointed out as Jewish in De Ceglie's report, but we meet Aldo Scavarda here for the first time. The twenty-year-old from Turin had trained with the Air Force and was just beginning an eventful career as a partisan.[4] According to what De Ceglie would report after the December 13 raid, Scavarda had come up to Amay for the day on behalf of attorney Reynaud, "of the Communist headquarters in Turin." That evening, Bachi told De Ceglie of the other rebels in the huts at Frumy. De Ceglie informed everyone that he would be going over to Arcesaz the following day "to collect some clothing" and would return on Monday the thirteenth "to take command of the camp." De Ceglie did go to Arcesaz the next day, but only to confer with Cagni. That afternoon he went to Aosta to report to Prefect Carnazzi, and on Sunday he was back in Arcesaz, where he informed Cagni "of the agreements and their orders from the boss." The second disastrous dawn was now just hours away.[5]

Meanwhile, Cagni and Bianchi were busy refining their plan. They spent December 10 getting to know the Italian rebels and the British ex-prisoners. The following day, "second lieutenant Cerri," aka Bianchi, organized an exercise in target practice in order to use up their munitions and give the Nazi-Fascists an even greater advantage in the coming raid. "The exercise went off without any problems and I was easily able to determine that only two of their automatic weapons were effective," he reported. On December 12, he told the Aosta prefect, "I proposed to get the group to dance, and made sure there was wine to be distributed, and a lot of it." The purpose, of course, "was to get them to dance and drink until late at night so that when the militia arrived at 3 a.m. they would be tired and unable to fight back."[6]

It's hard to imagine the partisans of Arcesaz dancing by themselves, all men; more likely the inhabitants of Graines, including young women, also took part. In any case, things were proceeding as the three spies intended until 9:30 p.m. that night, when a couple of valley dwellers appeared in Arcesaz to warn that a raid was planned at dawn. Now Cagni and his two fellow spies had to get out fast. But if we are to believe the report that Cagni made to Carnazzi, the leaked news of the raid did not raise the temperature of his sangfroid by even one degree. "While pretending to distribute weapons, I disabled some automatic rifles," he wrote, and "threw two Beretta machine guns and most of the remaining cartridge clips in the creek." It was already late at night when Cagni, Bianchi, and De Ceglio led a column of men down from Graines toward Arcesaz. The spies were only able to escape at 4 a.m. on December 13, and they heard "bursts of machine gun fire and shouts that told us that something critical had happened."[7]

That "something critical" was the attack on Arcesaz by Salò and German forces. In a memo written to Il Duce's personal secretary, Prefect Carnazzi would estimate the contingent was made up of 297 men, almost exactly the number Primo Levi would provide in *The Periodic*

Table: "they were 300 and we were 11, equipped with a Tommy gun without bullets and a few pistols."[8] Those three hundred were divided into two groups: the Republican National Guard, under the orders of Commander Domenico De Filippi, which climbed up from Verrès to Arcesaz, and the Border Militia, led by Centurion Ferro[9] ("centurion" was a rank in the militia), which came up from Saint-Vincent headed for Amay. Most of the attackers were thus Italians, but they were escorted by a set of German officers and soldiers, led by a Colonel Schmidt, local commander of German forces.[10] It was the first such Nazi-Fascist *rastrellamento*—house-to-house (to hayloft to hut) police roundup—ever in the story of the Resistance in Valle d'Aosta, and one of the largest that Italy had seen following the eighth of September.

The police left their vehicles outside Arcesaz and made their way on foot into town. They met no enemy fire, because most of the Casale band was still up at Graines. (The Rossi brothers, the founders of the group, had been warned of the forthcoming raid overnight and had left town; the Italian Resistance needed them, and their experience as partisan leaders was just beginning that December day.) The intruders, before climbing the hill for Graines to hunt down the men of Casale who were trying to disappear in the mountains, decided to search an inn in Arcesaz where they were convinced that rebels were hiding. They broke down the doors and windows, tossed in hand grenades, shot up the goatskins of wine in the cellar, and took what they could from the shop next door, while the terrified owners fled to the fields.[11]

There was just one person left inside the inn: the nineteen-year-old Internationalist Communist Giuseppe Carrera, one of the first to join the band of Casale. Now he was in a room on the second floor, unable to run. His ankle was twisted; he had hobbled down from Graines the night before to see the doctor in Brusson. The report of the Republican National Guard of Verrès tells the rest of the story. "It is unknown what took place in the room between Carrera and the militia, just as the circumstances of his death are unknown . . . Beside the door, bullet holes (from pistols and rifles) could be seen. Carrera must have been overcome by his many adversaries and was shot in the back of the neck with a pistol (presumably) at close range and struck on his right cheek with a knife as is also demonstrated by the attached medical certificate."[12] "Hacked with a dagger" was how a comrade would later describe the dead man's face.

Of the 186 partisans killed in the Valle d'Aosta during the twenty months of civil war, these were the first three. Fulvio Oppezzo, born in Cavaglià in 1925, listed chastely in the official record as "deceased" at Frumy. Luciano Zabaldano, born in Monforte d'Alba in 1926, also "deceased" at Frumy. And Giuseppe Carrera, born in Casale Monferrato in 1924, who "fell in battle" at Arcesaz.

The first journey

"At dawn on December 13, 1943, we woke surrounded by the Republic of Salò," wrote Primo Levi in *The Periodic Table*. He says nothing of Luciana Nissim and Vanda Maestro, who were arrested with him at the Hotel Ristoro along with Aldo Piacenza. He does mention Piacenza, and Guido Bachi, who was actually arrested somewhat later on Col de Joux. He also writes about his pistol, a tale that elicits pity for his naiveté as much as admiration for his daring: if found by the Border Militia, the weapon would have made him an armed partisan liable to be shot on the spot. "As they came in," he writes, "I managed to hide the pistol I kept under my pillow in the stove's ashes, a weapon that in any case I was not sure I knew how to use: it was tiny, all inlaid with mother of pearl, the kind used in movies by ladies desperately intent on committing suicide."[13]

Seventy years later, in 2010, Yves Francisco told a slightly different story to Erika Diemoz and me. He told us that he himself had awakened Levi and the two women in the early morning hours of a gelid December 13. He had come up to his aunt and uncle's inn that weekend to ski and was heading back down to his carpenter's job at Châtillon when he saw in the dark the outlines of twenty or thirty men of the Border Militia arriving. According to Francisco it was he who hid Levi's pistol. "The one all inlaid with mother of pearl?" I asked, a little thrill in my voice. "I don't remember whether it was inlaid with mother of pearl, but yes, the one Primo wrote about in his book!" he replied. "You see, I knew every inch of that inn." Francisco had seen that gun in its holster somewhere on the top floor, and he took advantage of the confusion to hide it in a crack in the rafters.

As Luciana Nissim recalled it, dawn began with dogs barking. The house was surrounded, and there was just time to toss some leaflets of the Partito d'Azione into the toilet. Then they had to quickly find something to put on. "Vanda and I wore ski clothes, with a leather jacket on top, as I recall," Luciana said.[14] Yves Francisco, too, was arrested by the Border Militia, on the reasonable suspicion that this vigorous young man might be a draft evader. His aunt, Maria Varisellaz, was also arrested; all the evidence suggested that the Ristoro was hosting partisans, Jews, and maybe even Jewish partisans. Maria's husband, Eleuterio Page, was able to flee when the Salò troops arrived. So did Cesare Vitta, a Jew from Turin who seems to have been staying not in the inn itself but in a frigid outbuilding; he was able to escape before the Salò police investigated.

Guarded by the militia, the prisoners were led toward the Col de Joux. The raid was a pincer action: the men of the Border Militia were supposed to meet the Republican Guard in the Val d'Ayas, rounding up any subversives they met between Saint-Vincent and Brusson. That was how Guido Bachi fell into their net. He had awakened peacefully in the farmhouse under Col de Joux where he was staying with his brother, had melted the ice in the pitcher on a sweet-smelling pinewood fire, and at about 9 a.m. had gone into the woods, armed with a pistol, to walk up to the huts of Frumy. But after a few steps Guido ran straight into the militia and its captives—the police singing lustily, the men and women of Amay gloomy—climbing the pass to get to Brusson on the other side. Arrested on the spot, Bachi joined the other prisoners. His position was worse for having been captured with a weapon.[15]

Supposing that Primo Levi's account in *The Periodic Table* is strictly true, it was at this point that Levi, marching under police escort from Amay to Brusson, swallowed "bit by bit" the "much too false" identity card in his wallet, and pretended to stumble so as to slip the notebook "full of addresses" in his pocket into the snow.[16] As for what happened when the prisoners arrived at Brusson, we can turn to the diary entry made by Bachi a year later to the day—in his jail cell at Aosta prison. At Brusson, he recalled, there was a bus belonging to the Republican National Guard waiting to transport them to the valley, and a handful of locals gathered to gawk at the chained prisoners. "I saw friendly faces as well as some who looked indifferent. One bunch of them was congratulating the militia men. 'These people should be eliminated,' I heard them say. 'Immediately. We are too good. Instead of shooting them like dogs, we treat them well; it's a waste of time and food to maintain them. Get rid of them now!'"[17]

Levi, for his part, remembered "several buses" ready to board the prisoners and their guards.[18] This sounds plausible, especially considering that their itinerary included the stretch between Arcesaz and the plain below. The prey taken at Amay were few, but many more had been captured around Graines. Yes, Francesco and Italo Rossi had managed to slip away, and so had various other young men who, after reorganizing under the Rossi brothers' command, would play a significant role in the Piedmontese Resistance. Nevertheless, the raid on Graines and Arcesaz had turned up a fair list of rebels, some fifteen. And the police did not only capture partisans; they also took some locals. Emerico Vuillermin, the owner of the hotel Croce Bianca at Arcesaz, which the partisans had used as their base, was arrested. So was Serafino Court, commissary of Brusson, guilty of having failed to inform the authorities that his territory hosted armed rebels, escaped prisoners of war, and fugitive Jews.[19]

Here began the first of three involuntary moves that Primo Levi would make during the next two and a half months—the first of the three stages on the road from Amay to Auschwitz, "a journey downward, toward the abyss."[20] This first stage, a transfer to the city of Aosta, was destined to weigh, in Levi's memory, almost as much as the third stage, from Fossoli to Auschwitz. The transfer was certainly less terrible, if only for the means of transportation: a bus[21] and not a freight car, something human rather than inhuman.[22] But it was the last moment when an extreme act of rebellion still remained conceivable, if not actually possible.

Primo Levi left two accounts of that journey from Amay to Aosta. The second one appears in *The Periodic Table*, written in the mid-1970s, and amounts to all of seven lines: "They made us get on and sit separately, and I had militiamen all around, seated and standing, who were not concerned about us and kept singing. One of them, right in front of me, had his back to me, and from his belt hung a hand grenade, one of those German hand grenades with a wooden handle and a timed fuse. I could easily have lifted the safety, pulled the cord, and done away with myself and several of them, but I didn't have the courage."[23] But a short story by Levi published in a magazine in 1949, titled "The Death of Marinese"—four pages, but still quite a bit longer than the later account—provides an earlier version of a similar trip. Its protagonist is different, though. And so is the outcome.

Again, pronouns matter. The narrative voice in the story is a "we" composed of the partisan companions of the fictional Marinese, who have managed to escape the police raid in which he is captured. The title figure, referred to in the third person, has much the same experience that Levi would describe in *The Periodic Table*: he is sitting on an open-backed truck surrounded by his captors, who are here German, and during the trip he sees he can profit from their overconfident distraction and grab a hand grenade from the belt of a soldier near him. Marinese, exhausted and feverish, seems at first unsure, unwilling. He resembles Primo Levi as Levi later depicted himself in the chapter "Gold," lacking the courage to end it all. But then—surprisingly, considering his gentle reputation among his partisan friends—Marinese experiences a sudden desire for vengeance, a need to "purify himself." So he grabs the grenade from the soldier's belt, keeping hold of it while they battle hand to hand. The explosion that comes blows four Germans to pieces and the partisan with them. His companions profit immediately. "The truck was left abandoned, and we were able to capture it the following night."[24]

This is far from that pearl-handled pistol hastily hidden in the stove. In "The Death of Marinese" Levi provides a counterpoint to actual events, giving us a December 13 both invented and deeply desired. Thus he uses the third person singular for Marinese. The first person would be false, because he does not wish to describe a fainthearted submission to the overwhelming force of the pursuers. He is writing, rather, of fear conquered, of a determination to "battle fiercely" and make good of this unexpected opportunity by voluntary sacrifice. Marinese acts without thinking of anything else, "not of mercy for himself, not of God," not even about "the memories of people close to him."[25] The story was an "episode" of the Resistance, or so Levi defined the piece when he sent it to editor Piero Calamandrei to consider for publication in *Il Ponte*:[26] an edifying episode likely to be appreciated by the readers of that review, so devoted to the Resistance martyrology that Calamandrei, more than anyone, kept vividly alive in postwar Italy.[27]

Beyond "The Death of Marinese"—a tale Levi never reprinted and which never appeared in any book-length collection during his life— the events of that December 13 also left another trace in Italian literature. A trace that came late, less a reflection of historical events than yet another imaginary and desired twist on them, as if Primo Levi's arrest needed to become, not only for himself but for others, something more memorable than the essentially ordinary procedure that it actually was. In 2002 the novelist Rosetta Loy published *Alas, Paloma*, a brief, vaguely autobiographical tale set in Brusson during the summer and fall of 1943. She writes of a young Jew named Ettore, who is at first vacationing in the mountain town, then trying to escape racial persecution. There is a scene where Ettore stands in chains "in front of the hotel Aquila," as the authorities prepare "to load him onto a truck along with two other young men suspected of being partisans." A small crowd of bystanders stands "outside the caffè in the piazza, observing the spectacle along with some others." Those others include Ettore's friends, young men and women who had played tennis and listened to love songs with him that summer—before the eighth of September, before their Jewish friend had to hide from the Germans, which still did not save him from being denounced by one of the locals.[28]

But Ettore's arrest is not just defeat, the beginning of the end. Marinese, in Levi's tale, makes a meaningful sacrifice with his death: Germans are killed and the partisans take control of their truck. Ettore, for his part, manages to use his arrest as a chance to pass the baton. Pirro, one of his friends in the piazza, locks eyes with Ettore as he's being taken off, and the captured man "sort of smiles" and shouts from the truck, in Piedmontese dialect, *A bsogna mostreje ij dent al luv!*—"We need to show the wolf our teeth!" The Germans force Ettore down into the truck, and Pirro swears he will avenge him. Going to his aunt and uncle, at whose home he is staying, he leaves a note on the table: "They took Ettore away and I've decided; I'm going to the mountains." Then he takes his knapsack and goes to find the rebels and join the Resistance.[29]

It is fiction, but only in part, for Loy's novel draws on the autobiographical account of a real partisan named Paolo Spriano. A student at the University of Turin and draft evader, class of 1925, Spriano (later the author of a six-volume history of the Italian Communist Party) really did take off from Brusson to join the partisans after seeing Primo Levi in chains in the town square. As "Pillo," a militant in the ranks of the Partito d'Azione, he fought the Nazi-Fascists between Turin and the mountains until the Liberation.[30]

White night

And then there were those Jewish refugees in the Val d'Ayas who were able to elude the hunters of human prey that mid-December. One of them had the same surname as Levi's mother: the attorney Vittorio

Luzzati, who along with his wife and children had fled to Brusson from Liguria around the middle of November. There they had found precarious shelter in nearby villages—sleepless nights on the hay in a barn in Vollon, anxious days in a room atop a stable—until they learned a raid was coming at dawn on December 13. A young priest, Don Carlo Ferrero, a seminary student from Rome staying in the mountains for health reasons, had taken the family under his protection, and he urged them to leave Vollon and hide in a cabin farther up the mountain, at the village of Estoul.

What happened next was recorded eighteen months later, at the war's end, in Vittorio Luzzati's own vivid account of how the family was able to survive the war. "We passed through Vollon," he recalled, his wife on a sled while he and the children walked. "Very, very cautiously we walked through Brusson, taking the high road." When they got to the edge of town, Signora Luzzati exchanged the sled for a mule and driver. "And there we began to climb the mule track, which was covered, like the countryside all around, with frosty snow. The landscape, lit up by a bright moon, looked magnificent, magical. The air was clear and crisp, and in the solemn silence of those mountains, in the midst of that immense expanse of soft white snow, we seemed to be in some unreal fairy world." Around 11 p.m. the Luzzati family arrived in Estoul, but found no trace of the contact that Don Carlo had said would meet them. "What to do then? With the help of the muleteer, and after having knocked on quite a few doors, we finally found a good man who gave up his bedroom to us, and there we slept the night."[31]

In his account Luzzati records how ordinary life in nearby communities was affected by the raid at Arcesaz. Word arrived in Estoul via a child who went down to Graines every day to attend elementary school. Fascist militiamen and German soldiers at Arcesaz had sacked and burned the town, and fired their weapons to drive some rebels out of hiding. The news, when confirmed, made a "huge and painful" impression on the Estoul villagers, and the first consequence was that the Luzzati family was turned out of the room they had agreed to rent. They had no choice but to return to Brusson. The popular fear was such that "the rare farmers we met on the way and begged for help, offering to pay, all declined, for one reason or another. All were afraid to do a good deed for some unknown people who might be anti-Fascists!" That night, clinging "to the icy mountainside step by step," the family managed to reach Brusson again. Slinking past the houses "as if bandits" they arrived at the rectory where, luckily, they saw Don Carlo. The good priest hid them until the early hours of morning, when he arranged to have them taken to the bus for Verrès, relying on a far-flung aid network that was supervised by no less than the Archbishop of Milan.[32] Eventually, the whole Luzzati family would manage to flee across the border to Switzerland.

We know far less about how Cesare Vitta, thirty-two, already cited as a guest at the Hotel Ristoro the night of the raid, managed to escape. All Primo Levi said was that Vitta was able to flee that dawn.[33] Slim documentary traces confirm his presence at Amay, but I was able to learn little about the circumstances and connections that had brought him to the mountains in the first place. After the Racial Laws were implemented, Vitta—a worker in a large factory supplying Fiat—had entrusted his family's legal interests to attorney Camillo Reynaud, the man who secretly maintained ties between the Partito d'Azione and the Col de Joux band from his office in Turin.[34] It's not clear whether Vitta was in Amay simply because he was Jewish, or whether his presence there also derived from political motives. The factory where he worked would later become a bastion of Turinese working-class opposition to the Nazi-Fascists,[35] but most likely Vitta had gone to the mountains to escape racial persecution. He had brought his wife (who was not Jewish) and their nine-year-old daughter with him, and lodged them not far outside town. After the roundup, Vitta joined them and returned to Turin. He would not be able to elude the Shoah: arrested in his home in June 1944, he was deported to Auschwitz that August, and did not survive.[36]

Emilio Bachi also succeeded, along with his cousin Paolo Todros, in getting away from Col de Joux without falling into police hands.

Todros, who was tipped off by a villager that a raid was coming, was able to remain in Valle D'Aosta for a year and a half, at times in hiding and at times acting as a partisan, until the Liberation.[37] As for Bachi, he had heard with his own ears the Border Militia men singing as they marched down to Brusson with their prisoners: Primo Levi, Aldo Piacenza, Luciana Nissim, Vanda Maestro, Yves Francisco, Maria Varisellaz, and, last and most unhappily, his own younger brother, Guido.

At that point Emilio raced down the hill to Brusson, getting there just before the police arrived. He hurried to the house of a young woman, Anna Ojoli, who had been romantically involved with Guido over the summer. "Anna sent her son to see what was happening, and after about a quarter of an hour little Paolo—he was about five at the time, I believe— came running back to say 'they're all in the piazza against the wall with their hands up, and there are a lot of soldiers in front of them!'" Not much later, word having spread that the town would be searched after the prisoners were taken away, Emilo Bachi decided to take his chances in the mountains. But rather than go down to Arcesaz and then up the valley to Estoul, he decided to head for a small gold mine "run by a worker named Nicolino." Bachi guessed that Nicolino sympathized with the partisans, and he wasn't wrong. "While the miners were getting ready to go down to Brusson, he kindly took me in and offered me the room he used as an office. There was a guard there who was something of a half-wit and spoke in a way I couldn't understand, but Nicolino said that he wouldn't make trouble, and that I'd be safe there."[38]

The elder Bachi brother thus spent that first night after the raid going back and forth between the mine office and a terrace "overhanging the snow-covered valley," the silence "broken only by a gunshot now and then." Emilio would never forget those "interminable hours of anguish" thinking about his brother and what would become of him. The next day he learned from the miners that the Nazi-Fascists had left the area, and decided it was safe to go back to Brusson. He spent another month in the valley with trusted friends. From time to time Anna Ojoli would come by to bring him news of Guido; he was alive, but a prisoner in

Aosta. On January 14, 1944, Emilio Bachi went down to Ivrea and from there to Milan. His Resistance was far from over.[39]

"There being no other charges against them"

It was a German city, the Aosta that, on the late afternoon of December 13, received the Turinese Jews of Col de Joux and the Casale rebels captured at Arcesaz, all of them in chains. Since October, the Platzkommandantur headed by Colonel Schmidt had been lodged in the high school near the station, the Wehrmacht infantry had occupied the army barracks, and the border guards of the Grenzschutz had settled into a villa on the hills.[40] The Italian forces had effectively melted away at the arrival of the German army—and not merely the parts of the Italian army that had dispersed upon returning from France after the armistice. The elite Alpine troops of the Fourth Regiment had also begun to disappear, slowly at first and then en masse.

Primo Levi and the other Jews were taken to the Cesare Battisti barracks, where the Border Militia was stationed. A few weeks later, Guido Bachi would be transferred to the Aosta jail to face charges—less as a Jew than as a partisan who had been captured with weapon in hand. But in the wake of the raid, the prefecture was mainly concerned with wiping out the rebels whose network reached from Monferrato to the Val d'Ayas. And so, hard on their brilliant feat of infiltration in the mountains, Cagni, Bianchi, and De Ceglie headed for the plain, following the trail that led back to Casale and those who had directed the partisan band of Arcesaz.

By December 16, Luciano Imerico, commander of the Republican National Guard at Casale, was already recording that Giuseppe Barbesino and two others—"guilty of contacts with rebel armed forces, of which they are members and organizers"[41]—had been arrested in and around Casale, thanks to the work of "three elements sent here by the Aosta prefect." After charges were filed, the three partisans were transferred to nearby Alessandria. The three spies from Aosta, as it happened, were also circulating there, no longer under military aliases—lieutenant and second lieutenant—but, to judge from a pass signed by Prefect Carnazzi, as distinguished university graduates, "Ingegnere Cagni, Dottor De Ceglie, and Dottor Bianchi."[42]

Within two weeks, Commander Imerico had also obtained statements from Federico Barbesino and Giovanni Cantele, who had taken part in forays up to Valle d'Aosta between mid-November and the beginning of December before turning on each other and filing mutual denunciations with the Republican Guard.[43] As a result of their testimony, other backers of the Arcesaz band would be exposed, including the Allara brothers of the Casale hauling company; Giovanni Conti, who managed the railway station diner; and half a dozen draft evaders who had taken part in trips between Monferrato and Val d'Ayas. Meanwhile, the three organizers who had been arrested on December 16 were moved to Aosta, apparently to test their confessions against the partisans who had been captured in the December 13 raid. Carlo Carretto, the old printer, was moved to Aosta as well.

The statements of those arrested were taken down by the public security commissioner, but according to unanimous reports after the Liberation, Cagni, Bianchi, and De Ceglie, under their phony military identities, were the ones who actually asked the questions. At least one of the Casale rebels, Giuseppe Barbesino, would accuse the three of torture. Others spoke of them as coldly determined and sometimes harsh, but never to the point of using pain as a routine technique to evoke confessions. Whatever the case, the reserve of the interrogated was quick to give way inside the Aosta headquarters of Salò power.

That was especially true of the sixty-eight-year-old printer Carretto. Despite a well-established anti-Fascist reputation (his name had figured on a list of "subversives" in Casale Monferrato as early as 1938), he was anything but tight-lipped in replying to his questioners. Interrogated on January 7, he denounced the Rossi brothers, saying they "went around collecting for their cause among the industrialists of Casale" after September 8, "calling themselves the peoples' commissars." He spoke at length about his own stay at Arcesaz in early December, when Giuseppe Barbesino had also come up, sent to remove the Rossi brothers from command "because there was proof that the Rossis, rather than carrying out the orders of the Casale Committee, had put together a band of crazies, were wasting funds and engaging in wild activities on behalf of Stalin." Of young Giuseppe Carrera, Carretto said, "I know him to be one of the founders of the Arcesaz group, and maybe the most fanatical; he wore a cap with a red star and urged them to strike like Stalin."[44]

Barbesino, whose interrogation was recorded on January 18, also proved loquacious under questioning. (As we shall see, his allegations of having been tortured are not without corroboration.) As proof of his patriotic sentiments, the ex-carabiniere—also ex-bankrupt, ex–brothel owner—spoke of his spontaneous request to enlist in 1935, when he was already forty-one, "as a volunteer in the Italo-Abyssinian war." He too talked about the Rossi brothers, who he said had squandered the money collected and refused to obey the orders of the committee in Casale. He described his trip to Arcesaz, his disagreements with the Rossis, and the decision to put the Graines camp under the control of "a certain Lt. Redi, only recently arrived," who however seemed trustworthy because of his "seriousness and preparation."[45]

Thus the double-dealing Cagni and the other trusties of the prefect of Aosta collected, one interrogation after another, pieces of the puzzle that the prefect would put together in a final report on how the local resistance was infiltrated and destroyed. The report was oddly slow to be written, not completed until early March 1944, but its outlines were sent in a January 11 memo from the prefect to Il Duce's personal secretary. It was a memo at once succinct and pompous, like other memos composed by Salò prefects in those first months of the civil war, aimed at impressing Mussolini and boasting of the meritorious works of anti-Fascist repression. Thus, "the rebel Giuseppe Carreri [sic]" had been killed during the December 13 raid. A dozen men had been arrested, and a large supply of vehicles, clothing, and munitions had been secured. At Amay, an impressive six rebels had been killed, and two of the escaped had fallen into a "deep ravine" and were "very likely dead." Five more rebels had been captured, "among them three Jews." The total spoils: six rifles, two pistols, eight hand grenades, food supplies, and "objects of value and money." In conclusion: "The band has been dispersed. The lifeline of the subversive organization in Piedmont is now in our hands."[46]

There is no trace in the Aosta court archives of the interrogations of Guido Bachi or Primo Levi, although we know the two were questioned. It's worth wondering what happened to those records. It cannot be ruled out that they might have been removed during some cleanup operation after the war.

Lacking the police reports, what we know about Levi's interrogations comes from his literary account of the events thirty years later: of the four pages in *The Periodic Table* devoted to his three months in Valle D'Aosta, the interrogations take up a good half. Levi's account in "Gold" rests on the contrast between the two main interrogators. There was Cagni, the "spy through and through," the "muscular sadist" who had been able to infiltrate the rebels at Arcesaz and capture the group on Col de Joux. And then there was an officer whom Levi calls Fossa, who was actually named Ferro: Guido Ferro, centurion in the Border Militia, the man who on December 13 had led the raid from Saint-Vincent up to Amay, and who had actually arrested Levi, Bachi, Piacenza, Nissim, and Maestro.

Were Fossa and Cagni the Salò versions of those familiar Hollywood types, the good cop and the bad cop? You might think so at first, reading *The Periodic Table*. "Every so often they came to take us for interrogation. When Fossa was asking the questions, it went all right. He was a type of man I had never encountered before: a Fascist by the book, stolid and brave, whom military life (he'd fought in Africa and in Spain, and liked to boast about it with us) had girded with solid ignorance and stupidity, but not corrupted or made inhuman." Fossa thought Levi was a careless young fellow who had ended up at Amay almost by mistake, dragged along by bad company. He seemed to doubt that a university graduate could really be a subversive. "He interrogated me because he was bored, to indoctrinate me, or give himself airs, with no serious inquisitorial intent. He was a soldier, not a cop. He never asked embarrassing questions, and he never asked whether I was Jewish."

Cagni's interrogations, on the other hand, "were to be feared." "He would begin the session by placing his Luger prominently on the desk, he would go on for hours without a break; he wanted to know everything. He threatened torture and the firing squad continuously, but lucky for me I knew almost nothing, and the few names I did know, I kept to myself. He would alternate moments of bogus cordiality with equally phony bursts of rage; he told me (probably bluffing) that he knew I was Jewish, and that was a good thing; had I been a partisan he'd have shoved me up against the wall and finished me off, but as a Jew, well, there was a camp at Carpi, and they weren't murderers; I'd be left there until the victory was final. I admitted I was Jewish, partly because I was weary, and partly because an irrational pride made me stubborn, but I didn't believe what he said at all. Hadn't he himself told me that this very barracks was going to come under the charge of the SS in just a few days?"[47]

Upon closer examination, though, it seems Levi's two cops were not playing a game between the good Fossa/Ferro and the bad Cagni. Ferro was not even a policeman. He was as Levi presented him: a complex human tangle of mercy, tolerance, and cynicism.[48] Whereas Cagni was both good cop and bad in one; he was duplicity incarnate, not only as a false partisan but as a real inquisitor. Otherwise, what is most striking in those two pages is the way Levi accounts for his capacity not to spill the beans under questioning by Cagni: "Lucky for me." So, too, begins *If This Is a Man* ("It was my fortune . . ."), where Levi argues, ironically, that it was an advantage to have been deported to Auschwitz only in 1944, when the Germans had decided to lengthen the average life span of the prisoners to be eliminated.[49] *La fortuna* is thus twice invoked by Levi—to explain how he was saved from the shame of informing, and then how he was saved during the inevitable selection.

Inside the Battisti barracks, it was difficult for Levi to communicate with Bachi and Piacenza. The walls were too thick for a voice to pass, and sounding out coded messages on them was enough to drive a man mad: "it took an hour to beat out a sentence." Centurion Ferro made sure the exercise periods in the yard were taken separately, so the captives couldn't talk to each other. It was a "painful" ban, Levi would recall thirty years later, because it prevented them from talking about their ugly secret; they were unable to "exorcise that still so recent memory."[50]

That much they had in common. But Levi's legal status was beginning to look quite different from those of Bachi and Piacenza. Cagni, who had infiltrated the group, knew Bachi was the head of the Col de Joux band; he was destined for the firing squad as a partisan captured with a weapon on him even before his fate as a Jew was considered. Nor could Piacenza pretend he was a bystander, for Cagni had seen him at work in the Val d'Ayas and knew he was Bachi's right-hand man. Whereas, as far as we know, Cagni had never encountered Levi before interrogating him at Aosta. De Ceglie, to be sure, had met Levi, Nissim, and Maestro at the Hotel Ristoro, where the spy had stayed under the name of Second Lieutenant Meoli. But apparently he never realized that Levi was a partisan, not merely a Jew in hiding.

In any event, that was what the investigators concluded: a Jew in hiding. Whatever may have been the tenor of Levi's interrogations by Cagni and Ferro, he was not suspected of partisan activity. Piacenza, questioned on January 11 and asked to explain the presence of three Jews at Amay, confirmed the interrogators' lack of suspicion by saying nothing of that nighttime expedition in search of weapons at Chambave. He said nothing of what Levi the partisan had done, whatever it amounted to. Regarding Nissim and Maestro, Piacenza said "they had moved up to Amay to escape internment as Jews. They knew the group were partisans, and once or twice had baked some sweets for them. From what I know, Signorina Nissim, who had studied medicine, treated Berto at the inn in Amay." And Signor Levi? "Levi was up there for the same reasons as Signorina Nissim."[51]

As late as January 1944, under interrogation in an Aosta barracks, Piacenza—who during the Russian campaign had seen firsthand the terrible evidence of the Final Solution to the Jewish problem—still believed that Levi risked graver consequences if he were identified as an active partisan rather than as a Jew in hiding. He was unable to see that the German occupation had made Salò Italy a hunting ground like Eastern Europe, just one more place on the continental map of extermination. Piacenza thought he was doing his friend a favor to describe him as a Jew, someone totally innocuous on a political or military level. And if the men of the Social Republic perceived any ambiguity in Levi's status, they were free to simply not concern themselves with the fate of those Jews arrested under Police Directive Number Five and sent to the Fossoli concentration camp at Carpi.

Prefect Carnazzi, an ardent anti-Semite who had spent two years heading the National Fascist Party at Aosta, did not likely suffer many doubts in handling the case of the three Jews captured at Amay. Before me sits a copy of his final report to the special tribunal for crimes against the state and to the chief of Public Security, in which he details the infiltration and dismantling of the bands of Arcesaz and Col de Joux and spells out the charges against dozens of rebels, both those detained and at large, including all the protagonists of this story. Those five pages thick with names, events, and accusations include, at the bottom of page two, the following lines: "At the Hotel Ristoro, managed by Eleuterio Page but effectively run by his wife Maria Varisellaz, were lodged three individuals of the Jewish race in hiding following the recent racial measures: Dottor Levi, Primo; Dottor Nissim, Luciana; and Dottor Maestro, Vanda. There being no other charges against them, they were transferred to the Carpi concentration camp."[52]

The report is dated March 7, 1944, a date that invites reflection. It had taken Carnazzi nearly three months to write it, and during that time events had moved forward for those three individuals of the Jewish race. Ten days before, each one of them had had a number tattooed on his or her left arm at Auschwitz.

Halt that train

Primo Levi, Luciana Nissim, and Vanda Maestro reached the Aosta train station on January 20, 1944. From there, with a small guard detail, they left for the Fossoli camp, the second step on the road from Amay to Auschwitz. Also on that train were some Yugoslav Jews who had fled to the countryside near Aosta between 1941 and 1942, and who had been authorized to remain there after February 1943, when most of their fellow Yugoslavs had been sent to the Ferramonti internment camp in Calabria. The Eisenstaedter and Lausch families came from Croatia; Davide Steinlauf and Samuele Zelikovics were Croatians as well. They had been arrested on the Canavese plain at the beginning of December. Like Primo Levi, they were transported first from Aosta to Fossoli, and from there to Auschwitz. None would return.[53]

Sometime between December 13 and the beginning of the new year, Primo Levi's cousin Ada Della Torre—with whom he had formed close ties in Milan the previous year, when the group of Piedmontese Jews working there began to meet and define themselves as anti-Fascist— learned of his arrest. Determined to halt the infernal machine of deportation, she contacted Silvio Ortona, who had also been one of their group in Milan. (After the Liberation, he would become her husband.) Following the eighth of September, Ortona had immediately set out for the mountains above Biella, near Ivrea, where he began a partisan career that would take him to the highest ranks of the Garibaldi Brigades. Who better than he, thought Della Torre, to find a way to save Primo Levi?[54]

In January 1944, Ortona was a novice but determined young partisan. He had been born in 1916 and therefore had done military service before the Racial Laws of 1938; he knew how to use a weapon. Right around the time when Della Torre contacted him about her cousin, Ortona, leading a small company of Italian rebels and Australian ex-POWs, had boldly tried to blow up the lines of an electric power station at the entrance to the Aosta Valley. The group did not succeed—they had too little dynamite and not enough expertise—but the effort alone suggests how intrepid he was.[55] Intrepid enough to come up with a plan (a rash plan, frankly, or at least premature in terms of the military and political capacities of the Italian Resistance)[56] that he and Ada hoped might rescue Primo from what promised to be imminent deportation.

Their plan was this: an exchange of prisoners. They had to find a way to capture a Fascist and then arrange negotiations with the Salò authorities, agreeing to free their prisoner if Primo Levi were freed. The necessary manpower would come from the combined forces of Ortona's Biella rebels and the rebels of the Canavese plain; Ada had contacted this latter group through the husband of her sister Irma, Olivetti manager Riccardo Levi, who was engaged in clandestine activity. Ada's brother-in-law, fearing such a plan would prove suicidal, was unsurprisingly skeptical, but she was not discouraged. The project was concrete enough that a victim was chosen: an Olivetti employee who was a firm supporter of Salò, lived in a house at the edge of town, and would be easy to capture because his habits were very regular. The commando team was also chosen: a group of partisans sent by Ortona from Biella, led on site by Riccardo Levi's most faithful political disciple, the Olivetti draftsman Mario Pelizzari.[57]

Pelizzari, nom de guerre Alimiro—the same Alimiro who as far back as July 1943 had been going around Ivrea chipping the fasces off the facades of public buildings; who on September 8 was up in Val d'Ayas helping Jews secretly cross the border into Switzerland. Alimiro (and "he was immediately enthusiastic," Della Torre would recall many years later)[58] was the one to head the commando group that was charged with capturing a Fascist and saving a Jew. But alas, the plan came too early, before the partisans were ready (and the Nazi-Fascists willing) to deal with something as sensitive as a prisoner exchange—and it matured too late, given the speed with which the prefect's trusties dealt with the Jews captured at Amay. The grim news of Primo Levi's deportation from Aosta reached Ada on January 20, 1944. Soon the train carrying him from Aosta station had passed Ivrea and was beyond the Chivasso rail junction outside Turin, traveling east.

4

Passing the Torch

Primo Levi's pistol

WE WILL NOT FOLLOW THAT TRAIN CARRYING PRIMO LEVI
beyond the Italian border, through Austria and Czechoslovakia, to
Poland and the *Judenrampe* at Auschwitz, where the wagons came to a
halt and the first selection took place, where old women, children, parents, sons and daughters disappeared "treacherously, before we knew it."[1]
For this is a book about the *partigia* in Valle d'Aosta, not about deportees to the death camp. We must therefore be prepared to let go of Levi
and his two Jewish friends captured with him at Amay, Luciana Nissim
and Vanda Maestro. We must do without them for an entire year and a
half, until the summer and fall of 1945, when the saved of the camps
will make their separate ways home.[2]

We will not linger, either, over the month the three prisoners spent
in the camp at Fossoli, from January 21 to February 21, 1944, before
another dawn, this one snowless, came upon them "like a traitor, as if
the new sun had made common cause with men to destroy us."[3] That

one would bring their departure in a freight car for Auschwitz, after those strange weeks of captivity that were so much freer than the time they'd spent in the Aosta jail. "What I remember is a sunny place," Luciana would say half a century later, recalling the camp at Fossoli. She and Vanda were still wearing the windproof jackets and mountain clothes they'd put on the day they'd been arrested, and thought they looked "rather nice in trousers and boots, very strong."[4] It was an almost idyllic internment, and Levi's biographers have detected hints of a romance with Vanda at Fossoli, while Luciana (who was romantically tied to Franco Momigliano, then a partisan in Val Pellice) seems to have become attached to Franco Sacerdoti, a Neapolitan Jew who was also interned there.

But before we leave these deportees there are two documents, two letters, that we must read. The first was written by Nissim on February 21, after the Fossoli prisoners were told they would be leaving on the following day, and sent to Momigliano by way of a non-Jewish friend of theirs, Bianca Guidetti Serra, in Turin. It is a message of fond farewell from a woman to the man she has loved. "Dear one, it is finished. Do not forget me, remember that I believed in the best and truest, that I sought the just and the good. Remember that for a year you've been my raison d'être, and that all I saw was through your eyes, and I lived only because you were alive." But it is also a message from an anti-Fascist who has been captured to one who is free and able to combat the enemy. "Once, when I thought it might be true, I told you that I was passing you the torch. Now that is certainly true," she wrote, adding: "It's a pity for us three, isn't it? But perhaps all of you will not suffer too much . . . Sweet, faraway love of once upon a time, do not suffer! I thank you for what you have been. I must go . . . do not forget this day, ciao, ciao, ciao." "*Morituri te salutant*," she signs off in Latin, and urges the partisans to "make the flame burn brighter."[5]

It is a powerful letter, not least because of the way Nissim moves back and forth between the singular and the plural—a mixture of one and all, both involuntary and inescapable. As if an intimate love affair

between two Italian Jews that began during the years of racial persecution, then was wrecked upon the shoals of deportation and the German
occupation, must perforce become a story of war, sacrifice, and revenge
to inspire all the other Jews of their generation.

That impression is borne out by the second message, written by
Levi and signed by him, Nissim, and Maestro. Placed on a postcard
printed with the Fascist slogan VINCEREMO ("we will win"), it is dated
February 23, when the transport from Fossoli to Auschwitz was halfway
between the Italian cities of Trento and Bolzano. Mailed by some merciful person in the town of Egna, the postcard made its way to Turin to the
address, once again, of Guidetti Serra. "Dear Bianca, We are on our journey in the classic manner—give our best to all—the torch passes to you."[6]

One of those who took up the torch was Emilio Bachi. After leaving
the Col de Joux just in time on the morning of the raid and spending the
following night in a gold mine above Brusson, Bachi had been hidden
by friends at a village farther north in the Val d'Ayas. The Allied landing at Anzio, toward the end of January, seemed to many to promise
that Rome would soon be liberated, and Bachi (under the assumed
name of Emilio Bertolani) and his wife and daughter decided to travel
in disguise to the capital. It was a daring trip, by train from Turin via
Genoa to Florence, and from there by way of a Salò military truck, brav-
ing aerial bombings and brushes with the bribe-seeking border and
customs police.

Helped by the Partito d'Azione's clandestine network, Bachi was able
to obtain ration cards for his family, all the more essential because a
second daughter was soon to arrive, and because Rome in fact would
not be liberated for another four months. Until then, the Bachis lived in
the Pensione Rubens on Via Borgognona, along with "a motley crew of
others".[7] Sicilian Fascists who had fled the island when the Allies landed,
anti-Fascists from the North, Jews in disguise like the Bachi family. It
was a precarious existence in suspended animation, as another Jew
lodged under a false name in the same pensione recorded in his diary.
There were "long, painfully endured hours" in the common dining

room, "playing cards and smoking," or "wandering through the darkened rooms like uneasy specters, sleepy and impatient, an ear tuned to the muffled guns."[8]

In Bachi family memory (or legend), it was thanks to the shared toilet of their lodgings that Emilio Bachi got to know the author of those lines: Giorgio Bassani. For toilet paper the guests had to make do with squares of old newspaper, and when Bassani left sheets of a clandestine paper to signal the presence of an anti-Fascist among them, Bachi left pages from another. Yet it was only after Rome was liberated, on June 4, 1944, that the two guests in hiding revealed themselves to one another. Thereafter, Bachi was able to offer his services to EIAR radio, which had become the voice of free Italy. He was then assigned as liaison officer with the American army, and remained with the Allied Military Government in Florence until the spring of 1945.[9]

In the meantime another denizen of the Col de Joux, Yves Francisco, had gone over to the Resistance. Arrested at Amay as a suspected draft evader, not as a genuine rebel, Francisco had been released from detention in Aosta when he promised to enlist with Salò. He did so but soon deserted, and hid up in the hills between Amay and Frumy again from January to April 1944. "Bitterly cold" months, Francisco recalled, "although it scarcely snowed at all after Christmas." His chance to join the partisans came that spring when he managed to connect with "Marius"—the partisan Gino Tordoni, energetic founder of a band near Verrès and a character out of Victor Hugo.[10] (There was some of the novelesque in Francisco's tale, too, and yet each time I doubted what he told me, other sources verified his account.) Marius and his group had climbed the trails to the Col de Joux pass and gone down to Graines in search of a hidden cache of partisan weapons. Francisco, when he saw the partisans go by, simply joined them.

There was another weapon too that had escaped the Nazi-Fascist raid of December 13: the pearl-handled pistol Primo Levi said he had kept under the pillow in his attic room at the Hotel Ristoro. "I have no idea where it even came from; a pistol with a cylinder, a tiny cylinder that would fire five meters, no more," Levi told the Italian writer Ferdinando Camon.[11] Francisco, who had hastily stuffed it into a crevice in the rafters during the raid, hadn't needed it himself: he had his own rifle, stolen from the Salò stocks when he deserted. But during the first year of the Resistance the shortage of arms was the worst of problems for the rebel bands; every weapon was welcome, even an amateur one. Francisco mentioned it to his uncle Eleuterio Page, who as manager of the Ristoro recovered the pistol and scrupulously consigned it to his cousin Edoardo Page.

Edoardo, a former captain in the Royal Army, would play a leading role in the partisan movement, rising to the top ranks of the Aosta Resistance. If the traces of Primo Levi's pistol were eventually lost, the same is not true of Edoardo Page.

March 1944

On February 18, 1944, Mussolini ordered the death penalty for conscripted men who didn't present themselves to the Salò military. If captured, draft evaders were to be shot within three days as "deserters before the enemy." In reality the decree was not systematically applied; the Social Republic, no matter how much it wished to please its Germany ally, lacked the means and organization needed to put tens of thousands of young Italians before the firing squad. The capital punishment decree was mostly a threat to promote compliance, and to some extent it worked, particularly in those parts of occupied Italy far from the Apennines and the Alps where it was hard to disappear. The hills and the mountains, on the other hand, were friendly territory for draft evasion as well as outright resistance.[12]

Faced with the military and political weakness of Republican Fascism, Prefect Carnazzi invented something new: the "Alpine Musketeers," an autonomous volunteer battalion. The idea was to link politics with military action, so that those who joined the Party automatically signed up for the Musketeers, no age limits observed.[13] "Young and old, recruits and veterans, all can join the above-mentioned battalion at the service of Il Duce," read an appeal from the prefect to "the men of Aosta and the Canavese" in the local Salò weekly. The one "indispensible prerequisite" for enrollment was *"Fede, Fede, Fede"*—"faith, faith, faith" in the Fascist creed. And Carnazzi did not stop at conscripting the diffident; he also promised judicial pardons and civic glory to "mountain dwellers" who had been led astray by the partisans, as long as they stopped taking "Red money" and surrendered themselves and their weapons.[14]

The birth of the Alpine Musketeers made news beyond Aosta; in March, *La Stampa* carried a notice on its front page.[15] That same month the Musketeers took part in their first military operation, a meticulous raid on the upper Canavese ordered by Prefect Carnazzi and led by Republican National Guard commander Domenico De Filippi, who had headed up the raid in the Val d'Ayas. Some 250 men, a mix of militia members and carabinieri, hit Pont Canavese, Sparone, Ribordone, Cuorgnè, Prascorsano, Valperga, Castellamonte, and Castelnuovo Nigra between March 2 and 10. The Canavese towns became battlegrounds, as sturdy bands of rebels sought to retaliate after every strike. While all this was going on, Carnazzi would report, the Musketeers were engaging in a diversive action near Pont-Saint-Martin "under unceasing mortar fire," handling it "brilliantly . . . thanks to the ardor of the participating ranks."[16]

De Filippi's report on the raid, somewhat less rhetorical than the prefect's, suggests how deadly such conflicts could be. Nine rebels were killed in the raid, five were wounded, and forty-four were arrested. Five foreign POWs were also taken, plus eight "hostages"—that is, parents, siblings, wives, and in-laws of those partisans who were able to escape capture. In terms of war materiel, De Filippi and his men recovered four trucks, three automobiles, two pickups, one "motorized wagon," one "light motorized van," and a motorbike. The Social Republic lost a militiaman and two musketeers. Seven of their men were wounded, including one whose name is familiar to us: Second Lieutenant Domenico De Ceglie, one of the three spies who months before had infiltrated the band at Arcesaz, now injured at Prascorsano during a "violent" enemy attack.[17]

The other two spies working for the Aosta prefecture, Alberto Bianchi and Edilio Cagni, joined the Canavese raid as well. Upon returning to Aosta, Cagni filed his own report, emphasizing the trio's contribution to the success of the mission. At dawn on March 3, when the column led by De Filippi left for Sparone, Cagni had positioned himself as a natural rebel-hunter, "seated on the headlamps of the Commander's transport." At Ribordone, he writes, he and Bianchi were shot at, but were not in the least shaken. "We saw several young men running away," and "we grabbed four of them." Cagni's most heroic moment came the following day at Prascorsano, in the fighting that left De Ceglie gravely wounded. "Five meters behind us I saw a civilian who was calmly aiming his gun and firing at us. I stopped him with a blast from my automatic rifle that finished him off." On March 6 at Castelnuovo Nigra, Cagni shone once again, when he was summoned by Bianchi because "there were two suspect individuals in a house." When he got there, Cagni found the two "in possession of arms and some very interesting documents," and he "undertook to interrogate them. One was the leader of a group of twenty rebels who had fled two days previously, so we took them both to the town square with four men from the border militia and had the two elements shot by firing squad."[18]

Resistance historians have bequeathed us the names of the three partisans whom Cagni boasted of eliminating, all of them quite young—in their twenties, as the victims almost always were on both sides of the Italian civil war. The man killed at Prascorsano was Domenico De Palo, born in Friuli in 1923 and a carabiniere before he began to fight for the cause of national liberation. One of the two men executed at Castelnuovo Nigra was a local boy: Flavio Berone, born in 1924 at Rivarolo Canavese, nineteen years old when he died. The other partisan shot in the town square, Livio Colzani, was born in 1921 near Milan, and was serving as an army telegraph officer at Favria Canavese on September 8. For most the armistice had been an invitation to return home, but Colzani had chosen to stay where he was and join the partisans instead.

While the soldiers under Carnazzi's orders were combing the upper

Canavese for rebels, other Salò forces, with the aid of some German pla-
toons, were moving up the valleys of lower Canavese. They carried out
a harsh and thorough sweep from the plain up to the mountain bluffs.
Hundreds of partisans were captured, dozens of them shot.[19] Countless
houses were destroyed, and stables and barns were torched. It was clear
that the Germans and their Italian allies meant to put a stop to all possible solidarity between the local people and the partisans. Other raids
followed in the valleys near Cuneo and Pinerolo. Finally, at the end of
March, the Piedmontese military wing of the National Liberation Committee collapsed in Turin. At a clandestine meeting in Piazza Duomo
on March 31, all five national committee members in the military wing
were arrested by police. Captured alongside them was their coordinator, General Giuseppe Perotti, as well as other important anti-Fascists.[20]

It was a paradoxical month. Even as many thousands of workers in
Turin and nearby towns laid down their tools and defied Nazi repression with a huge general strike, the partisans suffered repeated military
calamities and the destruction of their regional leadership. Following
the March 31 arrests, the Turin section of the Special Tribunal for Crimes
Against Fascism needed only two days to bring the members of the
National Liberation Committee to trial, their guilty verdicts written in
advance.

The Perotti trial, as it was called, began in the Turin Court of Assizes
on the morning of April 2, Palm Sunday, and concluded the following
afternoon. "The courtroom was like a military camp," one account
described it. "Kids armed to the teeth sat on the sills below the high windows, swinging their legs. There were weapons on all sides, and now
some more policemen came in. Some of the cops, machine guns at the
ready, were dressed in civilian clothes."[21] Provincial chief Paolo Zerbino
was present, as were party chief Giuseppe Solaro and Guido Buffarini
Guidi, the interior minister from Salò. On the other side, many judges,
lawyers, and clerks made public their support of the defendants. But
testimony meant nothing in a case in which, it was rumored, Mussolini
himself had ordered sentences that would set an example.[22]

We are particularly interested in the Perotti trial because two of our cast of characters—Prefect Carnazzi and his trusty subordinate Edilio Cagni—came expressly from Aosta to appear in the courtroom. Although the public prosecutor had not included them in his brief list of witnesses, the two were able to take the stand as volunteers, each bringing his own rock to the general stoning. Carnazzi spoke against Perotti, accusing him of having incited an officer of the Aosta Railway Engineers to desert his post after September 8. Cagni testified against attorney Cornelio Brosio, a member of the Piedmontese military committee. A fellow defendant summed up Cagni's appearance: "A slight, insignificant, colorless little thing came forward. He was rather fussily dressed, the way provincials are."[23] Basing his testimony on the interrogations he had conducted in Aosta in January that year, Cagni accused Brosio of being one of the secret financiers of the Casale partisans at Arcesaz.[24] "The deposition produced by this witness caused great excitement. His was the most dramatic testimony," the partisan recalled.[25]

At dawn on April 5, eight of the fifteen captured anti-Fascists were put before the firing squad, paying with their lives for their leadership in the Piedmontese Resistance. (Brosio was spared, being sentenced instead to two years in prison.) Two days later, the body of a partisan who had been tortured to death was taken from Turin's jail and buried in the woods somewhere south of the city, buried so well it was never recovered. It was Emanuele Artom, the Turinese friend of Primo Levi who had thrown himself into the Resistance struggle. Artom's band, including several other Turinese Jews, among them the young doctor Giorgio Segre and Luciana Nissim's beloved Franco Momigliano, was also caught up in the roundups of March 1944.

Momigliano and Segre were able to escape the raid, while Artom was tortured for many days in a barracks at Luserna San Giovanni, where an armamentarium of anti-Semitic stereotypes was deployed to deride him.[26] "Captured Jewish bandit," reads the caption of a photograph published in a collaborationist paper. The photo shows Artom, his face swollen and battered, sitting on a donkey, with a broom under his arm and a ridiculous hat on his head.[27] The Nazi-Fascists never tired of their old truism: the Jew was worthless because he made a ludicrous soldier, and he made a ludicrous soldier because he was worthless.

Free zones

The ferocity of the winter raids selected out those partisans more technically prepared and with better organizational skills.[28] And so, across German-occupied Italy, the spring of 1944 brought forth a more experienced, "elder" generation: those who, if only for having survived winter's hardships, were ready to place their hopes in the future. What's more, of course, spring was the partisans' natural ally—when leaves begin to return to the trees, when the underbrush grows thicker and its denizens no longer have to endure the bareness of their habitat, the inescapable transparency of winter.

Among the elders, those who had gone into the mountains back in the autumn of 1943 held almost mythic status. They were people like the Rossi brothers of Casale Monferrato, who perhaps had achieved little of military importance but had stuck it out. The leaders of the Casale band admitted that after the raid of December 13 they had gone through "a brief period of disorientation." Their escape from the Val d'Ayas had been more like a rout; the partisans who had gotten away were at first dispersed between mountain and valley, and some had been captured and deported to Germany.[29] When the band's base on the plain was demolished by Commander Imerico, they had trouble reorganizing. Hidden away in the Canavese, the Rossi brothers were for months unable to do more than keep in touch with their fellow rebels scattered throughout the hills, waiting for better days and collecting good news from various fronts around the world: the Allied assault on the Gustav Line, drawn across Italy somewhat south of Rome, the prospect of an imminent landing in France, and the Red Army's advance on the eastern front.

After the Casale partisans were dispersed, it was mostly local men who kept the flame of the Resistance alive in the Val d'Ayas. There were the ones led by Marius—the band Yves Francisco had joined—who when spring arrived settled in the high pastures above Arcesaz and Brusson. And there were those under the leadership of Riccardino, born Riccardo Joly, who had grown up in the fields below. It was these two bands who led, for better or worse, the boldest Resistance action yet in the region: the occupation of the town of Verrès on May 1—Italy's traditional Labor Day until the Fascists established another. Unfortunately the wild, carnivalesque celebration on that forbidden date was ill planned and counterproductive. What should have been a premeditated action became a stunt, and when the Nazi-Fascists reacted with predictable harshness it was one the partisans paid for dearly. Bands that came together spontaneously and were ruled by the bright ideas or hasty orders of a charismatic leader were prone to such behavior; they lacked the careful division of roles that the larger partisan movement— then becoming an organized resistance—could have provided.

About sixty of Marius's men, Yves Francisco among them, left their mountain huts on the afternoon of April 30. They requisitioned a truck and a couple of buses and headed down the valley, disarming the Republican garrison at Challand-Saint-Victor and taking more weapons from the guards of a hydroelectric power plant. As they drew near the castle of Verrès they joined with Riccardino's band, about forty men, to attack the headquarters of the Republican National Guard and the barracks of the Forest Militia. They didn't have to shoot much. The Salò forces responded only weakly; Francisco soon had his hands on the 9mm Beretta of a carabiniere. By 9 p.m. that evening, the partisans controlled Verrès, occupying the railway station and setting up checkpoints on the roads into town. The following morning, when the incredulous population came out on the streets, people were shouting "Verrès is free!" The red flag, "now the emblem of the partisan detachments, flew from the bell tower."[30] The only sour note was the hand grenade that fifteen-year-old Pietro Sassara, the son of a Fascist, tossed from the family balcony toward the crowd of celebrants. When the partisans chased him he was able to escape, but his mother and his sixteen-year-old sister were dragged to the square to have their heads shaved before the crowds.[31]

One hundred men took Verrès on April 30, and one hundred of them lost it on May 1: paraphrasing Beppe Fenoglio in "The Twenty-Three Days of the City of Alba"[32] is perhaps the best way to describe those twenty-four hours. At dawn Salò launched its counterattack with overwhelmingly superior forces. There were two truckloads of Republican National Guardsmen from Aosta, and two companies of Ukrainian soldiers under German orders sent from Ivrea by armored train. The bands led by Marius and Riccardino held the bridge over the Dora River against the trucks but were unable to stop the soldiers on the train. By evening Nazi-Fascist mortar fire had forced the partisans to flee to the mountains, and reprisals were under way in the valley. Two captured partisans were shot on the spot, and four civilians were killed in the following two days.[33] The entire enraged Sassara family—the two women who had been humiliated, the fifteen-year-old grenade thrower, and his father— went house to house, pointing out which of their fellow townspeople to sack, inspect, and assault in revenge.[34]

The occupation of Verrès looms large in anti-Fascist memory, and Yves Francisco's eyes still shone, seventy years later, recalling those epic hours of liberation. But the Nazi-Fascists were able to profit from the disorganization of the two bands to undertake a broad raid that would strike all the partisans hiding out in the Val d'Ayas and nearby areas. Major roadblocks were set up at the summit of Saint-Vincent, because a report informed Carnazzi that the rebels were following the mule path from the Col de Joux down to Amay, and that "at present, in the abovementioned mountains, there appear to be about two hundred armed men."[35] As a result it was not just the bands led by Marius and Riccardino that faced the consequences of their antics but also those of Edoardo Page and others.[36]

As for Prefect Carnazzi, his bags were packed. On orders from Rome he was to be transferred from Aosta to a more sedate job as a director of the National Agency for Maternity and Infancy at Pedregno, near his native city of Bergamo—a virtual holiday. He would soon move on to the Turin office of the Government Commissioner for Piedmont, then become prefect of Asti as of January 1945. At his side remained Edilio Cagni, who followed him all the way, shadowing Carnazzi's entire career in Salò affairs. But Alberto Bianchi and Domenico De Ceglie, Cagni's two companions who with him had made up the backbone of under-cover operations in Aosta, would both stay behind. De Ceglie, wounded during the raid in upper Canavese, stayed in the hospital.[37] As for Bianchi, he would continue to be active in the role that particularly suited him: agent provocateur.

May 18, 1944—a holiday, the feast of the Ascension—was a critical day for the Aosta Resistance: the notary Émile Chanoux, the guiding force and charismatic local leader of the Catholic partisans, was arrested.[38] Just how his arrest came about still remains murky today. But one thing we do know. The man who knocked at Chanoux's door that morning, pretending to be an officer of the Badoglio government; the man who blocked his flight over the balcony, and led him out hand-cuffed while his five-year-old daughter clung to her father's trousers, weeping—that man was Alberto Bianchi.[39]

That same morning Bianchi would also knock on another door in Aosta: that of Lino Binel, municipal chief engineer and Chanoux's right-hand man in the clandestine resistance group. "An elegant young man was shouting, 'Under arrest, you are under arrest,'" Binel would later recall, after returning from deportation to Germany. "Bianchi, one of those officers who had put himself at the service of the Gestapo, was charged with my arrest, and to make himself sound important was shout-ing, 'You listen to Radio Londra!'" (Radio Londra was the name given to the BBC's Italian-language anti-Fascist broadcasts, dear to opponents of the regime.)[40] That afternoon, Bianchi was the only Italian we know to have been present when SS officers interrogated Chanoux, leaving him so badly beaten that he could not walk from police headquarters to his cell in a nearby barracks. The next day Chanoux would come out of that cell a corpse, found hanged on the bars of the window, having chosen suicide or perhaps having been "suicided."[41]

After Chanoux's death and Binel's arrest, other members of the provincial Liberation Committee rapidly left town, escaping to Switzerland. The leadership of the Aosta resistance was now scattered. At the end of May the Fascists and the Germans mounted Operation Hamburg, coordinated raids that methodically combed the region. Columns of Nazi-Fascists invaded the Valtourenche, the Val d'Ayas, and other local valleys. When the partisans headed farther up the mountains, the militias unleashed a reign of terror in the villages, arresting young men, sacking houses, burning barns, and destroying huts in the pastures. Although it did not bring military victory over the partisans, Operation Hamburg further damaged relations between rebels and civilians. As the raids went on, the locals' caution toward the partisans often turned to outright hostility.[42]

In early June 1944, extraordinary news from central Italy and northern France began to arrive in Valle d'Aosta. Rome had been liberated and the Allies were landing in Normandy. History was now leaning to the side of the anti-Fascists. The Italian Resistance gave birth, at least formally, to a partisan army, the Volunteers for Liberty Corps. In Valle d'Aosta as all across occupied Italy, fewer conscripts were stepping up to serve Salò, while the partisan bands were expanding. During the summer of 1944 the Republican National Guard experienced a slow but steady rate of desertion. At Nus, Antey-Saint-André, and Valtournenche, carabinieri and militiamen were walking out of their barracks to join the rebel bands. The Germans and the Fascists controlled only the central valley from Courmayeur through Aosta to Ivrea, while most of the lateral valleys had become "free zones" controlled by the partisans.[43]

When in August they learned that Florence had been freed, along with Paris and Marseilles, the partisans gained new confidence and energy. Their high spirits masked just how tenuously they controlled the free zones. These were still only anti-Fascist enclaves in a region that was largely controlled by the Nazi-Fascists. Worse, what the partisans considered free did not correspond to what the valley dwellers wanted. How could a zone be called "free" when their food stocks were forcibly removed, their animals commandeered, and their most valuable goods (butter and fat, salt, wood for winter) dealt out by the rebels as if they didn't belong to the villagers? How could locals look kindly on these men who, by attacking the Germans and the Fascists, brought deadly fury down on *them*? The partisan movement grew rapidly in the summer of 1944, but the conflict between most of the mountain population and the "idealists," the "elect few," was intense, as one professor and rebel wrote in those days about his fellow partisans. The rebel of Valle d'Aosta was "a tragic Don Quixote figure," he said. "The craven 'good sense' of the many despises the 'madness' of the few who have mortgaged their youth to a desperate venture."[44]

Had it not been so serious, the war between the rebels and the Nazi-Fascists in Aosta might have resembled a game of cat and mouse. Lacking control of the lateral valleys, the Germans and the Fascists could not stop the partisans who ventured down from the mountains, carrying out sabotage and taking potshots at the enemy. The train line running to Aosta and from there to Turin, the phone lines and the high tension wires, the bridges on the Dora, and the hydroelectric power stations were targets that the "bandits" hit repeatedly, almost as if mocking their opponents. Nor could the Germans or the Fascists stop the partisans from attacking individuals: isolated soldiers, informers, commissars, the enemy's women. The Nazi-Fascists met these guerrilla actions with reprisals against the civilian population. On July 18, for instance, the Republican Guard and the Border Militia responded to a failed rebel attack at Cogne by killing two partisans, then laying waste to two hamlets in an operation personally conducted by the commander of the Border Militia, Major Guido Ferro.[45]

Ferro: that is, "Fossa" of *The Periodic Table*, the man who had led the raid on Amay and who had seemed to Primo Levi, during the interrogations in the barracks at Aosta, to exemplify the benign type of Fascist.

A soldier, Levi had thought, who had grown accustomed to the ignorance and stupidity plentiful in military life, but who had not been corrupted or made inhuman.[46]

Alimiro

The disastrous autumn of 1944 began early at Saint-Vincent, in the first days of September, just before the feast of St. Gratus, the patron saint of Aosta as well as of Amay. A German raid killed four partisans, all in their twenties, all locals. Giuseppe Thuegaz, a farmer and partisan leader from Saint-Vincent, would later recall how "at dusk one beautiful and sad evening, September 4," he and Edoardo Page had transferred the four bodies to the chapel of St. Gratus at Amay. "The next day, feast of the patron saint, instead of cheerful songs and ceremonies we held the funerals of the dead partisans: Dagnès, Torrent, Ravet, and Pellissier, four men who died for freedom!"[47] Eight more partisans captured in the German raid were shot in the following weeks.

In the chronicles of the Resistance in Valle d'Aosta for autumn 1944, nearly everything that took place was bad. Raids came one after the other, partisan attacks were met by reprisals, the free zones were recaptured, and the Nazi-Fascists regained almost complete control of the territory. One by one the Germans retook Val d'Ayas, Valtournenche, the Valsavarenche, the Champorcher, and the Cogne Valley, the last a free zone that in July had been the closest thing in the region to a partisan "republic." In November, when British general Harold Alexander, commander of Allied forces in the Mediterranean, urged the partisans to cease fighting through the winter, the rebels' morale sank. Nor were they helped by the amnesty that Mussolini proclaimed at the end of October, which offered draft evaders born between 1916 and 1926 the chance to surrender themselves and their weapons without being charged, conscripted into the Salò forces, or deported. The conditions were so forgiving that some eighty percent of the rebels in Valle d'Aosta gave up their weapons.[48]

Had the cat got the mouse? In the mountains and in the lateral valleys, the rebels had almost disappeared, taking refuge across the border in Switzerland or in France, now free. But on the hills behind Saint-Vincent and Verrès, several hundred partisans held out. Led by tough commanders like Marius, they readied themselves for a second winter of Resistance. Down on the plain there were also determined partisans. One of these, operating in Ivrea and vicinity, was Alimiro: the Olivetti draftsman Mario Pelizzari, who had been part of the aborted plan to exchange Primo Levi for a Fascist Olivetti employee. By the winter of 1944 Alimiro had advanced in the Resistance and was the local political coordinator for the Partito d'Azione.[49] He had become an expert in guerrilla actions: attacks on power stations, bridge and railroad sabotage, ambushes of enemy convoys on the road.

In May and June 1945, just after the Liberation, Pelizzari hastily wrote down an account of his partisan years, which would remain unpublished until after his death in 1977.[50] Sitting down to read *Alimiro's Memoirs* at the library of the Institute for Resistance History in Turin, I got a surprise a few dozen pages into the book. "In October 1944 I decided to stop and inspect an Olivetti truck carrying typewriters to Monza for the Germans," Pelizzari wrote. "During this operation, it was decided to inspect the baggage and the documents of some of the passengers. We were astonished to find that one of them was Lt. Bianchi, commander of the Republican police forces under Police Chief Piero Mancinelli of Aosta. The lieutenant was taken into custody. In his bag we found three pistols, four hand grenades, a switchblade knife, and brass knuckles, as well as a pass under a false name. Taken to a farmhouse in preparation for transport to the detachment, he tried to disarm his guard with the excuse he needed to relieve himself. But as there were two men guarding him, the other fired and shot him dead. So died the man who had betrayed poor Chanoux, pretending to be a partisan, then denounced him to Mancinelli. We thus obtained a pack of interesting photographs and letters."[51]

Historians are not always seeking what they find, just as they do not always find what they are seeking. When I picked up *Alimiro's Memoirs* I had not expected to come across a description of the capture and demise of Bianchi, the man who with Cagni had infiltrated the band at Arcesaz, at the hands of the very same partisan who had dreamed of saving Primo Levi from the train to Auschwitz. I also eventually had to accept not finding the "pack of interesting photographs and letters," which Pelizzari said he still had after the Liberation. What I wouldn't give to get hold of those papers, even today. I'd like to see what Alberto Bianchi looked like, a man whose photograph I've never been able to locate. I'd like to see what other photographs he had with him—snapshots, perhaps, from the civil war. I'd like to know what letters he'd received in that year he spent as a professional collaborator in Valle d'Aosta.[52]

Were there, for instance, letters from the young woman who seems to have been Bianchi's companion during the civil war? In January 1945, three months after Bianchi's death, a woman showed up at Palazzo Cisterna in Turin, where the Special Government Commissariat for Piedmont was headquartered, asking to see Edilio Cagni, Deputy Prefect Carnazzi's trusted aide. It was "a young lady I'd seen with Bianchi in Aosta, name of Rosetta," Cagni would later recall. "Word was going around that Bianchi had been shot," and the young woman begged Cagni to find out whether it was true. "My investigation turned up no positive trace," Cagni said.[53] Like so many girlfriends of men who disappeared during the civil war, this Rosetta, whose surname I do not know, would long be uncertain whether to grieve for a dead man or keep up hopes of seeing him alive.

But Alimiro knew about Alberto Bianchi's fate; he had arrested him and seen him die. "The discomfort, the danger, the scaffold, the firing squad, the ruthless pursuit of your spies do not dismay us. Sooner or later those spies will pay, and pay dearly," wrote Alimiro in a letter datelined "In the snow, November 16, 1944," and addressed to the Fascists of Ivrea. "Those broad, free, sociological discussions of ours, aimed at a better world for all, temper us and make us fighting soldiers," the rebellious Olivetti draftsman went on, in a style all his own. "We are near to the final tally . . . Do not be misled by any setbacks; you must pay, and you will pay. That is how we are made."[54]

In Resistance legend, however, Alimiro is revered not for the capture and death of Bianchi but for the sabotage of the railway bridge over the Dora in the heart of Ivrea, carried out on the night of December 23, 1944. It was a bridge of considerable strategic importance. Trains loaded with coal passed over it, heading up toward the Cogne ironworks; trains loaded with steel destined for the war industry in Germany passed in the other direction.[55] The Allies had decided to take out the bridge by aerial bombing. But the bridge was so central that bombing it was likely to leave houses destroyed and civilians dead. Alimiro therefore took on the task of sabotaging the bridge, so that it would collapse without exposing Ivrea to the danger of bombardment.

Piero Calamandrei, distinguished jurist and one of the founders of the Partito d'Azione, told the dramatic story in a commemorative speech at Ivrea in 1995. Under cover of darkness, Alimiro and another partisan slid down "the precipitous river bank" below the bridge, which was guarded by German sentries. "Holding their breath," the "miraculous equilibrists" slunk along under the metal structure. "The dogged acrobat Alimiro would cling to that iron truss for two hours, like a spider on the ceiling, as the Dora roared beneath him." He had to feel with his fingers for the right spots to attach the explosives, seeking not to betray his presence with the clink of a hammer or the rasp of a file, as the sentries paced just a few inches above his head. At last the detonator was ready and the two partisans disappeared into the darkness. A few minutes later there was "a gigantic boom" and the bridge "shuddered, flew up and fell down. The steel from Cogne would pass no more, and the city was saved."[56]

The road to Casale

When a massive Nazi-Fascist force bore down on Cogne in the first days of November, ending the thrill of its brief period as a "free republic," hundreds of partisans were forced to flee the area.[57] Among them was that young carpenter from Verrès we've come to know, Yves Francisco. But unlike most of the others, Francisco decided not to cross the mountains into France. Instead he returned to Amay, staying briefly with his aunt and uncle at their hotel, and from there set out for Switzerland across the Plateau Rosa glacier.

This chapter of his picturesque Resistance was part of what Erika Diemoz and I heard in person so many years later, sitting in Francisco's living room. By November 20, 1944, there was snow already on the Col de Joux, and quite a lot more on the mountain slopes, below the Plateau Rosa and across to Zermatt. Francisco couldn't make it across without skis, but he remembered a pair of skis belonging to Primo Levi that had been left at the Ristoro after the December 13 raid on Col de Joux. "Beautiful skis, damn it—ivory-edged!" the old partisan recalled, with indestructible Kandahar bindings. Thus equipped, Francisco, along with a captain in the Alpine Corps and a Czech deserter from the Wehrmacht, made his way through a high-altitude snowstorm to reach neutral Switzerland.[58]

Guido Bachi, too, had owned a nice set of skis. But his were borne off during the raid, along with his "heavy socks of Scottish wool," by a member of the Border Militia. The Italian civil war was also this: a struggle for possessions, for material goods. And all the better if they came with value added, like the "alligator-hide wallet" that was also taken from Bachi that morning, with "about 9,000 lire inside" (roughly $5,400 today).[59] Still, although the Salò militiamen robbed him, Bachi fared better than the other Jews arrested just before. Unlike Levi, Nissim, and Maestro, Bachi had been captured gun in hand, and so punished not as a Jew but as a partisan. Awaiting trial by the Special Tribunal, he spent the entire period between January 1944 and April 1945 in the Aosta jail. There Bachi—an accountant by trade—somehow managed to get into the good graces of the chief warden, who assigned him the job of keeping the books for the prison canteen. The warden even rented a piano and sent his daughter to take music lessons from Bachi, a talented pianist. This too was the civil war: mercy alternating with cynicism, conviction with opportunism, waiting for history to determine who would be victorious and who defeated.[60]

The Jews of Turin joined the Resistance in numbers well beyond their share of the population, hoping to sway that verdict. They fought in the mountains, in Valle d'Aosta, in the hills around Cuneo and Pinerolo, Asti and Biella and Monferrato, in the Langhe and the Canavese. They fought on the plain in every role and in formations of every political party.* Some of them would become major partisan leaders; Silvio Ortona, whom Primo Levi's cousin Ada Della Torre had approached for help when Levi was arrested, rose to be commander of the Garibaldi units on the mountains above Biella.[61] Others, like Massimo Ottolenghi, had more clandestine roles, assisting Jews in hiding or serving as liaisons between mountain and city. Beginning in the spring of 1944 the women of the Jewish community also began to play a more prominent role. Della Torre kept up contacts between Biella and her friends in Turin with the anti-Fascist movement Partito d'Azione. Primo Levi's sister, Anna Maria, who had returned to Turin after hiding her mother at Borgofranco d'Ivrea, worked as a partisan courier for Giustizia e Libertà. The circle in Turin also included Bianca Guidetti Serra (later a leading attorney), the friend to whom Levi and his two companions had sent word of their departure for Auschwitz, and the future historian Paolo Spriano, then a university student: two young people who were more than capable of carrying the torch their Lager-bound friends had passed.

That torch would also be carried by the other victims of the December 13 raid, the Casale band. After several months in the lower Canavese, the Rossi brothers resumed activities, as new recruits arrived with the spring. When the Resistance was restructured as the Volunteers for

* Translator's note: Each of the three main political parties of the Committee of National Liberation had its own partisan formations. The Partito d'Azione was represented by partisans of the Giustizia e Libertà movement; the Italian Communist Party organized the Garibaldi Brigades; and the Socialists had the Matteotti Brigades, named in honor of murdered Socialist deputy Giacomo Matteotti. Although all the groups shared the goal of liberating Italy from German occupation and the Salò government, they also had their political differences.

Liberty, the band would become a battalion, then a brigade, and finally a division of the Matteotti Brigades. They would suffer some terrible losses, beginning with the death of their commander, Italo Rossi, who fell in battle on June 29, 1944. In January 1945 one of their brigades was slaughtered at Casale, and the following month the head of the Rossi family, Commissar Oreste, was brutally murdered by the Nazi-Fascists. "They ordered him to shout 'Long live Il Duce,' and instead he shouted, 'Down with Il Duce!' And so they gouged out his eyes, split his skull, and finished him off with three bullets to the temple."

In spring some of the companies moved west to take part in the liberation of Turin, and some went east to free Casale Monferrato.[62] The latter were led by Bruno Rossi, now eighteen, the third brother from that working-class family of Casale partisans. He was among the very first partisans to enter Casale and to accept the surrender of the German military garrison.[63]

5

———

Justice and Revenge

Freedom going by

NINE-YEAR-OLD GIAMPAOLO PANSA, SITTING ON THE STEPS OF A hairdresser's shop in the center of Casale, had stopped reading the book that sat on his lap, *The Three Musketeers*, and was watching, wide-eyed, the scene unfolding before him. The Germans were gone and a great partisan commander was riding into town. "Bold and daring, with a splendid mustache," the man sat atop a jeep, wearing a borrowed English uniform and a black beret with a red star. "My father said to me, 'Do you know who that is?' I looked at the man's face, struck by the mustache. And I thought of Dumas's novel.

"'Porthos!' I said.

"My father: 'Porthos, my foot! That's freedom going by.'"[1]

Freedom wore the black mustache of Pompeo Colajanni, the legendary partisan known as Barbato. A Sicilian attorney and Communist, Barbato had been on the ramparts throughout the twenty months of the Resistance, rising from a cavalry officer to commander of the Garibaldi

Brigades in the district of Monferrato and the liberator of Turin. But the young Pansa would also play a role in Italian history. Although he was just a boy, he had an unusual ability to size up people and things, as if he already had the stuff of the special correspondent he would later become. Pansa would never forget Barbato's ceremonial entry into Casale or other spectacles he saw in 1945, both before and after that dramatic April day.

Among the first scenes that stuck in Pansa's memory, encouraged by the anti-Fascist mind-set of his youth and education, was one he had witnessed three months before the Liberation. A partisan known as Tom (Antonio Olearo) and twelve members of his band—one of the Matteotti Brigades—had been captured near Asti and dragged barefoot through the snow to Casale. There, the Fascist paramilitary Black Brigades chained them to one another with barbed wire and made them march down the street while onlookers jeered and slapped them. "Their feet were a fleshy pulp; bloody, violet, blackish and putrid yellow," Pansa recalled. Tom and his men were tortured in jail and shot the following day at the target range. Their bodies lay on the ground for two days, unburied. "The memory comes back sharper each time," wrote Pansa in 2009: the barefoot rebels, their corpses in the snow. "Those images summed up my civil war, and for some time seemed to obscure others that came later."[2]

The images that Pansa's memory later turned up—half a century or more after the Liberation, when the postwar culture of anti-Fascism was coming under fierce attack[3]—were deeply hostile to the Resistance, a vision of a liberation that was too brutal to be considered virtuous anymore. He remembered Fascists in cages, exposed to the hatred and scorn of the crowds. He remembered the women who had sided with the enemy, their heads shaved, forced to stand in shame in the town square. And then there was the settling of accounts between Communist, Anarchist, and Internationalist groups. Beginning in the 1990s Pansa, a journalist with a penchant for writing popular history, would process those repressed memories into a series of novels and nonfiction accounts that would reshape Italians' views of their recent past.[4] Despite their sloppy scholarship, those books played a large role in undermining the so-called anti-Fascist vulgate.[5]

Another witness of the Liberation in Casale was a priest well known in town, Father Luigi Frumento, rector of the Collegio Trevisio boarding school. On April 25, he wrote a few months after the Liberation, "the city rose up, every citizen was carrying a gun." "The students, given permission to go home to their families, came out in mass to join the partisans," he wrote, and "they looked quite tough with uniforms and weapons (you can imagine our worries)." The Liberation was a popular insurrection; it was also an eleventh-hour opportunity to join the Resistance, while "from the hills the first partisans were beginning to arrive," partisans like Bruno Rossi who hadn't waited until that moment to fight Nazi-Fascism.

As the partisans "took over the Castello and demanded surrender from the few Germans and Salò republicans on hand," Father Frumento could finally relax. For twenty months he had concealed in the Collegio several officers from the disbanded Royal Army, disguised as teachers, as well as a writer who had fled Turin, one Cesare Pavese. Denounced by two of his students, Father Frumento had been forced to go down to Fascist headquarters to defend himself against the leading figures of collaborationism in Casale: "those who now have been condemned to death, that is, the leading exponents of all the dirty deeds carried out in this town: Commander Imerico, Major Fornero, and Sergeant Barbano" of the Republican National Guard.[6]

Sentenced to death right after the Liberation, those "brutes" who had spread terror in Casale and all around the Monferrato countryside, men about whose destiny Father Frumento seems disinclined to shed a tear? Perhaps they had been, in the kind of hasty trials that fixed themselves indelibly in young Giampaolo Pansa's memory. "All the fury and the grief of the civil war" was there in the crowd pushing up the steps of the court, Pansa recalled later; the people "driving into the courtroom, striking and shoving, shouting, swearing, blaspheming against this or that

Fascist handcuffed inside the cages," while the weeping mothers of dead partisans "brandished photographs of their sons . . . the only ones at peace in that stormy sea swollen with rage and demands for justice."[7] The collaborators were indeed condemned by the courts, but they were never put to death: not Luciano Imerico, not Carlo Fornero and Lorenzo Barbano, not any members of the Black Brigades tried for the massacre of Tom's band.

Imerico, sporting a series of honorifics before his name, was in fact destined to expire in his own bed—"in the comfort of his Faith," according to the obituary notice published in La Stampa in July 1966, "his high and uncontaminated ideals" enduring "now and always" in those who had loved him.[8] He had been collecting honors from the Fascist regime as far back as the 1920s, becoming a Knight of the Order of the Italian Crown in 1931[9] and officer of the same order in 1936.[10] And then there were all his other roles, all the steps in the provincial Fascist's model career—early member of the Blackshirts; coach of various town sports teams, rising to "special commissioner" of the Casale Football Club; centurion, then seniore, then commander of the militia. It was a path that kept ascending to the day of the armistice, when Imerico chose the side of Salò and collaborationism.

One of the few war criminals in Monferrato who did pay with his life was Major Wilhelm Meyer, the German base commander at Casale. Meyer was held responsible for the slaughter of ten civilians in the Monferrato hills in October 1944; among his many misdeeds, this was considered the most contemptible. The victims, farmers who had nothing to do with the Resistance, were murdered along with their anti-Fascist parish priest, Don Ernesto Camurati. After the Germans surrendered at Casale, the Garibaldini traced Meyer to a prison camp near Asti. In May 1945, they took him to the village where the massacre had occurred; after a cursory people's trial, the Wehrmacht officer was taken behind a hedgerow and killed. His body was buried in a field beyond the cemetery, to avoid contaminating sacred ground. Years later the corpse was exhumed and a coroner ruled that the cause of death was a fractured skull, due either to a series of bullets fired at the back of the head or a blow from a blunt object.[11]

The liberation of Casale was also fatal to someone of quite another stripe: accountant Mario Acquaviva, a veteran anti-Fascist who had spent years in prison under Mussolini for being a Communist. A Communist, but a dissident from the Italian Communist Party, Acquaviva was one of the leaders of a small Trotskyite party, the Communist Internationalists. On July 11, 1945, two men approached him on the street and shot him in the chest and abdomen, killing him. The killers were never identified. Some pointed a finger at orthodox local Communists, who probably hadn't forgiven Acquaviva for his opposition to Stalinism.[12] But Acquaviva may also have been the victim of a third-party vendetta aimed posthumously at his disciple, an Internationalist whom we've already encountered, Giuseppe Sogno.

Sogno and Giuseppe Carrera had been among the very first to take up arms in Casale after the eighth of September. From their base at Carrera's home at Via Mantova (Sogno lived next door), the two nineteen-year-olds took part in the first excursions from Monferrato to the Val d'Ayas. Part bandits, part rogues, they were in any event staunch rebels against Salò and the Germans. When Carrera was killed during the December 13 raid at Arcesaz, Sogno managed to escape to the hills with the Rossi brothers. In 1944 he joined Tom's band, by then part of the Matteotti Brigades. During the January 1945 raid in which that band was captured, it is possible that Sogno was taken prisoner first, and under torture revealed the whereabouts of the others. What we do know is that he was spared the public gauntlet at Casale and was not among those shot the following day at the firing range—facts which have fanned suspicions that he had indeed betrayed the band.[13] The fact that he remained in German custody and was shot a few days later did not dispel rumors among the partisans after the Liberation that he had been responsible for the deaths of Tom and his men. Nor was his death sufficient to dispel the rage orthodox Communists harbored against Internationalists such as Mario Acquaviva, who had first inducted Sogno into the Resistance. Acquaviva, transported to a hospital after being shot, had just enough time to whisper a single comment to his wife: "So you see what the party centrists are capable of!"[14]

Quick-handed

The Italian civil war was too lengthy and too cruel to end quickly and painlessly. Freedom may have come on April 25, but the hunt for war criminals large and small went on well into May and June. Democratic Italy was baptized as Fascist Italy was crucified. This was more than a settling of accounts for the twenty months of the Social Republic, for the errors and the horrors of a puppet state serving the worst ends of the Führer in Berlin; this was the bill to be paid for twenty years under the regime of Mussolini, years of bullying, violence, and oppression. Those twenty years help to explain the rage, the hatred and brutality, the Dantesque retaliation visited on so many Fascists by their anti-Fascist opponents. Revenge was savored with the same intensity as the justice that had been so long in coming.[15]

In Valle d'Aosta, police and carabinieri reports documented daily disappearances and bodies washing up on the banks of the Dora. "Probable homicide," the prosecutor's register recorded from time to time; a hundred or so Fascists died in summary executions in an eighty-kilometer stretch of the Aosta Valley.[16] Those who were captured by the partisans were luckier. They were handed over to the custody of the Anglo-Americans, who would transfer them to prison camps in the south. When the trucks loaded with Fascists in chains drove through local cities and towns, they often tasted the fury of the crowds along the way. Tullio Aymone, then a boy living in Ivrea, never forgot the scenes. "The memories of their atrocities were so sharp, and the accumulated hatred so great, that we would stand by waiting to throw stones at them while the townspeople—even our own mothers—looked on."[17]

Some one thousand Fascists from the Piedmont province of Vercelli were rounded up by the Garibaldini between the end of April and the beginning of May and herded into an improvised concentration camp, the Novara soccer stadium, where angry crowds came to vent their scorn. Several dozen—perhaps fifty or sixty of those captured—suffered a worse fate. Partisans from the 182nd Garibaldi Brigade took them from the stadium to the Vercelli psychiatric hospital, and on May 12–13, in one of the bloodiest massacres in the "long Liberation," they executed them by a variety of methods.[18] "The blood of the vanquished," Giampaolo Pansa called the carnage, a phrase that would later catch on and define a new, revisionist version of the Liberation. In Pansa's telling, it became a cauldron of personal and collective vendettas, of shameful punishments, summary executions, and secret acts of slaughter. Although nothing was invented in that telling (at least not by Pansa himself), every act was made to carry the same weight, without any consideration of the specific contexts from which those acts of revenge had sprung.

Major Guido Ferro—Centurion Fossa of *The Periodic Table*—was also one of the vanquished that May. My research did not turn up much about Ferro beyond the circumstances in which he dealt with Levi and the Col de Joux band: the raid of December 13 and the interrogations at the Cesare Battista barracks in Aosta. The partisans considered him guilty of war crimes in 1944, but when his case came to trial in 1946 the Special Court of Assizes in Aosta was unable to prosecute him because he had already been shot.[19] Along with five others, Ferro was executed on May 21, 1945, on the shoulder of the road out of Verbania, on the shore of Lake Maggiore.[20] He was forty years old at his death.

I did learn that when Major Ferro died he was resident at Luino, on the eastern side of the lake, as were two of the other people killed with him. I also know that in the weeks leading up to the Liberation, the shores of Lake Maggiore had been a bad place to be discovered by Fascists. They "were shooting people freely in those days," writes the Luino native and anti-Fascist Piero Chiara; "they were looking for people to put up against a wall." Fitting, then, that Chiara should describe for us

Ferro's death: "He and the rest of the group were made to stand by the wall of a cemetery, and after he lit a cigarette, he was shot while tossing away the match."[21]

In *The Periodic Table*, Primo Levi would dedicate to Ferro's demise one of those wistfully ironic comments of his. "It is strange, absurd and sinisterly comic, given the situation at that time, that he lies now for decades in some out-of-the-way war cemetery, and I am here, alive and substantially unharmed, writing this story."[22] But contrary to what Levi imagined, Ferro did not lie for long in an obscure graveyard. His remains were soon transferred to the Langhe in Piedmont, the district of his birth, part of a great coming and going of corpses that characterized postwar Italy.[23] On December 9, 1945, his death was announced in *La Stampa*, in one of those obituaries in which the families of dead Fascists were compelled to euphemism. "The brief existence of Major Guido Ferro was cut short by a tragic incident at Unchio di Verbania on May 21, 1945. Grief-stricken and bereaved, we make the doleful announcement after the funeral has been carried out. His wife Ortensia Alfiere, children Gianfranco, Pierluigi, and Emmisa, father Giovanni, mother Luisa Ferro Picollo, sisters Tina, Gemma with her husband Gino Giordanengo and young Chiara, in-laws—family all."[24] So many relatives in mourning; such a sorry need to deploy the term "tragic incident" to conceal the blood of the vanquished.

The Langhe district was another dangerous place for a Fascist during the Liberation. "All of them, you must kill them all," an old Langhe farmer in one of Beppe Fenoglio's novels urges the partisans; "anyone who's not soaked in blood up to his armpits on that glorious day had better not come to me and claim to be a great patriot."[25] Almost as if they had been listening, the partisans who liberated Asti on April 25 set up a people's court that very afternoon.[26] In the next few days fifteen collaborators were sentenced to death, and all the sentences carried out.[27]

At the head of the partisans' list of war criminals stood Cesare Augusto Carnazzi, who had been prefect of Asti during the last three months of Salò. "Carnazzi and his killers will all meet the same end," the partisans had promised just before the April 25 uprising.[28] This vehemence was not surprising, given what Carnazzi and his trusted aide "Lt. Redi"— Edilio Cagni—had done in the region between January and April 1945.[29]

As soon as Carnazzi was installed as Asti's prefect that January, and Cagni designated head of the political police, the prefect had made it clear he would pursue the draconian measures ordered by Salò and maintain pressure on the partisans.[30] And Carnazzi made a point of showing how tough he was, going so far as to denounce the local German command for having allowed "one of the most notorious rebel leaders" to open negotiations for an exchange of prisoners.[31] On March 16, after partisans launched a bloody attack on a troop train near Villanova d'Asti, Carnazzi fined the mayors of seven towns along the rail line 200,000 lire each for "local population acquiescence" to "Fatherland negationists."[32] On April 15, even as the Nazi-Fascist universe was beginning to collapse around him, he telegraphed those seven towns again, reminding them the fines were "long overdue" and ordering an "immediate reply with proof of payment."[33]

On the evening of April 24, Carnazzi took the lead of a column of Fascists fleeing from Asti to the north. With him were his young wife and Cagni, his constant companion. Before leaving town, Carnazzi had ordered the local director of the Banca d'Italia to provide him with twenty-five million lire, which he distributed to high Salò officials and soldiers, officers, and militiamen of the Republican National Guard and several auxiliary police forces. Carnazzi, Cagni, and friends were able to distance themselves from Asti just enough to escape the avenging justice of the first few days of Liberation. But on April 28 partisans stopped the column of cars in nearby Lombardy. Carnazzi was taken back to Asti and jailed there on May 4. He would be tried not by an improvised people's court but by a Special Court of Assizes, one of the state tribunals set up after the war, in which the judging panels combined lay citizens with professional magistrates.

The saved and the drowned

Asti's special court started working its way through the various cases on June 4. That same week Primo Levi sent a long letter to Bianca Guidetti Serra from a transit camp at Katowice, Poland. Entrusted to a messenger leaving for Turin, it was the first letter he had been able to write to his friend since the previous year, when a Turin workingman had helped him get word from Monowitz, the Auschwitz subcamp where he was a prisoner, to Bianca and, through her, to his mother and sister.[34] It is a letter worth quoting at length, for it allows us to see Levi in real time during the longest stretch in that long odyssey home from the camp, the journey told (filtered by memory and shaped as literature) in *The Truce*.[35]

"It is unfortunately certain that VANDA MAESTRO has died," Levi wrote, employing the graphic emphasis and verbal terseness of a time when the question of whether someone was alive was too urgent to permit circumlocution. "LUCIANA NISSIM left in September for [the camps of] Breslau, and perhaps she has been saved." At Katowice there were some one thousand Italians, "counting war prisoners, politicals, and those arrested in [Nazi-Fascist] roundups," and they were treated benevolently both by Russian soldiers and by Polish civilians. "We are not doing badly here," Levi insisted. But, he added, "Do not believe what I wrote from Monowitz; the year under the SS was atrociously hard, what with the hunger, the cold, the beatings, the constant danger you would be eliminated as unable to work. I will bring home (I hope) the number tattooed on my left arm, which documents an infamy not ours, but of those who must now begin to pay."

In the first weeks after the Liberation, before Primo Levi's letter from Katowice arrived in Turin, relatives and friends had fervently hoped that both Luciana Nissim and Vanda Maestro would be among the saved. Despite the news spreading about the atrocities that the Germans had carried out, the women's political companions in Turin had not lost hope that the two young deportees would come back from Poland and join them in tasting the excitement of the Liberation, "these days of radiant happiness." "Luciana and Vanda," said a notice in the paper of the women's section of the anti-Fascist movement Giustizia e Libertà, "we await you still."[36]

Luciana Nissim would indeed return. An inmate-doctor in the Birkenau infirmary until August 1944, she had been given the rare opportunity to leave Auschwitz and work in a forced labor camp at Hessisch Lichtenau, in Germany, one of the numerous camps connected with Buchenwald. In April 1945, when the Americans moved into western Saxony, Nissim had traveled east with them, working as a doctor in a refugee camp near Leipzig, and when rail service began to resume in the ruins of Germany Nissim slowly made her way back to Italy. On July 20, she arrived in Biella, near Ivrea. Her sisters and parents, she found, had also escaped the Final Solution: at first by hiding in the Val d'Ayas under the protection of a parish priest during the winter of 1943–44, then by emigrating to Switzerland with the help of a Catholic organization that assisted Jews.[37]

As for Vanda Maestro, her friends in Giustizia e Libertà awaited her in vain. "Vanda went to the gas, fully aware and conscious, in October," Primo Levi wrote in *The Truce*.[38] His Turin friend Franco Tedeschi, the fiancé of Primo's sister Anna Maria, did not survive either. He had been arrested at Luino, where he was trying to find someone to take him over the border to Switzerland. Deported to Auschwitz, he lived long enough to be transferred to Mauthausen, where he died in March 1945. And Franco Sacerdoti—whom Primo, Luciana, and Vanda had met among the Jews in the transit camp of Fossoli, and with whom Luciana had become involved—succumbed during the death march following the German evacuation of Auschwitz, ordered on January 18, 1945.[39]

In Italy, as everywhere in the parts of Europe that had been occupied by the armies of the Third Reich, the first weeks and months after Liberation were full of frantic searching for those caught up in the Final Solution. False reports abounded. Sacerdoti's friends, for instance, heard that he had been hospitalized at Bolzano on the way back home, only to deduce, after long silence, that this was not true. In some cases the details would only emerge years or even decades later.[40] Cesare Vitta, the metalworker from Turin who had succeeded in escaping the Border Militia during the raid at Amay, was initially thought to have survived Auschwitz. "It appears that Cesare Vitta, who was with us in the mountains, is alive," wrote Primo Levi to his friend Bianca. Likewise, in the first systematic accounting of deported Jews,[41] Vitta was listed as "seen January 18, 1945, during the evacuation and alive at Katowice."

Few of those evacuated made it alive to the Katowice transit camp, however.[42] And in fact, under Vitta's name in the accounting there is a second entry correcting the first: "died after the Lib." Exactly where and how, we do not know; this is the case with nearly all victims of the Auschwitz death march. In July 2012, I looked up the number of Cesare Vitta's daughter Carla in the Turin phone book. Carla had been eleven in 1945. When she picked up the phone, I introduced myself, apologized for intruding, and asked her what she could tell me about her father's death. Carla Vitta recounted everything she had learned from her mother, but there wasn't much. "The liberators were getting close, the Americans I think, but I'm not sure . . . And so the Germans made the prisoners walk, and then they shot them, including my father. One of those poor devils told my mother: a man from here in Turin who had pretended to be dead, and so was saved."

The Jews deported from Turin numbered 246. Of them, twenty-one survived.[43] The exact figures were not known in 1945, but as the months went by the enormity of what had happened came into focus, the human cost of the Final Solution among Italian Jews as well as those in the rest of Europe. Through all of 1946 and even into 1947 the columns of *La Stampa* were filled with such death notices, timely or delayed depending on the supply of reliable news. They ensured, at least, that Italians would not forget that difficult place name, Auschwitz. Sooner or later, all the Jewish families of Turin—Segre, Luzzati, Norzi, Levi, Foa, Vitale, Diena—were compelled to publish that black-bordered announcement in the paper, with the name of some relative departed through the chimneys of the Birkenau crematoria.

On October 17, 1945, Primo Levi finally returned to Turin following his lengthy voyage home. He stepped off the train together with Leonardo De Benedetti, who had shared the absurdly long journey that began at Katowice and went through Belorussia, Ukraine, Romania, Hungary, Czechoslovakia, Austria, and Germany before arriving in Italy. De Benedetti was a Turinese Jewish physician old enough to be Levi's father, and the two had become close after Levi lost his inseparable companion from Monowitz, Alberto Dalla Volta, who was swallowed up by the death march.[44] Levi stood in for the son De Benedetti had never had.[45] The older man had been transported to Auschwitz (on the same train as Levi) along with his wife, Jolanda. The two had been separated on the *Judenrampe* that February 26, 1944, but De Benedetti, unaware she had been gassed the same day, still harbored faint hopes on his return to Turin twenty-two months later that she might have miraculously been saved.

Primo Levi, meanwhile, still knew nothing of the destiny of his mother and sister. And the two women, who had survived in hiding between Ivrea and Turin, had received no news of Primo since July 1945, when they got his letter from Katowice. Three months had gone by, plenty of time to lose hope. But now there he was, standing at the door to the apartment on Corso Re Umberto 75, alive, astonishingly alive.[46]

In what physical and moral state was the twenty-seven-year-old who arrived in Turin that October day? Along with later recollections and documents, we also have the vivid postscript to the July letter that Levi had written from Katowice. After asking about his friends Guido Bachi and Aldo Piacenza and reporting (wrongly) that Cesare Vitta was alive, he provided this portrait, embellished perhaps to reassure his family, but still striking, of one of the saved of Auschwitz.

"I am whole and sound, by now fatter than when I was at home, but still not as strong. I'm dressed like a tramp, and I may not have shoes on when I get back, but in exchange I have learned German and some

Russian and Polish, as well as how to look after myself in many circumstances, how not to lose courage, and not to break down during moral
and physical suffering. I have a beard once again to save on barbers, and
I know how to make cabbage and turnip soup, how to cook potatoes in
many different ways, all of them without any seasoning. I know how to
assemble, light, and clean a stove. I've practiced an unbelievable number
of trades: bricklayer's apprentice, shoveler, dustman, porter, gravedigger,
interpreter, cyclist, tailor, thief and fence, nurse, stone-splitter, and even
chemist!"[47]

Fascism with a human face

At times coincidence in human affairs seems more intensely charged
with right and wrong than any work of literature. So it was on that October 19, 1945. Primo Levi returned from his hellish voyage, embraced his
family in Turin, the Jew saved. And that very day, the Special Court of
Assizes in nearby Asti began the trial of Cesare Carnazzi, the anti-Semite
under prosecution.

Not that the former prefect recognized the charges of collaboration
against him. When he was interrogated by the public prosecutor before
the trial, Carnazzi denied any wrongdoing. He had "merely, and exclu-
sively, dealt with the administrative side" in serving the Salò government,
he said. He had never employed political agents, had never participated
in raids against the rebels, knew nothing about the torture of detainees.
In February 1944, when Mussolini himself urged the creation of the
Alpine Musketeers, he had "employed every means" to prevent that corps
from taking on "a political and antipartisan role." During the winter
of 1944–45, when he was in the office of the special commissioner for
Piedmont, he had never "carried out active police actions." And in the
following months, while serving at Asti, Carnazzi said, he had never
been involved in raids against the partisans.[48]

But the documents assembled during the investigatory phase con-
tradicted him. They showed he had had extensive dealings with the

informers Cagni, Bianchi, and De Ceglie; that he had seen the Alpine Musketeers as an antipartisan instrument; and that in general he had tirelessly collaborated with the German occupiers. Between the autumn of 1943 and the spring of 1944 he had proved "rather rigid with regard to the Jews," in the euphemistic words of the Salò police commissioner who served in Aosta during that period.[49] And the raid at Arcesaz could not have taken place without Carnazzi's order. There were even those who insisted they had seen the prefect himself in the Val d'Ayas on the day of the roundup.[50]

Among them was Guido Bachi, the founder and leader of the partisan band at the Col de Joux, who had seemed destined for execution because he'd been captured on December 13 with weapon in hand. Instead he spent fifteen months in the Aosta jail, doing bookkeeping and giving piano lessons to the warden's daughter, without ever facing trial before the Salò Special Tribunal, and had managed to escape from jail just a few days before the Liberation. In response to a prosecutor's request, Bachi wrote that after his capture he had recognized the prefect of Aosta among those carrying out the raid. And the raid had not only resulted in several rebels being referred to the Special Tribunal, Bachi noted; it had meant deportation to Germany for some others. "Among these was Dottoressa Maestro Vanda, deported because she was Jewish, who lamentably was killed in the gas chamber of a concentration camp."[51]

At the same time, the assembled documents and evidence provided investigators with little, if any, proof of war crimes directly attributable to Carnazzi. In that sense he was typical of most Salò high functionaries tried in special courts after the Liberation: too guilty to be let off, yet not guilty enough to go before the firing squad. Carnazzi's lawyer struggled to show that the prefect had not acted to further Salò's military and political objectives. But the prosecution struggled too, hard put to prove the gravest charges against Carnazzi under the wartime military criminal code—article 51, aiding the enemy, and article 54, giving intelligence to the enemy, both capital crimes.

The Special Courts of Assizes provided speedy justice; that was explicit in their founding order, which called for "a brief investigatory phase" and an "express ruling."[52] Carnazzi's trial followed the formula, opening at 9 a.m. on October 19 and handing down the sentence on the afternoon of October 20. In the special courts, justice was somewhat rough and did not always observe formal standards of proof. The goal was to punish rather than try to redeem or rehabilitate.[53] The investigatory phase of the trial, performed by magistrates, was generally done by the book, but the verdict and sentencing were subject to political pressures, for jurors were chosen from lists supplied by the National Liberation Committee in each province. Procedure tended to follow the rules, and the president of the jury was always a career magistrate, yet the National Liberation Committee front essentially determined the outcome, since four out of five jurors were direct or indirect participants in the Resistance.[54]

Questioned by the president of the court about the acts of collaborationism he was accused of, Carnazzi continued to deny any involvement. What about the three spies sent to infiltrate the band at Arcesaz and prepare the December 13 raid? According to Carnazzi they answered to the German local command, "while I hesitated." It was true that he had been present in the Val d'Ayas during the raid, he said, but he had arrived there only after the roundup was complete and had acted to prevent "any further reprisals." Why then were the leaders of the Arcesaz and Amay bands sentenced to be tried by the Salò Special Tribunal? "I did so merely to prevent the Germans from deporting or shooting them." Why had they carried out a raid in the upper Canavese in March 1944? That was just a face-saving operation to placate extremist Fascists in Valle d'Aosta who had accused Carnazzi of being "too tame"; that's why, when the raid was over, he had ordered the prefecture's chief press officer to put out a "pumped-up" news release. How was it he'd agreed to serve as prefect of Asti just a few months before the Liberation of 1945? "It was my belief that by remaining at that post I could perfectly carry out my patriotic duty, and I believe I have."

We know from what we've seen of Carnazzi up to now that his replies were specious, and it is hard not to feel some disdain for a high Salò official who, faced with his political, military, and moral responsibilities, lacks the decency to admit to even one of them. Yet the life of the thirty-one-year-old Carnazzi was in the hands of jurors, who, although they had sworn to act "with rectitude and impartiality," came from the ranks of the Resistance and might therefore have found it difficult to render a neutral judgment. Perhaps that's why Carnazzi decided to deny anything and everything.

At the same time, even some relatively influential anti-Fascist and Piedmont Resistance figures, such as the Fiat manager Aurelio Peccei, judged Carnazzi fairly indulgently. In the autumn of 1944, when Peccei had been detained and tortured by Fascists, he had benefited from Carnazzi's "courteous" behavior, and his family considered it possible that the Salò official may have played some role in Peccei's release.[55] Another partisan, who had been a prisoner in Aosta at the same time, said he considered Carnazzi to be "violent" and "impulsive" but not necessarily "malicious." In his view the prefect "was somewhat dominated by his advisors," Cagni, Bianchi, and De Ceglie.[56] Even Guido Bachi didn't really make Carnazzi look very guilty. He told the court that when the prefect questioned him at Aosta after the Amay band was captured, Carnazzi "proved incapable of interrogation," a comment that probably didn't strike the jurors as strong evidence against him.[57]

Other witnesses' testimony also put Carnazzi in a softer light. If some interrogations in the basement rooms of the Aosta prefecture were rough enough to have left prisoners "in a bad way," Carnazzi had never been present during those sessions.[58] Not only that, but when Police Order Number Five was issued and Italian and foreign Jews were to be arrested across Salò territory, Carnazzi had been almost kind to those captured in Aosta. "Especially with the Jews, but also with other prisoners, he ordered they be lodged in hotels rather than in the jail," the former police commissioner testified.[59] "They were sent to the Hotel Corona," the head jailkeeper at Aosta's Torre dei Balivi jail confirmed.[60]

Another witness who must have impressed the jurors was Guido

Usseglio. A leading Turin physician, Usseglio was in his forties when he joined the Resistance, first undercover in the city and then as leader of a band in the countryside. As commander of a Giustizia e Libertà division, Usseglio had led his men to the center of Turin, liberating the Fascist Party headquarters.[61] At Carnazzi's trial Usseglio told the court how in the autumn of 1944 the Nazi-Fascists had arrested his brother Sebastiano, convinced they had got their hands on Guido himself. The partisan took the risk of coming down from the mountain to the Piedmont Government Commissioners Office, meeting there with Carnazzi to inform him that they had arrested the wrong man and offering to take his brother's place in prison.

"I went to see him in Turin, and I found an open, fair-minded, and decent person who immediately gave me the impression I could trust him," Usseglio told the Special Court of Assizes, his words a reminder that Resistance justice did not always simply mean revenge. The winners of the civil war could also supply the losers with a warrant of humanity. They could even supply them with a warrant of dignity, recognizing that the choice of a Fascist like Carnazzi to fight to the end alongside the German ally might have its noble side. "During that long meeting he said to me that we were enemies, yes, but also Italians, and when I invited him to join us in the mountains, he said he could not, he had given his word . . . He also said, 'we cut each others' throats serving two masters, why can't we stop it?' . . . And not long after, my brother was freed."[62]

After hearing Usseglio's testimony the jurors were probably not surprised when the president of the court read out several other statements the defense had provided in Carnazzi's favor, including those of the bishops of Aosta, Asti, and Ivrea. Upright and honest: that's how Monsignor Paolo Rostagno, bishop of Ivrea, had found Carnazzi when he served at Aosta. The young prefect had not demanded outright backing for Salò from the priests; he had asked only that they keep their parishes calm to avoid German reprisals.[63] The two other bishops also wrote in support, very much in line with the general request made by Pius XII's apostolic nuncio in those same days that the special courts of assizes show clemency toward the veterans of Salò.[64]

From Resistance to clemency? Independently of what the Catholic hierarchy urged, the postwar climate was changing. By that autumn the "Northern wind"—the drive to revolutionize Italy after the war—had started to subside, and with it the popular fury that in the weeks after the Liberation had driven proceedings of the people's tribunals, military tribunals, and special courts of assizes to be so ruthless. To be sure, Fascists still faced being put on trial; across the north of Italy the special courts went on functioning beyond the six months of operation initially foreseen, and they continued to serve up sentences, sometimes severe ones, against collaborators. But as time went on, the magistrates with their technical procedures began to outweigh the political force exerted by the jurors, and formal justice began to overwhelm revolutionary justice.[65]

At Asti that afternoon of October 20, 1945, Cesare Carnazzi benefited only in part from this change of climate. The court ruled that he had backed the "pseudo Social Republic" with "fanatical zeal," and found him guilty of both capital charges against him. As prefect of Aosta, Carnazzi had manifestly favored the "German invader," directing "a police bureau dedicated to espionage" and instituting the volunteer Alpine Musketeers corps, as well as overseeing an "undetermined number" of raids like those on the Val d'Ayas and the upper Canavese. As prefect of Asti, Carnazzi had coordinated "all reprisal actions" against the partisans with the German command, "assisted by the notorious Redi (that is, Cagni), whom Carnazzi took with him from Aosta and Turin."[66]

The public prosecutor requested the death penalty: the defendant was sentenced to be shot in the back, the most humiliating of military punishments.[67] But despite finding that Carnazzi was guilty (and that the defense lawyers had offered "no serious proof" to the contrary), the court nevertheless granted him the benefit of "extenuating circumstances." He had demonstrated "a few second thoughts," the jury ruled, especially during the final days, "softening his stance against the approaching liberators . . . although lacking the civil and moral courage to join them in the work of saving the Nation." The court reduced the two sentences of capital punishment against Carnazzi to twenty-four years of prison on each charge, effectively a sentence of life imprisonment.[68]

Ladislao Gerber

That same afternoon Carnazzi's lawyers delivered an appeal motion to the court clerk.[69] His case thus began to follow the course that nearly all the cases of collaborators would take during the time of Italian epuration (or rather non-epuration, as it would prove to be). The defense would appeal to the Court of Cassation on the basis of alleged errors of legal form and substance, and in most cases the higher court would repeal the sentence—either because it was one of many verdicts that did in fact have technical faults, or simply because the Northern wind was abating, softening the force of popular opinion and allowing even the defeated to hope for pardon.

To read Carnazzi's appeal is an instructive experience. It is a leap into the world of post-Fascist law, a world both juridically lucid and ideologically murky. When his lawyers latched onto errors of legal form in the sentence, they simply did their job in assuring that their client received a fair trial. But Carnazzi's defenders also attacked the substance of the sentence. Using arguments that were often specious, they sought to flatten and deny the political and military nature of the crime, making collaborationism seem meaningless and insignificant. In essence, Carnazzi's lawyers argued not only that the ex-prefect was not personally responsible, but that collaborationism couldn't be attributed to an ex-functionary of Salò at all: that collaborationism itself did not exist.

The lawyers even objected when Carnazzi's accusers called the house-to-house raids *rastrellamenti*, as they were commonly known. Properly, they claimed, the term had a more restricted meaning. A *rastrellamento* was a war maneuver, cleaning out any hostile enclaves left after tanks advanced into enemy territory. But Carnazzi was no military man, so how could he be responsible for such maneuvers? That he had carried out police raids was merely part of his job as prefect. "We ought to agree that the prefect was duty-bound . . . to uphold public order." And it was just for that reason that he had created the Alpine Musketeers, and had occasionally ordered other "repressive or preventive actions . . . and in any case if he had dealt with arrested persons it was to save them from German clutches by exploiting every procedural loophole until the procedures themselves dissolved into nothing."[70]

In their appeal Carnazzi's lawyers also pointed to his "infinite good deeds during those twenty months" and to the "large sheaf of declarations and testimony" presented at his trial from bishops, ordinary people, university professors, partisan chiefs, and high-ranking magistrates, an outpouring of "unanimous consent."[71] Curiously, the lawyers did not emphasize that among the statements defending Carnazzi was one "signed by members of the Milan Jewish Community" substantiating the deposition made by "Rosa Gerber, daughter of Salomone, aged 33, born in Budapest and resident in Milan." That is to say, Carnazzi's lawyers did not think it particularly significant that the list of people writing on his behalf included Jews who had escaped the Final Solution. This lack of interest itself eloquently testifies to how little Italians knew about the death camps in the fall of 1945. But it is a lack of interest that we must put right, for the case of the Gerber family shows Cesare Augusto Carnazzi in a surprising light.

That Carnazzi was an anti-Semite, at least in his official role, seems clear. Back in 1942 he had informed the then-prefect of Aosta that hundreds of Croatian and Yugoslav Jews interned at Saint-Vincent and in the Canavese were wrongfully occupying housing meant for Turinese summer guests. In December 1943, as prefect, he put the firm of Camillo Olivetti, a Jew, on the Salò blacklist as the local Communist nucleus. And then there was the striking nonchalance with which he deported Primo Levi, Luciana Nissim, and Vanda Maestro, "there being no other charges against them" aside from being Jewish. So it comes as some surprise to find in the archives the statement presented to the Asti Special Court of Assizes by the Gerber family, testifying to the help these non-Italian Jews had received from Carnazzi.

The letter, dated Milan, August 7, 1945, is signed by seven members of the Gerber family: Salomone and Enzia, the parents, and the children, Oscar, Rosa, Elena, Ladislao, and Agnese. They are identified as Polish by birth, Jewish in terms of religion. The family had taken refuge in the town of Gandino in the Lombardy region, east of Piedmont, and there the armistice had found them. The men in the family took to the mountains so as not to be captured, but in the autumn of 1944 the twenty-two-year-old Ladislao was arrested by the SS "during a raid" and "condemned to death by the Germans" as a Jew and as a partisan. At this point his sister Rosa turned in desperation to Carnazzi, then directing the National Agency for Maternity and Infancy. Carnazzi, the letter went on, "took in the Signorina Rosa Gerber and warmly pursued the matter with the Italian and German authorities," finally obtaining a repeal of the death sentence and even Ladislao's release. "The undersigned . . . deeply moved, affirm their everlasting gratitude to Dott. Cesare Augusto Carnazzi for his kind and generous actions that saved the life of a young man, for no personal gain but merely out of great benevolence," the letter concluded, and it was countersigned "in perfect knowledge of the above" by nine other members of Milan's Jewish community.[72]

The Jewish partisan saved by the anti-Semitic prefect: it sounds like pure invention but it is not, or not entirely. Certainly this episode that ended well deserves the same detailed reconstruction as all the deplorable stories—about Carnazzi himself, the spy Cagni, Centurion Ferro, Commander Imerico, and all those Italians working for Salò who played their part, large or small, in the elimination of European Jews. So often our retrospective thoughts about the Shoah follow a binary logic: there were perpetrators and victims. Maybe bystanders are allowed as a third group.[73] Yet matters can be more complicated,[74] and the case of Carnazzi is a reminder. The functionary of Salò was a model of the banality of evil but also of the banality of decency, although we should note that the Gerbers' experience reflected the unusual circumstances that permitted Gandino, a town of five thousand people, to harbor dozens of non-Italian Jews during the German occupation.

Salomone Gerber and Enzia Rosemberg were born in Poland in the 1880s but met in Budapest, where each had emigrated, and there had their five children. From Hungary they had come to Italy in 1938, hoping to go on to the United States, but when they were unable to get visas for all seven family members they decided to stay, although they were put in civilian internment camps when Italy entered the war. Salomone and Oscar were sent far to the south in Calabria, but were eventually given permission to rejoin the rest of the family in the foothills of the Bergamo Alps. They settled in nearby Gandino, where a large community of Jews was interned—German, Austrian, Czech, Yugoslav, Polish, and Hungarian. In those days Gandino was a humble town that lived off modest farm enterprises. The internees supported themselves as best they could; many processed remnants of leather and fur.[75]

For the Gerber family as for other Jews, real trouble began with Police Order Number Five of November 30, 1943, when persecution became a matter of life and death.[76] But while as early as December Jews in nearby areas were being detained (and would soon be deported to Auschwitz), not one of the Jews living in Gandino was ever arrested apart from Ladislao Gerber. More than fifty, possibly sixty former internees lived inside the town limits for the entire German occupation, protected by a tight aid network. At the town hall, the registrar of births and deaths provided them with false documents. The inhabitants of Gandino hosted them in their own homes, in a silent and effective response that crossed class barriers: among the hosts were an elementary school teacher and a municipal doctor, a baker and a math professor, farmers and Ursuline nuns. Their help became a real rescue operation when Jews with recognizably non-Italian surnames—Zeitlin and Kerbes, Hacher and Lowi,

Gottlieb and Gerber, Kuschlein and Dubienski—were hidden away from German eyes in the mountains above town, in shepherds' huts and hunting blinds.[77]

According to what the inhabitants of Gandino have committed to collective memory, Ladislao Gerber was arrested on August 28, 1944, when the Germans carried out a door-to-door search without warning. Ladislao's sister Elena was able to confirm the circumstances when I spoke to her by phone in July 2012. Then ninety-three, but lively and gifted with the voice of a woman twenty years younger, Elena told me about the German "raid" of the house the family had been renting in town until that unlucky day. (Afterward, the town notary offered them a hut in the mountains; "the parish priest sent bread up to us once a week," she said, "and the Fascists never said a word, although they knew, every-one knew.") When Ladislao was sent to jail in the city of Bergamo, his sister Rosa decided to approach Carnazzi. Clara Klein, a young Hungar-ian Jew who had worked as a pediatrician at the Bergamo hospital, and who perhaps for that reason knew the director of the National Agency for Maternity and Infancy, helped her arrange the meeting.

"I remember Avvocato Carnazzi very well," Elena Gerber told me. "He was a good man . . . For what he did, for saving Ladislao, he wouldn't take anything. No fee, nothing at all." So was Carnazzi, the prefect who diligently applied the rules against Jews, also a Fascist with a human face? It appears so. On October 20, 1945, Rosa appeared at the Asti Special Court of Assizes to confirm in an oral statement what her fam-ily had written in their letter. "My brother was arrested by the Germans because he professed the Jewish religion, was a Polish subject, and also belonged to a partisan formation," Rosa Gerber told the court. "I con-tacted Dott. Carnazzi . . . My brother's death sentence was annulled and later he was released on Carnazzi's recognizance."[78]

When I read back the Gerber family letter to the now elderly Elena Gerber, the letter she and all the other members of the family had signed, she corrected the document on two points. First, she denied that her brothers Oscar and Ladislao had ever joined the partisans.[79] They remained hidden in Gandino and the mountain huts, she said. And on the matter of Ladislao having been condemned to death by the Germans, Elena Gerber denied that too. ("That's wrong, from what I know.") It may therefore be that the Gerbers, wishing to emphasize the merits of an official who was facing the death penalty, had heightened the drama somewhat in their postwar statements. It may be, but the essential point remains: Cesare Carnazzi did intervene on Ladislao Gerber's behalf. With his help, the young stateless Jew returned to the protection of the people of Gandino—six of whom were recognized by Israel in 2004 as Righteous Among the Nations.[80]

6

Body of Proof

"Two or three that I don't recall"

WHEN THE PARTISANS CAPTURED CARNAZZI ON APRIL 28, EDILIO
Cagni was taken prisoner as well. During his industrious career as a
collaborator, he had worked in three of the provinces of Piedmont—
Aosta, Turin, and Asti—so before charges could be filed the first question
was which jurisdiction would try him. At first it seemed that he, like
Carnazzi, would be sent before the Special Court of Assizes in Asti, the
city in which he'd initially been arrested and detained. But the police
commissioner of free Turin wanted the "war criminal Cagni" to be tried
there for his role in the Perotti trial of 1944, during which he had testified voluntarily against the resistance leaders.[1] The memory of that dramatic event, and of the farcical trial that had condemned eight of the
accused to the firing squad, was still too fresh for this request to go
unheard. At the same time, free Aosta also wanted to try the phony Lieutenant Redi, that factotum in Prefect Carnazzi's private police who had
been so busy between the autumn of 1943 and the spring of 1944.[2]

By early June the police in Aosta released a detailed report denounc-
ing Cagni. It was written by none other than Guido Bachi, who had
been so grievously duped by Cagni when the latter infiltrated the Casale
band. It had been Bachi who'd asked Cagni, or "Lt. Redi," that he send
"sub-Lt. Meoli"—the spy De Ceglie—over to assist his own group at
Col de Joux. Now, the man Cagni had conned was to have his hour
of revenge in a free Italy.

Bachi did not hold back. One day in December 1943, he recalled,
he and Aldo Piacenza had met the leaders of the band at Arcesaz, and
one of them had introduced Bachi to three army officers who said they
had fled Aosta because the German police were after them. Cagni, Bianchi, and De Ceglie were presented under their false names and ranks.
"I noticed right away that the one who had the most authority was
Cagni," Bachi wrote. "At my request" De Ceglie was placed with the
group at Amay as Bachi's "subordinate." Just a few days later, both bands
collapsed during the raid carried out by the Germans and the Salò
militia in league with the three spies.[3]

During the interrogations at Aosta, Bachi went on, "Cagni was always
the most obstinate accuser, and he often threatened torture and at times
he carried out those threats." This was in effect just what Primo Levi
would write thirty years later in *The Periodic Table*. "For example," Bachi
wrote, "Sig. Barbesino of Casale . . . had to be admitted to the infirmary"
following his interrogation, and Bachi saw at first hand "the suffering
he had endured." Furthermore, with the backing of Carnazzi, Cagni
had ordered the arrest of Bachi's wife, on the charge of passing on political information when she visited Bachi in jail. Cagni had also tried to
trap the Turinese attorney Camillo Reynaud, who was the contact
between the partisans at Amay and the political leaders of the Partito
d'Azione in Piedmont. Cagni had shown up at Reynaud's office "pretending to be a partisan"—in fact, pretending he had been sent by Bachi,
then in jail, "to procure weapons and money" for the rebels who had
escaped capture in the raid. (Reynaud sensed something odd and did
not fall for the ruse.) "From what I know of Cagni I believe he is one of

the most dangerous exponents of Republican Fascism, both intelligent and capable, but criminal in the gravest sense of the word," Bachi wrote.

There would be nothing to add to that had his statement not also included a notable description of a conversation from December 1943. After the phony Lieutenant Redi had taken over command of the Arcesaz band he met with Bachi, head of the group at Col de Joux. "I informed him," Bachi wrote of Cagni, "that two members of my group were unwilling to take orders, and proposed they be transferred to the group at Arcesaz. But Cagni did not agree and he offered me a revolver so that (the words are his) 'you can eliminate them in the quickest way possible.' I opposed his methods and I did well, because four days after that meeting, a raid against Arcesaz and Amay was carried out and I saw with my own eyes that the presumed army officers in our bands were Republican spies."

I sat there reading and rereading that statement by Bachi until the truth struck me. The aftermath of a civil war is this too: a time of reckoning when the victors can insinuate that the losers are guilty of things done by the victors themselves. The episode Bachi mentions, as we know, refers to those two hotheads unwilling to submit to discipline, Fulvio Oppezzo and Luciano Zabaldano. Now the Liberation had come and Bachi, to fortify the case against Cagni, denounced the advice he said the spy had given him: to resolve the problem with a revolver. But he did not mention what had happened after that advice: the snowy dawn of December 9, the mysterious "Berto," the "Soviet method," the two young men outside the hut at Frumy, the Beretta machine gun. The anti-Fascist Bachi wrote his statement as if the brusque method suggested by the Fascist Cagni had not been, in fact, diligently applied by the partisans of Col de Joux.

On June 21, the Turin police came to transfer Cagni to jail in the Piedmontese capital.[4] They did not yet have Bachi's denunciation, and when they first questioned Cagni he argued that he had no criminal responsibility because he had been merely a functionary of the Salò government. It was true that he had worked directly for Carnazzi in Aosta, he said, but "in the press office." He claimed he had never taken part in Nazi-Fascist raids or been part of the Black Brigades. He had been forced to testify against Perotti and company by Prefect Carnazzi, who in turn had been ordered to appear by his own superior. In court, Cagni said, he had limited himself to supplying basic information. In Bergamo and Asti, serving with Carnazzi, he had been a mere bureaucrat. Really, he'd done nothing seriously blameworthy in those twenty months after the Royal Army had disbanded and he began to receive a salary ("3,000 lire a month") from the Social Republic. On the contrary, "although the events I have described might make it seem I was a Fascist, I would like to say that several times I helped partisan leaders by supplying false documents and weapons."[5] In short, Cagni took advantage of the fact that his accusers did not possess all the information they needed, presenting himself as collaborationist small fry, someone who had ended up in the anti-Fascist nets almost by chance.

By the next time Cagni was interrogated, on July 13, his investigators were somewhat better informed. They now had the statement Bachi had made to Aosta police, and they had arranged for him to formally identify Cagni as the agent provocateur who, along with Bianchi and De Ceglie, had provoked the raid of December 13. However, they still did not have the self-aggrandizing accounts sent by the three spies to Carnazzi after the raid was over, the records of the rebels' interrogations, or the report Cagni filed regarding the March 1944 raid in the Canavese. They lacked, in short, the documents that eventually would nail down Cagni, Bianchi, and De Ceglie as willful collaborators. Without that evidence, on July 13 Cagni was once again able to offer a wonderfully naïve version of his role in the infiltration of the partisan bands at Arcesaz and Amay.

This was the story he told: in December 1943, when the German commander at Aosta decided to comb the area around Brusson for rebels, Prefect Carnazzi was concerned the Germans might also attack "the pacific population," and so he had sent Cagni to the Val d'Ayas merely to "identify those areas controlled by partisans." When a woman working at the bar in Verrès introduced him to some of the rebels, Cagni had followed them "half-heartedly" toward Brusson. Once he arrived at their camp, he said, he did nothing to impress them. "I sat in a corner drying off from the rain," and "frankly I cannot today reconstruct the circumstances that led me, an outsider who had only arrived in the area two days before, to be named head of the partisan formation." Then, at the request of "a certain Bachi," he had arranged to send a young man who had just arrived at Aosta, De Ceglie, "to Amay, where I vaguely knew there was a small band of partisans." Warned by a local farmer that a raid was imminent, Cagni said, he had "distributed weapons to everyone." The Nazi-Fascists prevailed, but "no partisans were captured," in part because Carnazzi and Cagni himself had tried to discourage the Germans from pursuing the rebels. Returning to Aosta, Cagni had seen a handful of fairly harmless people taken in the raid: "a certain De Furia and his wife, a certain Carretto, and two or three that I don't recall."[6]

A way with words, a strategic "I don't recall" here and there: during the Liberation, these would not suffice to keep justice from being done. Even as Cagni was insisting on his unlikely reluctance as a collaborator, Guido Bachi was telling investigators about those two or three prisoners whose names Cagni couldn't recall. In the Col de Joux raid, Bachi said, those captured from the Amay band had included Bachi himself and Aldo Piacenza, both sent to be tried by the Special Tribunal, plus three people "deported to Germany": "Dott. Levi Primo (presently on his way back from Germany), Dottoressa Nissim, and Dottoressa Maestro Vanda (the last passed away after her deportation to Germany)." Why they had been deported, the Jewish Bachi chose not to say. He seems to have thought the three deserved justice as Italian anti-Fascists before they were counted as Jewish victims.[7]

Lions and lambs

After several months of indecision, the Aosta Special Court of Assizes prevailed over the courts of Asti and Turin, winning the right to try Cagni there first.[8] The months-long dispute over the venue would redound in Cagni's favor, not only because the public and private passions of the civil war were waning as time passed, but also because by the fall a passionate new cause had begun to occupy the anti-Fascists of Valle d'Aosta: the question of whether their region should remain in Italy under a special autonomous statute or secede from the country outright. The region's most distinguished Resistance veteran, the historian Federico Chabod, had managed to obtain autonomous regional status for Valle d'Aosta and was set to become its first regional president. In the way stood a newly formed separatist group, Union Valdôtaine, and various ex-partisans who wanted Valle D'Aosta to be annexed by De Gaulle's France.[9]

Nevertheless, the case against Cagni went forward. There was still a desire to try anyone who had been involved in the repressive apparatus of Nazi-Fascist power—functionaries in the prefecture and the police, bosses and militiamen in the Republican National Guard, officers and men of the Black Brigades, volunteers with the Alpine Musketeer corps, spies at the Cogne steel works, doctors and journalists at the service of the enemy, and the women who had collaborated as secretaries, inter-preters, informers, or mistresses to the Germans. Although the team of magistrates at the Special Court of Aosta was small they were hard-working, and managed to conduct ninety-nine trials between June and December 1945, plus another fifty-two the following year.[10] More than 250 defendants were tried, among them Cagni, who would appear in court in April 1946.

During the investigative phase Cagni's case involved several other people as well, including Alberto Bianchi and Domenico De Ceglie, sus-pected of complicity with Cagni under the same two articles of the wartime military criminal code that figured in the charges against Car-nazzi: aiding and providing intelligence to the enemy.[11] The investiga-tors turned their attention primarily to Cagni, however, because neither Bianchi nor De Ceglie could be found. A report filed in January 1946 with the Aosta police political department stated that "De Ceglie, at the time of surrender of the Social Republic, left Aosta for an unknown destination."[12] And a report on Bianchi tentatively reconstructed what became of him after he left Aosta in October 1944 to take part in special police training near Milan: "during the journey he appears to have been taken aside by partisan elements near Santhià and shot."[13]

In mid-January 1946, the deputy prosecutor in Aosta questioned Cagni closely and at length. But just as he had done when questioned in Turin in the summer of 1945, Cagni replied with a series of denials and alternative versions. "Redi" had not been a spy when he appeared in the Val d'Ayas in December 1943, he claimed; he'd been sent by the prefect merely to report "with a simple yes or no" whether there were any partisans in the area. He had found himself at the head of the Arcesaz band following a series of chance events, when he had no choice but to "go along with the fortuitous and unexpected way things developed in those days." Cagni also denied any responsibility for the arrests of Levi, Maestro, and Nissim, whose names he garbled in testimony. "I had no way of materially knowing that such persons existed, because no one had ever mentioned them to me." He suggested the accusation be directed at De Ceglie. In any event, he said, "I have never been to Amay."[14]

But it was not just the three Jews captured at Amay and deported to Auschwitz that Cagni had on his conscience, the court insisted. There was also the matter of Giuseppe Carrera, the nineteen-year-old partisan from Casale with a twisted ankle who was killed at the inn in Arcesaz, his corpse desecrated. The prosecutor at Aosta deposited in the trial record a letter from the boy's mother. Maria Carrera blamed "the Social Republican criminal Lt. Cagni" for her son's violent death, adding that "all responsibility for what took place falls on this monstrous assassin, against whom I demand justice to the extent of the law." Not long after the Liberation, in July 1945, she had filed charges against persons unknown for Giuseppe's death, indicating Cagni, then in custody in Turin, as the man who could supply "the name of the perpetrator of the murder."[15] Now, in March 1946, this aggrieved mother no longer sought to determine legal responsibility but to assign moral blame.

Another statement was put on record at the same time, also sent from Casale. It was signed by Alessandro Del Rosso, a tradesman who had served on the Casale Liberation Committee for the Socialist party. "The black brigand Lt. Cagni," Del Rosso said, had arrested him after breaking into his mechanic's shop a few days after the raid in the Val d'Ayas. "Pointing a revolver," Cagni had taken Del Rosso to the Republican Guard command for interrogation, and had threatened him and others, saying, "They're all lions here but they'll be lambs when we get them to Aosta." Cagni also searched Del Rosso's house. There he saw "on top of a cabinet, quite visible, a photograph of young Giuseppe Carrera (whose family lives ten meters away from mine) . . . and he pointed to that photograph before my wife and said, 'There he is, Carrera,' as if to say, 'There's your body of proof' "—that is, evidence of a connection between Del Rosso and the Resistance. Cagni knew very well who Carrera was, Del Rosso wrote, because Cagni had infiltrated the band at Arcesaz and guided the "assassin raiders," who after they killed Carrera had "hacked at his face with a dagger." And "that detail can be confirmed by photographic evidence," Del Rosso added, in effect neatly turning Cagni's "body of proof" against the spy himself.[16]

The proceedings against Cagni were set to open in the Aosta courtroom on April 12 when his defense lawyer, attorney Vittorio Chauvelot of Turin, appealed to the president of the court for a deferment. Procedural obstacles, he said, had kept him from meeting his client until just a few days before the trial was to start and had made it impossible to organize his defense. "Do not force me, esteemed Signor President, to merely pretend to be his defender," he wrote, adding that in the halls of justice, the word was that Cagni's judicial prospects were grim: "The death sentence is considered almost certain." The prosecutor, speaking of it, had "accompanied his words with an eloquent gesture." And not only were the charges extremely serious, but "the local mood likewise" made defending Cagni exceptionally difficult.[17]

Aosta was in a lynching mood in those first days of April 1946, saturated with politically explosive sentiment as the debate over Valle d'Aosta's future grew ever more contentious. On March 26 the city had seen the largest and boldest demonstration of the postwar period, which came close to ending in tragedy. Some two thousand demonstrators who wanted to see Valle d'Aosta annexed by France surrounded the palace where regional president Federico Chabod had his offices. The group broke in and the rowdiest among them occupied the president's office, calling for a direct popular vote on whether the region should secede from Italy. When Chabod refused this request, he was punched and kicked, dragged out onto the balcony, and nearly thrown off it.[18]

The violence continued outside. Carabinieri were assaulted and army tanks attacked; rioters broke into the Torre dei Balivi jail and obtained the release of three French journalists who had been jailed the day before. Even when the tempestuous day was over and calm returned to Aosta, the pressure from separatists did not let up. Bolstered by support from the government in Rome, Chabod managed to hold on to political control of the region, but he remained uneasy about the future. The separatists, he told Italy's prime minister, Alcide De Gasperi, were holding rallies, sometimes clandestine ones, in the woods and pastures of the Col de Joux.[19]

Such was the political climate in which the president of the Aosta Special Court agreed to Chauvelot's request to delay the Cagni trial until May 4. Meanwhile, Guido Bachi, taking advantage of the extension, sent a brief letter to the chief prosecutor. "Distinguished Signor Cordone, in discussing the Cagni trial with several friends, I learned they were eager to be heard as witnesses on May 4, and would therefore be pleased to be listed as prosecution witnesses. Both are survivors of the camp of Auswitchs and were arrested along with me in the raid of December 1943 carried out by Cagni."[20]

If the spelling of Auschwitz did not come automatically to an Italian in April 1946, even a Jewish one, readers will nevertheless know to whom Bachi was referring. The two survivors anxious to appear before the court were "Dott. Primo Levi" and "Dott. Luciana Nissim."[21] With those numbers on their arms, were they not also bodies of proof?

The witness Levi

Levi and Nissim, who had left Aosta in chains and were now returning to testify against those who had betrayed them, showed up at a moment when both were transmuting their experiences in the camp into words on a page. Luciana Nissim had just finished writing *Remembering the Death House*, which would be printed later that year.[22] Primo Levi was deep into *If This Is a Man*, having finished the chapters "Chemical Examination," "The Canto of Ulysses," and "October 1944," and begun to write "Ka-Be."[23] The occasion was charged for them both, but there is much for a historian to gain by examining how Levi in particular saw his role as witness in 1946—for it is as a witness above all that he came to be appreciated and understood in the later decades of the twentieth century. It was an image backed up by Levi's own statements, interviews, and conversations in the 1980s. At that point in his life, Levi, as one of the saved of Auschwitz, presented himself as a "witness by right and by duty."[24] He even sounded uncharacteristically proud of himself in that regard: "I am among the few in Italy who have borne witness."[25] Meanwhile, the literary criticism on Levi's works has emphasized this role to the point of cliché, treating him as one of *the* witnesses of the Shoah. Yet in 1946 Levi seems to have understood his role less, it seems, as Primo Levi the Witness; more like "the witness Levi" called before the court in Aosta.

For both the physician Nissim and the chemist Levi, their writing about the Lager was initially conceived as a matter of documentary evidence, if not actually scientific proof. Nissim's book was a revised version of a report she had sent to the Union of Italian Jewish Communities in Rome during the winter of 1945–46.[26] That report was one of the accounts received by the retired colonel Massimo Adolfo Vitale, who was collecting information on Jews deported from Italy under the German occupation. Not long thereafter Vitale would also receive a "Report on the Medical–Health Care Organization of the Concentration Camp for Jews, Monowitz (Auschwitz–Upper Silesia)," coauthored by Levi and

Leonardo De Benedetti, the physician who had made the return trip from Poland to Italy with Levi.[27] That report, published in the medical journal *Minerva Medica* later in 1946, is now considered by literary scholars a precursor of *If This Is a Man*.[28]

As early as 1945, when writing to Bianca Guidetti Serra from Katowice, Levi had defined the number on his left arm as a "document" he was bringing back to Italy. The same word, *document*, also appears in the opening sentences of *If This Is a Man*, where the author says his book "was written not to file new charges, but to supply documents for a cool-headed study of some aspects of the human soul."[29] The tattoo was the corporeal link between the victim who is made powerless and the executioner who must pay, proof incarnate of Nazi-Fascist guilt. Still, while Levi spoke of an intent "to document," there is nowhere yet an explicit reference to "bearing witness." He was simply providing crucial information; only later would he assume the public role of not allowing the Holocaust to be forgotten.

The word *testimone* ("a witness," a person who can testify to events) does not appear in *If This Is a Man*. The word *testimonianza* (a testimony, evidence offered by someone who is "bearing witness") appears just once in the first edition of the book, in 1947, and it appears in a painfully prosaic context, when Levi describes the barracks of the infirmary at Monowitz where inmates with dysentery were housed. "Precious evidence" is Levi's ironic way of referring to the proof ill prisoners must produce to show that their diarrhea is continuing, which earns them the right to remain in the barracks.[30] Only in the second edition of the book, published in 1958, does another instance of the word *testimonianza* appear, now with an entirely different and fully noble meaning. In a new chapter added for that edition, "Initiation," Levi recalls how, thanks to a "man of good will," the prisoner Steinlauf, he learned just a few days after arriving at Auschwitz that "even in this place one can survive, and therefore one must want to survive, to tell the story, to bear witness."[31]

In Latin, one of the words that means *witness* is *superstes*, survivor. Yet despite Levi's extensive knowledge of Latin from his schooldays, and

Steinlauf's wisdom transmitted in the camp, during the first years after his return from Auschwitz Levi does not seem to have made the connection between surviving, telling, and bearing witness. Or so at any rate suggests the richest source that historians have to reconstruct Levi's state of mind during the months he wrote and rewrote *If This Is a Man*: those wonderfully intimate letters he sent to Jean Samuel, the Pikolo of "The Canto of Ulysses," between the spring and fall of 1946. On March 23, Levi told his friend he was writing "poems, essays, even stories" (and that Samuel might be surprised to see one about himself), but that he had vowed "to never forget" and "hoped to collect all in a book in the end." In short, he meant to remember, to recount, but not necessarily to assume the public role of witness.[32] In another letter, dated October 29, Levi went so far as to write: "Auschwitz more or less forgotten, apart from when I look at the number on my arm."[33] As he was nearing completion of *If This Is a Man*, that number continued to seem to him the sole essential document, the alpha and omega of the "saved" of the death camp.

In fact Primo Levi in 1946 did not envision that in testifying about the Final Solution he would have to make legal judgments. In the preface to *If This Is a Man* he specifically said he had not written the book to formulate new charges. Especially in dealing with a situation as extreme as an extermination camp, he believed that a study of the human soul must avoid extremes, that it should record not "the heroes and the traitors" but the norm, "the average man, neither contemptible nor saintly."[34] As much as betrayal was a thread running through his language in that first book (dawn arrived "like a traitor" on the day the Jews of Fossoli were to be deported; parents and children disappeared "treacherously, before we knew it" on arrival at the *Judenrampe*; the very structure of the Lager, in which privileged slaves were given a hope of survival, was founded on the "betrayal of natural solidarity"[35]), nevertheless in Levi's book it is as if treachery took place without traitors. Few real figures of infamy were named and pointed out, apart from the spy Frenkl, who did evil for evil's sake.

In April 1946, a free man ready to travel to Aosta and give his testimony in the Cagni trial, Levi had already finished writing "The Story of Ten Days," which would be the last chapter of *If This Is a Man*. He had already put down on paper those days between January 18, 1945, when the Germans left Auschwitz, and January 27. Levi and two French prisoners with scarlet fever, a farmer named Arthur and a schoolteacher named Charles, had been abandoned by the Germans in the infirmary with other prisoners considered already dead; but the three were able to fight off their illnesses, organize themselves in the ruins of the camp, and come back to life. In the evening of January 25, Levi wrote, "around the stove, Charles, Arthur, and I felt ourselves becoming human again. We could talk about anything and everything. I loved listening to Arthur talk about how they would spend their Sundays at Provenchères in the Vosges, and Charles nearly wept as I described the moment of my arrest."[36]

In the first draft of "The Story of Ten Days" Levi said nothing more, nothing at all. There was not even a hint of Cagni, the spy at the Val d'Ayas who did evil for evil's sake. It was as if Levi the Witness and "the witness Levi" answered to different logics: one analyzing morality and human nature, the other eager for justice and revenge.

Day of judgment

The Italian postal service was surprisingly efficient in the spring of 1946. Guido Bachi's letter, in which he asked that two veterans of "Auswitchs" be added to the list of prosecution witnesses, was sent from Turin to the chief prosecutor of the Special Court of Assizes of Aosta on April 23 and arrived the next day. The Aosta court bureaucracy also functioned smoothly, and that same day the prosecutor asked the president of the court to include "witnesses Levi and Nissim" among those called to testify. On April 25 the clerk recorded that the request had been carried out.[37]

If Aosta was too troubled by tensions between autonomists and separatists to properly celebrate the first anniversary of the Liberation, the same was not true of Turin, one of the capitals of the Resistance. The dead were celebrated in what *La Nuova Stampa* called "a moving pilgrimage to the partisan graves." The Archbishop of Turin held a mass at the section of the city cemetery dedicated to the Resistance, while the veterans of the partisan bands held a rally in the central plaza. On the front page of the paper, meanwhile, was a story about the crime news of the day, the stealing of Il Duce's corpse from his tomb by some unidentified neo-Fascist militants.[38]

It was a year since the civil war had ended, but Italy still bore the scars. It could not have been otherwise: the world war and the German occupation had not only devastated the country, but had left deep fault lines that made grief itself divisive.[39] The approaching Italian constitutional referendum, which offered the country a choice between retaining the monarchy or establishing a new Italian republic, made for further tension. So did rumors that the winner of this referendum—whether it be the monarchy or a republican government—would celebrate with a general amnesty for all those who had committed crimes during the civil war. Yes, amnesty could be seen as a gesture of national reconciliation (as well as a measure to ease severe overcrowding in the prisons), but for a broad sector of democratic opinion the very idea that clemency could be extended to veterans of Salò and the Resistance alike was anathema.[40]

The way the jurors were chosen in Cagni's case highlights the political aspect of Aosta justice in the spring of 1946. The four lay "people's jurors" were officially to be selected by lot from a list drawn up by the local arm of the National Liberation Committee. In practice, the jurors in Aosta Special Court were all but handpicked, and in this case those chosen were decidedly anti-Fascists. Three of the four came directly from the ranks of the Resistance and were by now habitués of the courtroom. One, Silvio Gracchini, had been a major partisan commander. Another, Lino Melli, had been among the leaders of clandestine activities at the Cogne steel works. There was also Mauro Bordon, who had aided the partisans as an informer in the Valtournenche.[41] Although the rules stated that jurors must resist "any sentiment of aversion or favor," the presence of those three meant Cagni's fate was hardly in impartial hands.

When the trial opened on May 4, the first person called to testify was Cagni, the sole defendant present in the courtroom. (Alberto Bianchi and Domenico De Ceglie were being tried in absentia.)[42] Cagni simply repeated what he had already told the prosecutor when previously questioned: that he was present in the Val d'Ayas solely to transmit information, that his reports had purposely inflated his role, that it was not his job to interrogate prisoners in Aosta, and so forth.[43] His appearance was followed by that of dozens of witnesses, who came and went before the court with astonishing speed considering the seriousness of the charges: the collaborationism alleged against Cagni, Bianchi, and De Ceglie was punishable by death.

The witnesses appeared one after the other so quickly that the clerk did not always get their names and addresses right. Giuseppe Barbesino, the railway worker who accused Cagni of having tortured him—and who, by the time the trial took place, was mayor of Giarole Monferrato—was identified as "Barbesino Vincenzo," mayor of some place named Gerolamo d'Alba that is not to be found on any map. Attorney Camillo Reynaud, the Turin liaison to the partisans of Col de Joux, was "Vincenzo." Luciana Nissim was set down as the daughter of "Domenico," rather than Davide; was said to be a teacher rather than a doctor; and had her age recorded as thirty-three rather than twenty-six. Primo Levi was identified as an engineer, thirty-two years old, while he too was twenty-six. History was in a hurry to be written that spring Saturday in Aosta.

There were few surprises in the courtroom. Witness by witness the prosecutor composed a portrait of Cagni as a major collaborator, something more—and worse—than a mere factotum of Carnazzi. He was the prefect's dark side, his agent of evil, roaming through Valle d'Aosta and Piedmont via Turin, Casale Monferrato, and the Canavese plain. The most dramatic deposition of the day came from Maria Carrera, mother of Giuseppe, killed at the inn in Arcesaz on December 13. Just a few words, with an uncertain grasp on the historical sequence of events, but gripping: "My son before he was killed told me that up there was a suspicious type, a certain Cagni Redi, and once while he was eating he told me *I don't feel secure,* and then afterward I heard my son was dead in Brusson."[44]

Among the other witnesses testifying that day was Aldo Piacenza, who accused Cagni of having "damaged six hundred hand grenades" in the Val d'Ayas "so that we would be without munitions."[45] Six hundred grenades? That improbably high figure was confirmed in court by Ferdinando Trombin, who had joined the Arcesaz band at age eighteen, was captured in the December raid, and deported to a German prison camp.[46] Cagni's most tenacious accuser, Guido Bachi, also testified, and even got into an exchange with Cagni. What happened during the raid on Arcesaz "was not planned," Cagni said, interrupting Bachi's testimony. "That's not true; my impression was that it was planned," the ex-partisan insisted.[47]

The owner of the Hotel Ristoro, Maria Varisellaz, who was also captured in the raid, told the court of her confinement in the barracks at Aosta: "I was under arrest for 52 days charged with damaging the nation and having hosted Jewish persons."[48] One of them, Luciana Nissim, testified that the man calling himself Meoli (that is, De Ceglie) had come to Amay, where he studied the situation and informed Cagni, who in turn communicated with the German command.[49] Primo Levi's deposition was concise, practically telegraphic: "I was taken away and interrogated by Cagni at Aosta. I was identified by Meoli (De Ceglie), who supplied extensive information about our band and the National Liberation Committee."[50]

Many decades later, when I held in my hands that handwritten sheet recording Levi's deposition, my first reaction was disappointment. Was this all there was to it? The capture at Amay; the transport to Aosta; Cagni's interrogations, with his Luger on the desk; the transport to Fossoli; the journey to the lowermost rung at Auschwitz; the eleven months of a no-longer-human among no-longer-humans; the too long, or too brief, voyage of the truce—all this and more, reduced to just two meager sentences recorded by the clerk?

It took me a while to understand that the scene's power lay in its very terseness. Its weight came from the multitude of witnesses appearing in rapid succession before the special court, from the way Primo Levi's voice overlapped those of the many other men and women who were victims of Edilio Cagni's actions, largely unknown victims whose names generally do not appear in the annals of history: not just Trombin and Varisellaz, but Giuseppe Delchoz, farmer at Issogne; Emilio Prola, farmer at Verrès; Costanza Francisco, student at Verrès . . . [51] What mattered too was not so much what Primo Levi said but his decision to be present, with a surname so familiarly Jewish that even the clumsiest court clerk could not but pronounce it correctly; a man "already drowned," as he wrote in one of his "terse and bloody" poems of 1946, but perhaps saved for this too: so that he, number 174517, living proof of the crime, could appear at Cagni's trial.

It would be interesting to know whether the depositions of the two Jewish survivors of Auschwitz had any particular impact on the jurors in the trial. Most likely they did not; indeed, the deportation of the three Jews captured at Amay did not even figure in the twelve pages written by the judge justifying the sentences meted out by the court.[52] To the jury, Nissim and Levi probably appeared merely as just two among the victims of the "vast raid" in Val d'Ayas "that resulted in one dead partisan and 47 prisoners."[53] Nor did the court seem to give particular weight to the fact that Vanda Maestro, the third Jew deported, had been murdered in a gas chamber. If that Saturday in the courtroom at Aosta had any historical significance, it lay not so much in what Levi's testimony accomplished against Cagni as in what it did in the mind of the man then writing *If This Is a Man*.

In contrast to the dozens of prosecution witnesses there were only a few for the defense. Defense attorney Chauvelot insisted that some of his witnesses were not given a chance to testify,[54] but among those who did was Don Federico Bosticco, a priest who had worked with the partisans around Asti and mediated for them with the Germans. He gave credit to Cagni for having helped to exchange "eleven hostages," and oddly described the man as "meek."[55] Even odder was the deposition of Salvatore Balestrieri, a Sicilian army officer who had worked with a partisan division near Milan. Cagni, he said, had given the anti-Fascists information that allowed them to arrest a certain Baroness von Hodenberg, "a Gestapo director." And, he said, Cagni had further helped them "search for some gold bars belonging to the Interior Ministry" of the Social Republic and to the "famous" Paolo Zerbino, who had been Cagni's boss when he was a spy.[56]

The intelligence services had been so eager to recover the gold that they had let Cagni out of jail in Turin so he would have "the necessary freedom to conduct his inquiries." And, Balestrieri emphasized, the defendant "did not take advantage to escape." However, the recovery operation did not bear fruit, and Cagni was soon back in jail.[57]

Man and beast

The court records do not tell us at what hour that afternoon the Aosta Special Court of Assizes, after the procession of witnesses, heard the prosecutor make his closing statement, in which he asked for the death penalty for all three defendants. Afterwards, the defense spoke: a court-appointed lawyer for the two men being tried in absentia, and Chauvelot on behalf of Cagni. The judge then asked the sole defendant in the courtroom if he wished to make a statement, and when Cagni said no, told the jurors they could begin their deliberations.

The court records do not say how long those deliberations took, either. But we do know the session ended at 8 p.m. after the judge read out the sentences; it had taken ten hours altogether to determine the fates of the accused collaborators. Edilio Cagni was sentenced to be shot in the back, while his two sidekicks each got a thirty-year sentence and were banned from public office for life. The assets of all three defendants were to be confiscated by the state.[58]

Four days before the trial took place Cagni's lawyer had petitioned for transfer to a different jurisdiction, arguing that Aosta and its environs were hostile to the defendant. The president of the Aosta court had rejected that petition. Shortly after the trial, though, the appellate Court of Cassation asked whether local pressures might have influenced the judgment. Certainly not, the Aosta prosecutor replied. To begin with, he wrote, the composition of the jury ensured a fair trial: "perhaps in no other session of this Court of Assizes did the group of jurors chosen offer such a guarantee of impartiality." The jurors, "apart from one, had never before heard Cagni spoken of." As for the courtroom debate, it had taken place "most calmly and with little intervention from the public, which was very well behaved."[59]

Other sources, however, suggest that the atmosphere during the trial was not entirely pacific, and that the crowd was riotous at times.[60] Certainly a jury made up of former partisans was not likely to be impartial. As for the assertion that just one of them had heard of Cagni before the trial, it's hard to imagine that those jurors, who had served on numerous trials, could have been unaware of the existence of the man invariably known among Aosta anti-Fascists as "the notorious Lieutenant Redi." In short, the argument that Cagni, Bianchi, and De Ceglie received a fair hearing is difficult to credit.[61]

Indeed, the jurors, to judge by their written explanation of the verdict, had found the testimony presented in court somewhat superfluous, given the "firm structure of evidence" that had already been collected during the investigative phase of the trial. There were no two ways, they said, to interpret the documents from the winter of 1943–44, the reports sent by Cagni to Carnazzi after the "betrayal at Arcesaz" and the Canavese raid. Even supposing that some details in those reports had been inflated for effect, it was a "laughable attempt at defense" to suggest that everything Cagni had written was systematically exaggerated. "His full and undeniable guilt" was proved by the mass of "testimony and reports he personally had put his signature to."[62]

Did anyone seriously doubt that Cagni deserved to be judged by the wartime military criminal code, the jurors asked? Or wish to deny that the police role he played from the armistice to Liberation provided a direct advantage to the German occupier? Cagni himself had given blatant proof of that when he voluntarily appeared as a witness at the Perotti trial. In April 1944, Prefect Carnazzi's right-hand man had followed his boss to Turin precisely to build a case against anti-Fascist Cornelio Brosio, to accuse him of having funded the partisans at Arcesaz. "His zeal, his evident, calculated harshness and ruthlessness, his passion—and passion is the right word in his case—for the ignoble job he was doing, the tenacity with which he pursued and achieved his deplorable ends" had sowed the records of the Perotti trial "with documentation that requires no comment": so wrote the jurors in the Special Court of Aosta. Their language, as we can see, was not really juridical; they saw themselves more as the injured party than as impartial outsiders.[63]

Nor did the defense attorney's efforts to show that Cagni had grown more lenient between the winter of 1943–44 and the following one, or to establish his supposed absence of cruelty during interrogations, convince the jury. And if he had helped to deflect some Nazi crime, the jurors wrote, he had done so late in the game, when the direction of the world war and of the civil war were such that he could plainly see "the inevitable fate of the Italian Social Republic, and, sadly, of our poor country." They went on in a confusion of legal, political, and moral language: "Those acts of redress, essentially negative gestures, do not diminish his degree of responsibility, above all when we consider that even the most ruthless persecutors of their Italian brothers showed moments of humanity and merciful impulses at times. But these, fortunately, are part of the nature of all human beings, without which man would be nothing but a cruel and pitiless beast, prey to his most ferocious instincts."[64]

In the post-Liberation Italy of 1945–46, the sentences of the Special Courts of Assizes were often expressed in such terms; the jurors did not even try to conceal the partisan nature of their perspective. Such sentences would supply the collaborators' defense lawyers with many juridical hooks on which to hang their appeals, and the magistrates of the appellate Court of Cassation would find numerous technical points to invalidate lower court rulings. As the months went by after April 25, 1945, the mood of war gave way in criminal proceedings to the letter of the law. A sharp contrast became ever more evident between the logic of a fundamentally Jacobin justice system (that of the special courts) and one that might be called Thermidorian (a professional magistrature bound to guarantee state continuity rather than support the breach that the Resistance had been).[65]

Cagni's sentence was already vaguely anachronistic when it was issued. It came just one month before three major developments in Italian history: the referendum on the monarchy; the election of an assembly to draft a constitution for the new republic; and the general amnesty for political crimes. When the jurors at Aosta condemned Cagni to be shot, it was as if they thought the "Northern wind" was still blowing, that their side still had the power to overwhelm collaborators large and small. At the same time, when they granted Alberto Bianchi and Domenico De Ceglie the benefit of doubt, classifying them as mere underlings who carried out a superior's orders ("young men not much over twenty, who revolved about Cagni and were to some extent dominated by him"), the jurors administered their justice with discernment. Yet around them, both near and far, the wheel of history had begun to turn away from the direction it had taken just after the Liberation.

Cagni himself was too clever not to have perceived the change of climate, even from deep in his cell in the Torre dei Balivi. In fact, I feel certain the twenty-eight-year-old ex-spy did not endure a dark, Victor Hugo–esque "last night of the condemned" after he heard his death sentence read out. Most likely Cagni had already understood he would not end his days before a firing squad, was already confident he would come to a better end than those three young partisans of the Canavese— Domenico De Palo, Flavio Berone, and Livio Colzani—whom Lieutenant Redi had been so proud of eliminating one day in March 1944.

7

———

Role Play

Credit where credit is due

DURING WORLD WAR I, CARABINIERI SERGEANT MARTINO
Veduti earned not one but two medals for bravery in wartime. The first,
silver, was awarded in 1916 for having courageously disarmed a bandit; the second, gold, was given to him two years later for "exceptional
military capacities" displayed when he foiled a terrorist attack on a
powder magazine. Veduti had arrived after the fuse was lit, and when
he could not remove the explosive with his hands he ripped it out with
his teeth, thus preventing a catastrophic explosion.[1] The weekly *Domenica del Corriere* dedicated one of its celebrated cover illustrations to
this twenty-four-year-old "heroic sergeant."[2] It was the prime minister
himself who in 1918 pinned the gold medal to his chest. Three years
later Veduti would serve as standard-bearer when Italy paid tribute to all
the fallen who had never been identified, ceremonially transferring
the remains of the Unknown Soldier to the Altare della Patria in Rome.[3]

Eventually Veduti left the service and went into business. When the armistice came on September 8, 1943, he was fifty years old and had a family. But history was bearing down on him again: the ex-carabiniere with the gold medal soon found himself at the heart of rebel activity under German occupation. In December 1943 he was among those arrested at Casale thanks to the work of Cagni, Bianchi, and De Ceglie. Interrogated by the threesome, Veduti was not uncooperative. He told the police that Francesco and Italo Rossi had come to the sack factory that he managed in Casale, seeking bags to hold flour and rice for escaped officers and soldiers. At subsequent meetings, Veduti continued his account, the Rossi brothers and Giuseppe Barbesino had gone so far as to ask him to head up the clandestine organization. But the honored veteran had categorically rejected the proposals of "those people": "I maintained neither written nor telephonic correspondence with any of them, nor did I help them in any way; the sacks were paid for."[4]

Despite his denials and his willingness to name names, Veduti was nevertheless kept in prison, first in Alessandria, then in Aosta and Turin. Finally he managed to escape and join his son Melchior, a twenty-year-old draft evader fighting with the partisans in the mountains near Cuneo. And so it was that in the late autumn of 1944, Martino Veduti began a new phase of his life, directing an exceptionally effective partisan intelligence service on behalf of a division of Giustizia e Libertà.[5]

After the Liberation, Veduti was among those beating the drums of revenge. In a letter signed only with his code name, "V-14," thus without revealing his identity, he asked the partisan police of Casale, Alessandria, and Aosta to "strike in an exemplary fashion" the collaborators in their respective territories. And he asked that they search among the documents of the Alessandria and Aosta police and the prefecture to discover the names of all those who between 1943 and 1944 had played a role in "sending Veduti, Barbesino, and Devasi to prison and keeping them there for months and months," the guilty to include all functionaries, agents, and spies. When this information had been collected, the letter said, they should put it aside, and "Veduti himself"—although for the moment "lying in hospital" because of wounds sustained in the battle to liberate Cuneo—would take care of the "consequent coercive measures."[6]

The search for those documents would be successful. In July 1945, Veduti, now fully recovered and named special commissioner of the auxiliary police of Casale, sent the Asti prosecutor documents he believed would "enlighten the justice system" about "war criminal Carnazzi." These were the reports that "war criminals Cagni, De Ceglie, and Bianchi" had written for the Aosta prefect after having infiltrated the partisan band at Arcesaz and setting up the subsequent raid—reports we know well.[7] What is remarkable here is how much the hunt for collaborators could take on a personal, extremely partial character in Italy after Liberation. As we've seen, Guido Bachi also went out of his way to settle scores with Carnazzi and Cagni. He even played the detective, obtaining access to the Turin police command and prefecture to go through the Salò records in search of evidence to help convict his enemies.[8]

Both Veduti and Bachi appeared as prosecution witnesses in the Cagni trial. Now they decided to take a further step as Resistance veterans. Having worked to see that people like Cagni and Carnazzi were tried, and having seen them condemned as war criminals, the two, along with many other Italians, undertook to be officially recognized as anti-Fascist combatants. In the autumn of 1946, they applied to the Piedmontese regional committee assessing partisan status.[9]

The formal status of ex-partisan offered various advantages, including a demobilization allowance and pension benefits. In order to limit false claims, the Italian government sought to fix clear criteria for qualification, despite various difficulties both political and financial. As early as summer 1945 a dedicated ministry was created, and in December of that year a circular was released with unequivocal definitions. Those eligible for assistance included "partisan combatants" and "patriots," as well as those wounded in the struggle for liberation and the families of men who had died in that struggle. The category of "partisan combatants" included those who could demonstrate they had been part of regular formations for at least three months and had taken part in at least three military or sabotage actions. "Patriots" were those who had actively taken part in the fight for liberation but for a briefer time, or in activities less immediately military.[10] Nationwide, three-quarters of the requests made were accepted, with just about twice as many partisan combatants as patriots recognized.[11]

And so as 1946 and 1947 went on, the one-time "bandits" in the hills of Piedmont and Valle d'Aosta were conscientiously filling out forms and affixing tax stamps in hopes of gaining one of the qualifications. Martino Veduti asked to be recognized twice: as a fighter wounded near Cuneo, but also as a rebel with the Arcesaz band in the autumn of 1943.[12] Guido Bachi applied as a member of the Col de Joux band, which he designated "the patriot group of Amay." He also documented two periods of militancy: first as the commander of the group in Amay, and secondly inside the Aosta jail, where "as a stenographer for the Warden's office" he "maintained contact among and assisted political prisoners." The command of the Giustizia e Libertà division confirmed his claims, and Bachi earned the title of partisan combatant.[13]

Although Bachi had gained the rank of lieutenant as a reserve officer in the automotive corps of the Royal Army, when asked on the form to document his military service prior to the armistice he wrote, strangely, "none because exempted as a Jew."[14] Nevertheless, Bachi did not present the Col de Joux band as a group of Jewish partisans, as some other ex-partisans had designated it. Instead, he said, the patriot group of Amay "was not of Jewish nationality, first because 'Jewish nationality' does not exist, there being only Italian nationality, and second because the majority of the group was not Jewish, although some of those who joined were."[15]

Among them, of course, was Primo Levi, and in 1946 he too applied for the status of partisan combatant. He had the right, for even without being able to demonstrate his participation in three military actions, he was eligible under a clause that included those "imprisoned, sent into internal exile camps, or to concentration camps for more than three months following capture by the Nazi-Fascists for partisan activities."[16]

Levi's application said that his nom de guerre had been "Ferrero" (a name that figures in no other documentation from the period) and that he had been part of the First Mazzini Brigade (a Giustizia e Libertà formation which only came into existence in the spring of 1944, when Levi had already been at Auschwitz for several months).[17] Somewhere in the files, meanwhile, was the report made by Carnazzi in which he wrote that he was deporting Levi, Nissim, and Maestro as Jews, "there being no other charges against them." Still, the Piedmontese regional committee assigned Primo Levi, too, the title of partisan combatant.

Levi's was scarcely the only application that did not strictly adhere to fact in reconstructing a Resistance career. By its very nature, partisan life resisted certification. The rebels in the mountains and those undercover in the cities had not been interested in leaving signatures on their actions—rather, they had done everything they could not to. And in the waning of a collective adventure in which the *we* had been more important than the *I*, many partisans were uncomfortable with the post-Resistance bureaucracy, the need to supply backup information, signatures, and countersignatures in order to qualify for the status of partisan or patriot. The transition from the poetry of victory to the prose of civilian life—from the excitement of parading through town in celebration of victory to the boredom of standing alone in a queue in some public office waiting to file a request—was a hard one.

Only one category of ex-partisan was spared this transition: the Resistance dead, who would reside forever in the land of poetry. The war of liberation would eternally remain a heroic struggle only for those who would not enjoy its fruits. Such was the spirit of *Johnny the Partisan*, the Resistance novel Beppe Fenoglio worked on feverishly from the late 1940s until his premature death. The meaning of the Resistance, he believed, the only thing about it that was really honorable, lay in the partisans' willingness to pay with their lives to deliver Italy from evil. And this was true not just of the liberation of Italy in general but also of the liberation of smaller, local places: Piedmont, the Langhe, Alba, Canelli. For Fenoglio, honors to the dead at the local level bore a symbolic importance greater than any national honors. The posthumous medal conferred by the prime minister was less important than a plaque laid by the city council. Even better was the street named in a partisan's memory, a man's name imprinted on the land he had freed.[18]

Out of all that affixing of plaques and naming of streets that took place in postwar Italy, it would be only just to collect a few traces here of the partisans slain in this story. To begin with, there are those three men Edilo Cagni boasted of having done away with during the upper Canavese raid in the early spring of 1944. Domenico De Palo, the man in civilian clothes killed by Cagni at Prascorsano on March 4, is remembered in a plaque at the city hall of Ruvo di Puglia, the southern Italian town of his origins. As for Flavio Berone and Livio Colzani, whom Lieutenant Redi was so pleased to have put before the firing squad on March 6 at Castelnuovo Nigra, each has a street named after him in his birthplace: Viale Berone at Rivarolo Canavese, and Via Colzani at Seregno.

Giuseppe Carrera, killed in Val d'Ayas on December 13, 1943, was honored by the city of Casale with a street named after him in the same part of town where he had worked as a machinist. After the stretch named Via Giuseppe Carrera the street becomes Via Don Ernesto Camurati, named after the parish priest killed at Villadeati. That street meets Via Italo Rossi, named for the founder of the Arcesaz band, which in turn meets Via Antonio Olearo, honoring the head of the "Tom" band. Nearby are numerous streets named after heroes of the Risorgimento, Italy's nineteenth-century drive for independence. So the partisans of Casale share their eternal life with those who fought to unite modern Italy.

Bathed in tears

Just as the Risorgimento generated many legends of martyrs, the Resistance produced its own. There were the dewy portraits of grieving mothers, devastated by the loss of their sons yet proud of their sacrifice, and edifying accounts of the last acts of partisans aware they were fated to die for their country, always heroic and defiant to the end.[19]

Cagni's self-serving report on the events of Castelnuovo Nigra, for instance, is counterpointed by an account that Flavio Berone and Livio Colzani's fellow partisans compiled after the war. It describes the two trapped in a house surrounded by the Alpine Musketeers, the "grim hounds" of the Republican National Guard—who we know were Cagni and Bianchi—"lunging" at them and dragging them to the town square to face the firing squad. First Berone is shot, then Colzani is urged to name names in return for his freedom. "One of the men of Salò, the superior clearly, insisted more than the others; his false words were repugnant, slimy as a reptile. Livio raised his handsome head proudly, and said, 'I prefer the fate of my companion.'"[20]

The death of Giuseppe Carrera also inspired accounts of this kind: tales of the young workingman firing on the Nazi-Fascist enemy until he had but one bullet left and then killing himself to the cry of "Long live free Italy!" That was the version upheld in "A Brief History of the Partisan Movement Around Verrès," published by local partisans after the war. If not entirely reliable as history, that reconstruction of the raid at Arcesaz, along with the grief of Maria Carrera for her son, did unknowingly echo the rhetoric and stereotypes of a familiar Risorgimento theme: the mother of the martyr as mother of the nation. "The Fascists kept hacking at him, but his mother, when she arrived two days later to claim the body they had mocked, said to them, 'I would rather see him in this state than in your ranks!'"

Maria Carrera was fortunate to recover the body rapidly. Giuseppe's corpse was transferred to Casale, where the funeral took place as a subversive assembly, of the kind that twenty years of Fascism had forced on opponents of the regime.[21] The Salò police were in attendance; the gates of the cemetery were guarded; those on hand risked being arrested for siding with the Arcesaz rebels.[22] Still, other mothers of the fallen did not have even such consolation. The world war and the civil war prevented many from recovering the bodies of their offspring, whether on the partisan or Salò side, until the conflict was over. After the war, the families of the Salò dead would endure their suffering in silence. The families of slain partisans at least had the comfort of burying their children without shame, indeed seeing them honored as local and national martyrs to freedom.[23]

And even after the war it was not always easy to recover the dead. Often the locations of hasty burials were hard to find, and some bodies were never buried at all. A great writer on war, Mario Rigoni Stern, described such a scenario in a fine story called "A Boy from Our Parts." On the Asiago plateau in northeast Italy, the fellow partisans of a young man named Moretto are still searching for his body a year after the Liberation; but instead of finding it they keep coming upon other bodies, for which they arrange funerals. Still, Moretto's companions do not give up: they comb the woods, descend into gorges, climb down gullies with double ropes. Finally one of them catches sight of "a scarf at the mouth of a squirrel's nest" and recognizes it as having belonged to Moretto. The body itself is not far off. "On the truck, we covered it with fresh, damp flowers, and two days later there was a funeral not even a king could dream of."[24]

After the war, the leaders of the Italo Rossi Division of the Matteotti Brigades included Luciano Zabaldano and Fulvio Oppezzo in the official list of partisan losses, reporting December 10 as the date of death for Zabaldano and December 13 for Oppezzo. The report understandably omits the particular circumstances of their deaths, the fact that they were shot by their own comrades.[25] Indeed it would have been very strange if two years after the events at the Col de Joux, with so much water under the bridge and after a fight to the death against the Nazi-Fascists, the victors had recorded a passing incident in which a tiny band of unknown hotheads—those *partigia* of Primo Levi's poem—hastily finished off two undisciplined volunteers. What would they even have written? In what terms would they have explained the cruel fate of two immature boys who in the first months of the Resistance confused war with adventure, partisan struggle with anarchy? What words to justify a high-handed decision by inexperienced commanders, a spray of bullets from a Beretta to punish the bullying of villagers or the theft of a few kilos of flour?

Several documents from September and October 1945 attest to the difficulties of grappling with these circumstances. They are letters to regional and local officials written by Vincenzo Grasso, president of the association of political prisoners who had survived concentration camps. Regarding the "bands constituted around Saint-Vincent" in the autumn of 1943, Grasso wrote to the Piedmont National Liberation Committee, "we had two deaths, respectively partisan Luciano Zabaldano and Fulvio (surname unknown)." He added that he was "still awaiting further clarification from persons who were members of the bands, whom I am trying to contact."[26] A month later, when he was writing to the town secretary of Saint-Vincent, Grasso had Fulvio Oppezzo's full name and hometown. But despite "research carried out," Grasso's impression of the events was still hazy: "Between October and November 1943 at Amay, and more precisely at Fremi [sic], two of our partisans died after being wounded, more precisely wounded by a machine gun." It seems the veterans contacted by Grasso had not troubled themselves to enlighten him about exactly what had taken place.

Still, once the two young partisans had been identified their remains could be transferred to their places of origin. "We request you assist the Mother of Fulvio Oppezzo, a Partisan Fallen in this Town in December 1943, whose body has recently been recovered and rests in the Cemetery of this Town, who wishes to transport the body of her Son to Cavaglià," reads a message sent from the Saint-Vincent city government to the Piedmont National Liberation Committee on October 15, 1945, swelling with a characteristic overflow of capital letters. The message went on to talk of Zabaldano and of Sassi, the district of Turin that had been his home. "It appears that on October 17 Turin's National Association of Italian Partisans intends to transport the Body of Partisan Andrea Luciano Zabaldano from here to Sassi (his remains are also in this Cemetery) and therefore it might be expedient to transport the two in a single trip."[27] The archives do not record how the question was resolved: whether the two young men who had gone up to the mountains of Valle d'Aosta together, and lay together under the ground at Frumy, also accompanied each other down to the plain of free Italy, to be separated only at the crossroads of Ivrea.

A request for partisan status was undertaken on behalf of both men. In those documents, Oppezzo is described as "fallen near" Amay on December 13, 1943; Zabaldano as "fallen" in "combat" three days earlier.[28] In May 1946, the Piedmontese regional committee recognized Luciano Zabaldano as a fallen partisan. His family also kept a document from the Matteotti Partisan Association of Piedmont, which attested that he had "Fallen bravely with honor and glory in the Struggle of Liberation for the dignity of Italy, for Liberty, and for better Social Justice in the World."[29] Later, in 1948, as part of a further bureaucratic procedure to establish Zabaldano's rank, his partisan career was reconstructed with even more invention. The boy who died at Frumy in Valle d'Aosta was now a partisan active in Monferrato, and a group leader (equivalent to the military rank of sergeant) with eight men under his command.[30] Stripes were thus sewn onto Luciano's uniform, post mortem, that no one would have dreamed of awarding him in life.

The archives of the foundation that compensated partisans and their families contain a record of the death benefit paid to Zabaldano's relatives, a one-time sum of 20,000 lire.[31] A photograph on the certificate depicts a shy and boyish-looking lad, more adolescent than adult. That must have been a photo taken before autumn 1943—perhaps dug out of the bottom of a drawer—because in the small oval-framed photograph affixed to the partisans' memorial plaque at the Sassi cemetery, Zabaldano looks much more like a grown man. He was no more than seventeen, of course, but in this picture he is wearing a sailor's uniform and smiling directly at the camera, projecting physical strength and spiritual resolution.

The plaque, inscribed TO THE PARTISANS WHO FELL IN THE CAUSE OF LIBERATION, does not have much to say about the eleven young men from Sassi whom it honors: just names, dates of birth and death, and those small photographs in their frames. And yet these sober details reveal some important things. Most of the dead were very young, with eight of the eleven born in 1925 or 1926; the eldest was thirty-three. Two of them, brothers, share a surname; two others share a death date, having fallen in the same action. The plaque also points to the particular cruelty of the last few weeks of the war leading up to the Liberation. Seven of the eleven dead lost their lives in March or April of 1945. Zabaldano was the sole partisan of Sassi to have died before the end of 1943.

The plaque says nothing about Zabaldano's death at the hands of his fellow band members, his Soviet-style execution. We could even say it conceals those facts. Yet when I look at a photo of that monument, having studied at length what took place at the Col de Joux, I do not really think it hides anything or tells a lie. Did Luciano Zabaldano not die "in the cause of Liberation" just as the other ten partisans listed alongside him? That teenage boy who on the last evening of his life, at the Hotel Ristoro, had boasted of his Communist beliefs—was he not also a martyr of the Resistance?

The monster's tail

Sometime between February 1946 and October 1947, Primo Levi made a significant change to the last chapter of *If This Is a Man*, the chapter titled "The Story of Ten Days." In the previous draft, when describing how Charles, Arthur, and he—the least ill in the infirmary of Monowitz— had shared stories with each other in the days before they were liberated, Levi had said only that he told them of "the moment of my arrest." But in revising the typescript before publication, Levi added a few lines suggesting that he spoke at length to them of his experience at Amay. "Charles was near to tears," he wrote, "when I told him how the armistice had arrived in Italy, about the murky and desperate beginnings of the partisan resistance, about the man who betrayed us and our capture in the mountains."[32]

A single sentence, but too important to be passed over. Not merely because it represents the only reference in that text to what had happened before Levi's journey from Fossoli to Auschwitz; not merely because Levi was able to describe the beginnings of the Resistance in two adjectives, "murky and desperate," that are more vivid than whole volumes of history. Those few lines are also important because they contain a fleeting reference to that figure of evil, "the man who betrayed us," Edilio Cagni. The man against whom Levi and Luciana Nissim had decided to testify in the Special Court of Assizes; the man who, those two saved Jews perhaps hoped, would now be put to death.

But Cagni's time had not yet come. Nor was he finished betraying. As the Italian, American, and Swiss archives disclose, his story was at once the norm and an aberration among those collaborators who escaped the justice of war and were consigned to the justice of the courts. The norm, since many war criminals who received harsh sentences from special courts would evade those punishments for one reason or another. But Edilio Cagni's story was also unusual, because when an opportunity to survive came along he embraced it with all the intelligence, intuition, and cunning he possessed. The former Lieutenant Redi did not merely dodge the firing squad: he went on to play once again, under new bosses, the role of agent provocateur. A monster, brilliant and duplicitous, he was a master of the double and triple game.

From the point of view of his legal defense, Cagni was in good hands. His lawyer, Vittorio Chauvelot, had experience looking after war criminals: he had defended the head of the Turin political department of the Republican National Guard, and would soon represent Alois Schmidt, the SS captain who personified Nazi terror in Turin.[33] Cagni also had assistance from Tancredi Gatti, a Roman attorney and professor of criminal law (not to mention one of the subscribers of the *Manifesto of Racial Scientists* and author of articles such as "Libido, Rapacity, and Race-Hatred on the Part of Jews").[34] And after being condemned to death by the Aosta Court of Assizes, Cagni named Domenico D'Amico—a celebrated criminal lawyer in Rome who had already defended other Fascists[35]—as his personal attorney. Such a high level of legal assistance suggests that Cagni had, if not political, at least financial support from somewhere. The internal revenue office in Palermo, where he was resident for tax purposes, listed him as being "in a state of poverty," while in Genoa, his birthplace, he was considered "without means."[36]

Just before Cagni's case was heard in Aosta, Gatti had presented a motion drawing the attention of the cassation court, the high court of appeals, to the sensitive nature of the case. Cagni's trial, he argued, should be moved out of Aosta, for "legitimate suspicion" that the trial would not be impartial and for "grave reasons of public order." Gatti claimed that "unidentified elements, who evidently wish to silence probable revelations that Cagni is known to be in a position to supply, have several times threatened to eliminate the defendant in jail or even at the upcoming public hearing. The lives of the president of the court, lay jurors, and witnesses who may testify on behalf of the defendant have been unequivocally threatened."[37]

"Reliable sources, officers of the Royal Army, can attest that more than once prior to his arrest, Cagni was the victim of attacks and ambushes," Gatti went on.[38] Anti-Fascism in Piedmont and Valle d'Aosta was riddled with disreputable elements: such was the thrust of his reasoning. Therefore, he implied, the court had to transfer Cagni's trial far from any place where he had exercised his influence under Salò. It was a strategy shared by most of the lawyers defending Fascists charged with collaborationism; they hoped to make the trials into ordinary hearings, not special occasions—no longer urgent political events but judicial routine.

When condemned collaborators had their sentences overturned on appeal, the cassation court often did rule that the retrials had to be conducted in new jurisdictions. The court evidently wanted to blunt the menace many Fascists perceived in the weeks after the Liberation, when a kind of justice not very different from vengeance was the rule. And so, as the months and years went by, trials that had first taken place where the accused had committed their collaborationist crimes—crimes including torture, reprisals, and massacres—were now repeated at a distance, far from the spilt blood. Cases were no longer heard in Turin, Genoa, Udine, or Padua, where the civil war had been fought, but much farther south, in

Viterbo, Aquila, Perugia, or Bari. Italy regained its national juridical system, but the victims of Nazi-Fascism lost their right to justice.

The clearest signal that the spirit of the Resistance had cooled came in June 1946, when Justice Minister Palmiro Togliatti decreed an amnesty for many adherents of Salò. In theory the measure excluded all those who had committed "massacres, particularly vicious torture, homicide, or plunder" during the civil war. But in practice many hundreds of Fascists were released from prison, both those awaiting sentencing and war criminals already sentenced.[39] They included people like Ercole Righi, a top member of the Asti Republican National Guard during the German occupation, sentenced to twenty-four years in prison in October 1945. That summer, thanks to the amnesty, Righi was free to walk the streets of Asti once again. The ex-partisans of Asti were not pleased. And twenty-year-olds who had fought in the civil war like Beppe Fenoglio's Johnny, dreaming of the day they would be soaked in blood up to their armpits ("because partisan, like poet, is an absolute term that spurns any degree"), were more than ready to take up the struggle again.

Two such young men were Giovanni Rocca and Armando Valpreda. Rocca, a distillery worker, had been a Garibaldino commander during the Resistance, a partisan both intrepid and ruthless.[40] Valpreda had left Asti with a surveyor's diploma hoping to become a technician at the Cogne works, joined the partisans of Giustizia e Libertà, and came back from the mountains with a bronze medal for military bravery.[41] In the summer of 1946, Rocca and Valpreda responded to the amnesty as if the civil war had never ended, organizing an attack on Righi that put him in the hospital. Still not satisfied, they tried to hang him from a tree in the public gardens.[42] Now was the time to strike, they thought. At the National Association of Italian Partisans meeting in Turin in late July 1946, Valpreda spoke openly of mounting a new armed struggle against the Fascists. The ex-partisans of Asti, he said, would wait until the first national congress of the partisans' association, scheduled for early September in Florence, and if the tune hadn't changed by then they would take up arms.[43]

But the two young men soon became too impatient to wait even that long. In August they occupied Santa Libera, a mountain hamlet between Asti and Cuneo, creating a "free zone" like those of the Resistance in 1944. Hundreds of partisans from across northern Italy, many of them armed, quickly poured into the area. In the following weeks, all the tensions already emerging in the Resistance only a year after Liberation were made clear, as the left split itself apart in disputes and the protest cooled down.[44]

Less clamorous but more illuminating was the speech made at the congress in Florence by Mario Pelizzari, aka Alimiro, now one of the national leaders of the Association of Italian Partisans. In forceful terms, Pelizzari denounced partisan profiteering. There were some, he said, who after the Liberation had "taken to every sort of piracy": ex-partisans who had pocketed millions of lire from the war chests of their bands and who now owned factories, controlled cooperatives, drove luxury automobiles. Riffraff like "Piero Piero," said Pelizzari, calling out Piero Urati loud and clear by his nom de guerre. Urati, in turn, sent a telegram announcing his imminent arrival at the congress to refute the charges, and representatives of the Matteotti Brigade took up his defense. Still, Pelizzari's warning was stern. "If we want to oppose a government that's not working, we must clean up our own house first," he said. "If we don't, we'll be no better than the worst Fascist."[45]

But as 1946 came to an end, it was not just impeccable figures like Pelizzari who were questioning partisan ethics. To accuse partisans of having enriched themselves proved a convenient tactic for many. A Southern wind was now blowing strong in Italy, bringing together a sometimes silent, sometimes noisy majority made up of Christian Democrats, anti-Communists, monarchists, and Qualunquisti (who defined themselves as being against all parties), plus a minority of neo-Fascists grouped together in the Italian Social Movement.[46] What counted now was international subservience: the De Gasperi government was following the agenda of the Truman administration in Washington and that of the Vatican, while the Italian Communist Party fell in line with its Soviet elder.

Then, during the winter of 1946–47, the "Dongo gold" scandal broke. Near the end of April 1945, Mussolini and some of his Salò henchmen had fled toward the Swiss border with a supply of public money and gold, as well as other valuables. They were stopped at a partisan checkpoint on Lake Como, commanded by a fighter known as Colonel Valerio; Il Duce, though wearing a German uniform, was recognized; and at the town of Dongo, the henchmen were shot, followed by Mussolini and his mistress, Claretta Petacci. But the captured money and jewels were not delivered to the partisan General Command, and the subsequent fate of those Dongo riches turned into a dark legend. The Como National Liberation Committee itself launched charges against the partisans who had stopped the Fascists at Dongo; these were taken up by the military prosecutor of Milan and publicized by the local and national press. It was claimed that part of the Dongo gold went to the Italian Communist Party, the rest into the pockets of those who had captured Mussolini and company. And that was not all. Two partisans, a man and a woman, were said to have been killed by their companions after the Liberation because they'd been present when the spoils were divided up and had threatened to make the story public.[47]

In February 1947 military general prosecutor Leone Zingales ordered numerous arrests in connection with the events at Dongo. It was the beginning of an affair that would go on for a decade, until a long-awaited but inconclusive trial finally took place in 1957. But beyond its judicial side the affair also started a heated media battle between two opposite political poles. In September 1946 the most important neo-Fascist paper in the north, *Il Meridiano d'Italia*, had launched a campaign about "the mysteries of Dongo," raising questions not only about the missing money but about Mussolini's death. Who was the partisan who had shot Il Duce? The Italian Communist Party refused to name him, both for security reasons and to bolster a myth that Mussolini had been executed not by one but by all, by common will. With a great deal of digging, *Il Meridiano d'Italia* came up with a name and surname for "Colonel Valerio," the man at the Lake Como checkpoint by now presumed to have killed Mussolini; they reported that he was a little-known Communist from Alessandria, a bookkeeper named Walter Audisio.[48]

At this point the Communist Party decided to make a virtue of necessity, and presented their obscure bookkeeper to the world as a great hero deserving of a medal, the man who'd liberated Italy from Il Duce.[49] But by the time the party decided to identify Audisio, the *Meridiano* had already done its damage, publishing insinuations picked up in turn by the entire anti-Communist press. In the early months of 1947 the Communist paper *l'Unità* mounted a countercampaign, exposing illegal underground neo-Fascist organizations. The news was sometimes obtained by infiltrating the enemy side, a dangerous tactic in days when many ex-combatants were still trigger-happy.

Just days after prosecutor Zingales ordered the arrests in the Dongo case, *l'Unità* reporters Riccardo Longone, in the paper's national edition, and Manfredo Liprandi, in the Turin edition, began publishing a series of articles under the title "La coda del mostro": the monster's tail, as in the final lash. "Our source spent time in jail in Aosta and became a neo-Fascist functionary," the paper wrote, promising "revelations" to come: "we fear no murder threats from these neo-Fascist organizers."[50] "The only investigation of neo-Fascism backed by documents, code books, and photographs," another blurb in the paper boasted the following day, "our series alone goes deep into the traitors' background and organization."[51]

And here we meet Edilio Cagni once again. He is one of the protagonists in Liprandi's investigation, a diabolical figure who comes and goes in the six-part series, pulling the strings of neo-Fascist affairs all over Italy's northwest. The first article in the series was illustrated by a chart showing the organization of "Monte Rosa," a clandestine neo-Fascist division based in Turin and headed by Cagni. The story quotes ex-partisan Guido Piovano, who had profited from his detention in the

Aosta jail by gaining the confidence of someone who called himself "Italic Dreamer." This was "a certain Edilio Cagni whom I had already had occasion to meet at Dock Milano," a noted Turin hotel, Piovano told *l'Unità*.[52] Cagni himself had given Piovano a code book to find covert neo-Fascist radio broadcasts. "He took it out of a leather bag along with a notebook, a bag that seemed to be stuffed with stacks of thousand-lire bills," Piovano said.[53] According to the article, these meetings had taken place a few months before, in the autumn of 1946.

The third article of Liprandi's series featured a photo of a young man with regular features, a penetrating gaze, and a moustache and goatee à la d'Artagnan. The picture caption read: "Ex-paratroop officer of the Nembo Regiment Edilio Cagni, who calls himself 'Italic Dreamer.' Cagni is the local commander for Monte Rosa. He's reputed to be a hardliner."[54] In December 1946, the article said, Cagni had brought Piovano to a clandestine summit in a villa on the outskirts of Milan, where the two listened to an interminable speech by former Fascist boss Carlo Scorza.[55] Just a few weeks later, an all-out law enforcement action against Lombardy neo-Fascists made their fellows in Piedmont more cautious. Cagni and other area commanders decided to suspend their activities and wait for the situation to calm down. Piovano, who had infiltrated the group, passed all his documentation to Liprandi, who in turn passed it to the Turin Police Command.[56]

Manfredo Liprandi, thirty-seven, was a former partisan and seasoned journalist. During the German occupation of Turin he had worked tirelessly on the clandestine edition of *l'Unità*, and after the Liberation he had personally pursued Salò criminals who had escaped capture.[57] Decades later, another experienced reporter, Giampaolo Pansa, would recall Liprandi as "the best crime reporter" in postwar Italy.[58] There is every reason to think that his reportage on neo-Fascism in Piedmont was thoroughly researched, and none to suggest that someone with his experience chasing veterans of Salò would have made a mistake about the identity of that "Italic Dreamer" he named as Edilio Cagni.

No reason to doubt him, that is, were it not for the fact that Cagni, between October 1946 and January 1947, was supposed to have been far from the Dock Milano, the bundles of bills, or a Milanese suburb. Cagni was supposed to be in jail.

Our bastard

To be shot in the back by a firing squad: so the Aosta Special Court of Assizes had sentenced Cagni in May 1946. Attorney Chauvelot had immediately filed an appeal. As the decision on whether it would be granted loomed in November, Cagni's newly hired attorney, Domenico D'Amico, repeated the defense's request for a change of venue. He asked the court that any new trial "be held not in Piedmont but ideally far away from Valle d'Aosta: in Lazio, Umbria, or Naples, for example." There was "legitimate suspicion" that the Aosta trial had not been fair.[59] In Cagni's case there were particular concerns, D'Amico argued, because his client had recently been transferred to the Civitavecchia jail just north of Rome on orders of the Justice Ministry "for security reasons"—that is, to remove him from an environment held to be dangerous. "It would not be possible to return Cagni to Piedmont where he has not been forgiven . . . and has been threatened with murder."[60]

The second criminal section of the Supreme Court largely accepted the arguments made by Cagni's defense. The court annulled his sentence on the grounds that even though Cagni was guilty of providing intelligence to the enemy, mitigating circumstances had not been considered. It also transferred the new trial to Perugia in central Italy,[61] five hundred kilometers from Piedmont and even farther from Valle d'Aosta.

How could it be, then, that Cagni, officially transferred from the Aosta jail to that of Civitavecchia, was an active presence—as "Italic Dreamer"—in far-right activities outside any prison? How could he occupy the role of Turin commander of neo-Fascist forces? The possibilities are two. Either Manfredo Liprandi and Guido Piovano were wrong in naming Cagni as Italic Dreamer (but then why did the Monte Rosa organizational chart specifically mention him as its chief?); or Italic Dreamer really was Cagni, allowed for whatever reason to leave the penitentiary and burrow into the demimonde of clandestine neo-Fascism.

That second hypothesis is less fanciful than it might seem. Personally, I find it the more likely explanation: that the phony ex-Lieutenant Redi, condemned to death as a collaborator in May 1946, was able, for some time after his sentence, to circulate freely in Italy and play a role in the secret gatherings of the Far Right. I draw that conclusion from documents showing that in the autumn of 1945, when Cagni was supposed to have been in a Turin jail awaiting his sentence, he was in fact collaborating with American intelligence—the OSS, Office for Strategic Services—as an agent provocateur among Nazi-Fascists who had escaped capture. Somehow he had gotten out of prison, and had been able to move relatively freely from Piedmont to Emilia and from there to Liguria in order to carry out his mission. If he was permitted to do so then, why not later?

Let us not forget what Salvatore Balestrieri told the court at Aosta as a defense witness during Cagni's trial. He testified that Cagni had cooperated with the Italian intelligence services in pursuing the Gestapo leader Baroness von Hodenberg. The Cremona Division had agreed to release Cagni from jail so he could carry out his investigations. And as Balestrieri noted, Cagni had not used his freedom to escape.

Who was this so-called Baroness von Hodenberg, and how had Cagni assisted in her arrest? The Baroness's given name was Elizabeth Petsel. Born in Bremen in 1898, she was in her early forties when she was sent to Naples in 1941 by the Abwehr—German military intelligence—to make contacts in Italy.[62] She was tall, slender, blond, and wore just a trace of makeup: the classic Nordic female, come to seek adventure on the shores of the Mediterranean, it appeared. She spoke good Italian, and also French and English with a German accent. She went by a number of code names, but American counterintelligence knew her primarily as Annabella.[63] Until the winter of 1944 she recruited informers for the Abwehr between Naples and Rome; then she moved to Florence, where a collaborator, Captain Aldo Vannini, became her close aide and lover. As the Allies advanced, the two fled to Milan in the autumn of 1944. They spent the final days of Nazi-Fascism there, in the velvet and damask quarters of the Hotel Diana, before trying to escape across Lake Como after the Liberation.[64]

Among Annabella's circle was a junior Salò army officer named Ugo Perugi, arrested in the summer of 1945 by partisans in Turin and jailed in the Carceri Nuove. Edilio Cagni, who had also been arrested by the partisans and held in that same jail, approached Perugi, gained his confidence, and passed intelligence to the Americans via Captain Balestrieri, who dealt with the OSS as part of the intelligence service of the Cremona Division. Cagni, from prison, let it be known that he might be able to find Annabella. In late October 1945, then, the OSS had Cagni transferred to a cell in their Turin headquarters. Observed from a distance by American agents and by Balestrieri, Cagni went to see Perugi's wife, Albertina Porciani, and convinced her that he had escaped from jail. Her husband, he told her, could do likewise: there was a secure escape route to Switzerland, and they could take it along with other hunted Nazi-Fascists. Cagni spoke of a Salò treasure chest hidden somewhere between Geneva and Zurich, and convinced Porciani to join him in the search for Annabella.[65]

Later, Perugi's young wife—the OSS officers described her as "stupid" and "impressionable"[66]—told her questioners that she had been struck by Cagni's "mystical, almost ascetic nature" and by his "apparent sincerity."[67] In any event, in early November 1945, using an automobile provided by the Italian secret service and followed by another car with American agents, Cagni and the ingenuous Porciani drove from Turin toward the town of Copparo, where she believed Annabella and Captain Vannini were hiding out. They did not find them there, but learned from a confidential source that they were in a town called Carcare. And so the parties departed once again for the Ligurian coast, where they found the Nazi spy and her lover. Annabella, sure she could trust Perugi's wife, fell into Cagni's trap, believing in the offer to take them over the border to Switzerland. On November 9, she and Vannini were arrested, and soon placed in detention in Rome by the OSS. Cagni, meanwhile, remained "under protective custody" with the Turin headquarters of the OSS.[68]

That the American secret services were using Cagni with such ease should come as no surprise. Thanks to the enterprising young James Jesus Angleton, the OSS section for counterintelligence had expanded greatly in those months in 1945. The Truman administration had already begun to consider the Italian transition from Fascism to democracy in resolutely anti-Communist terms. For Angleton, the hunt for Nazi-Fascist secret agents still acting in Italy was an intermediate step in building a paramilitary network to protect the country from a pro-Soviet coup d'état (an operation code-named "Stay Behind").[69] To achieve his aim, Angleton recruited high-ranking ex-collaborators, beginning with Junio Valerio Borghese, chief of the infamous Decima Mas unit of marines, who had refused to recognize the armistice in 1943 and fiercely battled the Resistance.[70] At the same time the OSS was deploying Cagni in Turin, Angleton was complaining to his superiors about having to return Borghese, who had been in American custody for several months, to Italian authorities. According to Angleton, the Fascist's cooperation offered a host of benefits to the Allied cause, and he urged that everything be done to prevent the Italians from putting him on trial—a trial that might well cost him his life.[71]

He may be a bastard, but he's our bastard. Americans could be cynical in fighting the Cold War, happy to employ their former enemies. Compared to Borghese, Cagni was a small fish. But even in his case the OSS was clear about what they hoped to achieve. Two memos written in mid-November 1945 by the Turin OSS office to headquarters in Rome urged them to press Italian authorities for "the release of Subject," so Cagni could be infiltrated full-time into "a suspected Fascist movement developing in Piedmont and Lombardy." If it proved impossible to release him, the memos said, OSS command should at least try to affect the outcome of his upcoming trial before the Aosta court. "It is requested that your HQ direct a letter with regard to his cooperation to competent Italian authorities, so that it may be taken into consideration at the time of his trial."[72]

How reliable Cagni seemed to the Turin office of the OSS! Far more so than Captain Balestrieri, whose behavior during the capture of Annabella led American counterintelligence to "slowly break off association with him completely." The man from the Cremona Division had pocketed nearly half the 15,000 lire in expenses for the mission to Emilia and Liguria; he had also tried to make off with Elizabeth Petsel's ring and diamond bracelet and with Aldo Vannini's gold watch. But the Americans sniffed out his thievery, and all the valuables were put away in the OSS safe. Afterwards, however, Cagni had decided to cut his ties with his partner. "Dr. Eligio [sic] Cagni has broken relations as informant of Capt. Balestrieri," the Turin office of the OSS reported.[73] Ex-Lieutenant Redi apparently had principles of his own.

The story of the stolen valuables did not prevent Balestrieri from testifying on Cagni's behalf six months later during the Aosta trial, although his testimony didn't spare the spy a death sentence. We know what happens afterwards, and it all seems far less surprising now that we know about the OSS documents. "Italic Dreamer" gets to know Guido Piovano—the secret emissary of Communist journalist Manfredo Liprandi—in the Aosta jail. Condemned to death, Italic Dreamer nevertheless races around with Piovano that winter to secret neo-Fascist meetings between Turin and Milan. Piovano believes he is spying on Cagni, who doesn't seem to know he's been infiltrated by l'Unità. In reality, Cagni is spying on Piovano and Liprandi, who don't realize they have been infiltrated by the OSS.

How long Italic Dreamer worked as an informer for the American secret services, no archive I'm aware of allows us to say. It may be that l'Unità, with its investigation that put Edilio Cagni's name and photograph on the front pages, destroyed the new spy career of the former Lieutenant Redi. Certainly, during that winter of 1946–47, the "Post-War" was suddenly becoming the Cold War,[74] not only in Italy but internationally, and that shift made certain kinds of role play particularly dangerous. The chief editor of *Il Meridiano d'Italia*, Franco De Agazio, the man who orchestrated the neo-Fascist press campaign about the "Dongo Gold," was among those who would pay the price.

In March 1947, De Agazio was murdered by two men on a Milan street. The crime was the source of fervent media speculation; newspapers of various political stripes argued that it was a settling of accounts among neo-Fascists, or a Communist vendetta, or the result of some international connection directed either by Americans or by Soviet or Yugoslav agents.[75] Today it seems certain that De Agazio was killed by a commando of the so-called Volante Rossa, a "Red Squad" made up of Milanese ex-partisans who wanted to punish him for denigrating the Resistance.[76] Whoever committed the murder, though, it was immediately clear that the editor of *Il Meridiano d'Italia* was in deeper than had seemed. The night he died there was a letter in his pocket from the secretary of the neo-Fascist Italian Social Movement, asking De Agazio to undertake "an urgent and extremely important mission." The journalist was asked to cooperate with Turin neo-Fascists and with the Archbishop of that city to create secret anti-Communist action squads.[77] No mere political journalist, De Agazio was involved—or was being drawn into— budding right-wing diplomatic and military activities. In this game, political battles, investigative journalism, and subversive aims were all mixed up.

8

The Wind of Pardon

"Port of Shadows"

L'UNITÀ'S MULTIPART INVESTIGATION OF THE MONSTER'S TAIL and the Italic Dreamer had finished running two weeks before Edilio Cagni appeared in Perugia for his retrial, charged with "collaboration and espionage."[1] The trial opened on March 17 at 9 a.m. and, like the previous one in Aosta, was concluded quickly. By 8 p.m. the evidence had been heard and a sentence issued. But while in Aosta there had been dozens of witnesses, in Perugia there was just one. Of the score of inhabitants of Verrès and nearby mountain valleys who were summoned, none showed up. Neither did Lino Binel, Guido Bachi, Aldo Piacenza, Camillo Reynaud, Giuseppe Barbesino, Maria Carrera, or Salvatore Balestrieri. Out of thirty people called to testify, whether for the defense or the prosecution, the only witness in the courtroom was Ferdinando Trombin of Casale Monferrato.

If we are to believe the medical certificates received by the Special Court of Perugia in the days before the trial, Northwest Italy was in the grip of a widespread health crisis in March 1947. "Flu with bronchopulmonary complications," "rheumatic pain," "flu with fever," "progressive degenerative paralysis," "multiple abscesses," "flu with bronchitis," "flu with fever with bronchopulmonary complications," "sciatica," "serious cardiac disease"—nearly enough maladies to write a textbook of general pathology. Then there was the justification sent by Riccardo Avetta of Issime: "As the sole baker of bread in this Commune he cannot be substituted during the time necessary to reach Perugia and return." Aldo Piacenza, who had just earned a law degree, was unable to attend on account of "participation in state exams for employment." Two ex-partisans who had been among Cagni's most stubborn and severe accusers in the first trial were now also victims of the general malaise. Giuseppe Barbesino was "confined to bed with sciatica." And Guido Bachi sent a letter in his own hand: "I am sorry to say I am unable to appear at the above-mentioned hearing, being presently confined to bed with a serious case of flu."[2]

In 1947, Perugia was even farther away from Northwest Italy than suggested by the several hundred kilometers that separate them on the map. Rail connections were unreliable, and the roads were just as bad. To appear in court, a witness from Piedmont or Valle d'Aosta had to count on three or four days of travel coming and going. And that, of course, was part of the calculation made by the collaborators' attorneys when they pressed the cassation court to move appeals trials far from where guilty sentences had been issued. Put some Apennines between the two trials, and juries would be less sensitive to local demands for justice; and there would be no witnesses, or very few, in the courtroom. The war crimes of Salò would be related by the defendant, the judges, and the lawyers, and no longer by the victims.

Cagni, of course, did not consider *crimes* to be the right term in the first place. Asked by the president of the Perugia court to defend his actions under Salò, Cagni repeated the line of defense he had maintained since the summer of 1945. In both Aosta and Piedmont, he insisted, he had been a most benign Salò functionary. If no witnesses had showed up in Perugia on his behalf, it was because he'd been the bene-factor of so many people that he couldn't even recall their names. Only an absurd equivocation had landed him in the damning camp of the collaborators.[3]

Some prosecution witnesses, although they did not appear in Peru-gia, did send the court written statements. But there is a difference between hearing an account read out by a lawyer or a clerk and hearing it live from the victim. Maria Carrera, "mother of Partisan Giuseppe who fell during the liberation struggle at the hand of the accused Cagni," wrote in to tell once again how her son, on a return visit from the Val d'Ayas to Casale, appeared "oppressed by worry" because "a certain Cagni who appeared suspicious" had joined the band. She described how Giuseppe was betrayed: "my son, having resisted to the utmost, was wounded, and then massacred at [Cagni's] hands." She told of her trav-els to Brusson to claim the body, and the carabiniere of Verrès who had told her in private that "my son's assassin was Cagni."[4]

Thus Maria Carrera presented her account of what had happened at Arcesaz, perhaps naively thinking that her words were enough to con-vict, that the judges of Perugia would simply retrace the steps of those of Aosta. "I have already appeared at the trial in Aosta where Cagni was justly condemned to death and where he lowered his head before my accusations, in a gesture of acknowledgement." Or perhaps Maria was already resigned and knew that her appearance as a *mater dolorosa* in Perugia would not make a difference, that a change of climate had taken place in Italy between May 1946 and March 1947. Italy was now a Republic—and a Republic "born of the Resistance," as men of good will liked to say. But many Italians, perhaps the majority, preferred to think of the Republic as already detached from the tragic circumstances that had brought it into being, uncoupled from the civil war. A Republic brought by the stork.

Beyond the material difficulties of a journey from northern Italy to Perugia in 1947, this sense of the Northern wind falling and the South-ern wind rising may explain why so many prosecution witnesses obtained doctor's certificates for the second trial. Perhaps they knew that anything could happen at the Special Court of Perugia—far from any sea coast but still a "port of shadows" in the style of Marcel Carné's atmospheric 1938 film *Quai des brumes*, a place shrouded in fog and the unknown. Under such circumstances, Ferdinando Trombin was a determined if somewhat futile witness. Having testified against Cagni in the trial at Aosta, the twenty-two-year-old had come to Perugia to up the ante. During the raid in Val d'Ayas, Trombin now insisted in court, Cagni had been responsible not only for the death of Carrera ("who, seeing he had no chance, killed himself") but for "another seven assassinated, including two English prisoners and three Jews."[5]

Trombin, evidently, was somewhat wrong about everything. He was wrong in cultivating the heroic legend of Carrera's suicide, when even Giuseppe's mother knew he had been brutally shot. He was wrong to say that the Nazi-Fascist raid of December 13 had left seven others dead on the ground. Yet there is something wonderful about this young Quixote from Casale, tilting wildly at the counter-Resistance in that Perugia courtroom. He went far out of his way to testify for three of Cagni's victims not present that day, the three Jews deported to Auschwitz as a result of the raid. None had been killed in the Val d'Ayas, and if Trombin was referring to them he knowingly or unknowingly lied. Nevertheless, thanks to him, their capture and the death of Vanda Maestro, gassed at Birkenau in October 1944, were at least evoked in the courtroom.

It was now 1 p.m. "At this point, given the late hour, the hearing is suspended to be resumed at 4 p.m. today," the court transcript runs. The proceedings, that is, were halted for a leisurely lunch. When the hearing resumed, the public prosecutor made his concluding remarks, asking the court to recognize mitigating circumstances and calling for Cagni to be sentenced to thirty years in prison.[6] Defense lawyer D'Amico argued that the charges against his client had been extinguished under the national Togliatti amnesty.[7] The jury, made up of two magistrates and five lay jurors, then convened. The sentence followed the prosecutor's lead precisely: Cagni was given thirty years. (Because of a clause in the amnesty decree that reduced all penalties over five years by one-third, this thirty-year sentence was automatically lowered to twenty.) Attorney D'Amico immediately appealed once again to the Court of Cassation.[8]

The historical climate

We do not know whether Primo Levi or Luciana Nissim had timely news of how "the man who betrayed us," as Levi called him, had fared in court.[9] Nor do we know what they thought of Cagni's sentence in the previous trial, when they had traveled to Aosta to testify. The two veterans of Auschwitz by now had full professional and personal lives, and little time to brood on the "murky and desperate beginnings" of the Resistance. Nissim was a manager at Olivetti in Ivrea, as was her husband Franco Momigliano.[10] Levi was engaged to Lucia Morpurgo and was working as a chemist in a factory outside Turin. He had finished writing *If This Is a Man*, had the bitter disappointment of learning that the Einaudi publishing house was not interested, but had found a publisher in the smaller Turin firm De Silva.[11]

The book's first chapter, "The Journey," appeared in a weekly called *L'amico del popolo* in late March 1947.[12] At that same time, Colonel Massimo Vitale—who in 1946 had received the report on medical conditions at Monowitz from Primo Levi and Leonardo De Benedetti—proposed that the two survivors go to Warsaw as prosecution witnesses for the trial of the SS commander of Auschwitz, Rudolf Höss. As *La Stampa* would report, "survivors of seventeen nationalities . . . still bearing traces of what they had suffered" came to testify. De Benedetti was among them, speaking out against "the horrors and the evils" of which he was "a witness and often a victim."[13] Perhaps he savored Höss's sentence of death by hanging, read out on April 2 and carried out at Auschwitz two weeks later. Primo Levi, for whatever reason, chose not to attend the trial.[14]

In those times, trials against Nazi-Fascist war criminals took on different colors depending on the national and international context in which they were held. In Poland, the harsh and irrevocable sentences handed down to major criminals of the Third Reich who had escaped trial at Nuremberg served in part to mask the direct and indirect role that Poles had played in the Final Solution.[15] In Italy, judicial proceedings against Germans charged with the most heinous war crimes on the peninsula were assigned to the Allies, specifically to British military courts. These were heavily influenced both by incipient Cold War geopolitics (which meant the Western powers were less severe toward German war criminals than they had been before Nuremberg) and by the Italian government's hope that the Allies would not try high officials of the Italian army for wartime crimes in the Balkans.[16]

Thus in the spring of 1947, as Prime Minister Alcide De Gasperi, backed by Washington, prepared to push the Socialists and Communists out of Italian government, Nazi-Fascists on trial in Italy seem to have enjoyed a certain clemency—de facto if not de jure. In May, for instance, a British military court in Venice sentenced Albert Kesselring, Luftwaffe field marshal general and commander of German forces in the Mediterranean, to be executed by a firing squad. But the following month, after the Italian government said the death penalty was a "Fascist practice" that had been abolished in Italy by the 1947 constitutional convention, and after Winston Churchill let it be known he thought Kesselring's punishment was scandalously harsh, the sentence was reduced to life imprisonment.[17]

La Stampa ran just a brief report on the developments: "Death for Kesselring Commuted to Life in Prison." If that was enough for Field Marshall Kesselring—the incarnation of German terror in occupied Italy, responsible for the brutal 1944 murders of 335 Romans among many others—then it is no surprise that newspapers failed to say much at all about the rulings of the various courts as one by one they lightened collaborators' sentences from the first round of trials. That included the clemency for Cesare Augusto Carnazzi, initially condemned to forty-eight years in prison. In May 1947 Carnazzi was granted a new trial in the Special Court of Assizes of Milan. The court held him eligible for amnesty under the Togliatti measure, and he was released from jail in late June. From that day on the former prefect of Salò was a free man, although for a few more years one or another police officer continued to investigate him.[18]

Edilio Cagni's defense, as we have seen, also tried to invoke the Togliatti amnesty. But the Perugia court rejected the motion, ruling that proven "military collaborationism, in its various forms including killing and sacking . . . constituted an obstacle to applying amnesty." Still, the court granted Cagni the benefits of mitigating circumstances, with the spy winning credit once again for having supplied "important information toward identifying and arresting a high Gestapo official in Italy" and with having tried "to recover gold bars belonging to the Interior Ministry of the Social Republic" to return to the coffers of postwar Italy.

Cagni's lawyer, Domenico D'Amico, was the scion of a distinguished family of a strong liberal tradition.[19] Yet the kinds of evidence he offered in Cagni's appeal against the Perugia sentence suggested no such allegiance. Of course D'Amico was only doing his job as a lawyer in pointing to the absence of any material proof linking Cagni to murders and pillage. The death of Giuseppe Carrera? Not even the Aosta Special Court had ruled that Cagni was personally involved. The deadly raids in the Canavese? No victims were directly imputable to him. And one might even argue that D'Amico was only doing his job when he pointed to "Cagni's decent nature."[20] But the attorney went well beyond the legal issues in the case when he put forward a list of considerations that "by themselves" urged clemency for his client: "his good record, his youthful age, and, above all, the historical climate in which the facts he is considered responsible for must be considered."[21]

The historical climate: the phrase hints carefully at the civil war, the particular atmosphere in which Italy fought its war of liberation in 1943–45. But by 1947 that atmosphere had changed. Carlo Galante Garrone, Piedmontese magistrate and ex-partisan, observed that by focusing on the technical defects in the sentences handed down by the special courts, the high court had effectively cancelled the crimes of Fascism and simply freed war criminals.[22] Was there any prefect unable to prove,

Galante Garrone asked crisply, that he had acted against the Germans, "if only for a single hour in twenty long months of terror"?[23] Could all the Salò functionaries, he wrote with bitter sarcasm, really have been "unaware of what a Nazi-Fascist raid was"?[24]

Having followed Cesare Augusto Carnazzi's judicial adventures, in which the man who sent Primo Levi and his companions to Auschwitz in 1944 walked free in 1947, we cannot but sympathize with the ex-partisan's objection. But there was also something false, or at least something not fully acknowledged, in what Galante Garrone wrote. The justice handed down by the special courts in the months after the Liberation, before the Togliatti amnesty, was itself neither independent nor innocent. It was political justice, in which the transition from Fascism to democracy was meant to take place by means of punishment. It was a vindictive justice that simultaneously demanded new rights. Now, the appellate court, granting indulgence in many of its sentences, marked the beginning of a new season. It was the end of emergency and revolution, the beginning of an era of regulations and reaction.

Too late

In July 1945, soon after liberation swept through Casale, seven Fascist officers and soldiers judged guilty of exterminating the Tom band of partisans had been condemned to death by the Casale Special Court of Assizes. In a second trial some months later, the Special Court of Turin had confirmed the death penalty for six of the seven.[25] But even though the cassation court in turn had ruled this sentence valid,[26] it was never carried out. In 1947, hoping to profit from the new climate in Italy, the condemned began to write to Rome for reconsideration.

Enraged, anti-Fascist Casale rose up in early September to protest the wind of pardon. Like the rebels of Santa Libera, the anti-Fascists of Casale wanted to undo the months of Italian history after the Liberation and start afresh from April 25, 1945. For some, the zero hour went back even further, to September 8, 1943, when the most radical among them had inaugurated the struggle for a free world in Arcesaz. Indomitable, or naive? Stalwart, or maybe just pathetic? In a changing Italy, the partisan band from Casale was determined to ignite the Resistance once again.

This was no protest hidden away in the mountains, like the "free zone" of Santa Libera; it took place in urban Casale Monferrato, at the factory gates, where the alliance between partisans and workers had been the most revolutionary aspect of the war of liberation. "As this story is written, the city is paralyzed," reported *La Stampa*. From early morning, "when sirens announced the struggle had begun," workers abandoned their factories and shop gates were pulled down. Workers and partisans proclaimed that the general strike would go on until the president of the Republic, the prime minister, or the justice minister promised to reject all requests for pardon from Casale criminals and carry out their death sentences immediately.[27]

"Casale Occupied by a Thousand Partisans," *La Stampa* reported the following day. The Turin paper described a checkpoint blocking access to the bridge across the Po River, where "we find a group of young men wearing work trousers and jackets, with service caps or tricolored ribbons pinned to their lapels . . . Rossi's men." Commander Francesco Rossi of the Matteotti Brigades ("ranks and formations have been reconstituted overnight as they were two years ago") was in charge of the headquarters in the union hall. After lengthy negotiations by telephone, Rossi had authorized journalists to enter the city, so long as they were supplied with "appropriate passes." Beyond the bridge, the city was "impressively quiet." Factories, shops, hotels, offices: all were shut. But behind the "calm and the hush," a nervous suspense was palpable.[28]

In January 1946, when the Special Court of Turin had held the second trial against the collaborators of Casale, Francesco Rossi had been the leading witness against them. He wore the aura of Resistance legend about him, wreathed in memories of his own and his family's bravery. Both he and his brother Bruno had been partisan commanders; father Oreste and brother Italo were martyrs to the cause. At the Turin trial, he had brought into the courtroom not only a crowd of women in black, mourning for their sons, husbands, and brothers, but two genuine instruments of torture recovered from the Casale Fascist Party head-quarters: a pair of gloves armed with hooks and a metal whip.[29] Now, in September 1947, Rossi and his men were no longer disposed to delegate anti-Fascist justice to others. "One of those taking us around," *La Stampa*'s reporter continued, had told him: "This time we intend to put things right. Starting with war criminals: condemned to death three times by the people's tribunal, and then acquitted and set free . . . Either justice is done, in a serious way, or we will do it ourselves."[30]

Casale had not forgotten. People would never forget, the story went on, "that cold, fogbound morning of January 1945" when thirteen young men from the Tom band had been lined up against the wall and shot by local militiamen of the Black Brigades. The bodies had lain in the snow, and later their graves were profaned, their portraits ripped off, "the very gravestones shattered by hand grenades." The time to pay had come. Until a firing squad had taken aim at the backs of those Fascist criminals, Casale would continue to be occupied by partisans and workers. The general strike would go on until a delegation to Rome leaving that night came back: a delegation made up of "the mother of the fallen Italo Rossi," the mother of one of the martyrs of the Tom band, and Luigi Cappa, ex-commander of the Matteotti Brigades. Until that delegation received a promise from the highest authorities of the Republic that the Fascist collaborators would be shot without delay, Casale would remain composed, halted, waiting. "No wild behavior, no singing, no signs and signals." This was no theatrical performance. "The city is calm," observed the paper.[31]

La Stampa's correspondent, Giovanni Giovannini, found just the right tone to recount the unarmed battle of Casale, that final partisan blast without the submachine guns. He wrote of the "melancholy" that was already palpable the day after the strike began, although Casale was still under the control of "a mixed committee of partisans, relatives of the fallen, and workers." He wrote of the hopes that their struggle would expand nationally, perhaps even that weekend, when the Garibaldini partisans from all over Italy were to rally near Cuneo headed by "their commander Barbato." He wrote of the groups of men "waiting patiently" under the arcades of Via Mazzini or in Via Roma. "From time to time some person hurried by, and they would ask if there was any news. And without fail the passerby would shrug his shoulders."

More happened on the third day of the general strike, September 3. There was heartening news from the rest of Piedmont: demonstrations organized by partisans at Alessandria and Asti; a strike in solidarity proclaimed by the Lancia, Viberti, and Fiat autoworkers of Turin.[32] From Rome, Casale learned that Justice Minister Giuseppe Grassi had assured their delegation that he was opposed to pardoning the six Fascist criminals.[33] Then came the dispiriting word that Interior Minister Mario Scelba had ordered a battalion of carabinieri and police to move on Casale immediately. By nightfall, hundreds of agents were entering town. Francesco Rossi's twenty-year-old brother Bruno, who as a teenage partisan had been one of the first to triumphantly enter Casale on Liberation day, stood at the window of the offices of the National Association of Italian Partisans and read an outraged message over the microphone. The government in Rome, he said, was treating the partisans like common criminals.[34]

Giovannini reported the militarization of Casale with all the dry competence of the former army officer that he was. Through a partly open gate, he wrote, "this morning one can see numerous military trucks and armored vehicles, batteries of twenty-millimeter mounted guns, and light tanks lined up in the vast courtyard." Such a display of force lent the city "the air of an emergency," as did the store and factory gates still shut, with food shops only open at the request of the authorities. For the rest, the day went on as before, with groups of workers and partisans collected in front of the partisans' association and the union hall, "where by now all were accustomed to wait by the loudspeakers for news and developments." There was "fatigue in the air" and impatience to learn what the delegation would bring from Rome. "The most directly involved are obviously the cement-layers, now in their fourth day on strike. That means four thousand-lire bills they risk losing, for despite partisan assurances that no one is going to lose a penny in this strike, it won't be easy to get the money out of the owners, who say this matter has as much to do with them as oranges with apples."[35]

In fact, the workers of Casale no longer knew what to think or do. In a telegram from Rome, the secretary general of the national union federation, Giuseppe Di Vittorio, had suggested they suspend the strike. The justice minister had promised the union leadership that the Casale insurgents would get what they wanted. But when at lunchtime the delegation finally returned from Rome, rumors began to spread that Grassi was anything but decided. That afternoon, tensions began to rise. And at a rally that evening, Luigi Cappa, the ex-commander of the Matteotti Brigades who had made up one-third of the delegation, gave an incendiary speech.[36]

Cappa, like Bruno Rossi, was an old hand—at twenty-three. A railway worker, he had helped supply the early partisans with their first weapons, robbing a military transport in the Casale station just after the armistice in September 1943. "If you don't join the partisans, you're not a man," Cappa's father, a Socialist militant from just after the Great War, had apparently told his son. Cappa had joined the Rossi brothers in the spring of 1944, when the early members had regrouped in the Canavese. After Italo Rossi was killed, Cappa quickly rose to the leadership of the Matteotti Brigades. Following another year of actions in the Canavese and Monferrato, he would be commander in chief in the battle for the liberation of Turin.[37]

It was raining in Casale that evening of September 4, but not enough to keep people from coming to the piazza to hear Commander Cappa. Giovannini reported what he told the crowd: "In Rome the atmosphere is decidedly Fascist; the partisans are forgotten or more often called bandits. No one seems to know anything about the crimes of the Black Brigades. Even in Turin, even in the magistrature, there is rot; for twenty months the case of the six criminals lay ignored in the prosecutor's office." As for the justice minister, they could by no means count on him: he was a "huckster," saying one thing to the mothers of the fallen, another to the Roman press, a third thing to the president of the Republic. "At each of these remarks," *La Stampa* went on, "the crowd shouted, insulted, whistled, swore. And the elements seemed to want to participate in the fury of men; the rain poured down in torrents, the electric lights went out all over town, the microphone was silent. Violent flashes of lightning illuminated faces here and there in the crowd, people trying to stay dry under the arcades." Cappa could scarcely be heard as he announced the demands of the partisan leaders. The government of Rome had been sent a formal notice: the six Fascists had to be shot within a nonnegotiable period of fifteen days.[38]

The rest of the story can either be seen as a disaster averted in extremis, or as a classic comedy *all'italiana*. The president of the Republic said no to pardons for five of the six men,[39] and they were all confined to underground cells in Turin's Carceri Nuove reserved for those condemned to death.[40] The relatives of the condemned came to visit their loved ones during the so-called pre-death phase,[41] and the prison chaplain announced that he had comforted five Christians ready to meet their fate.[42] The firing range was readied for executions to take place at dawn the following day.[43] Then rumors began to circulate that the sentences might be suspended because the forthcoming Republican Constitution—which was not yet in effect—had outlawed the death penalty.[44] The five Fascists requested absolution under the Togliatti amnesty, and were transferred "in great secret" to a prison in Liguria.[45] The application for amnesty was rejected by Turin's Special Court of Assizes.[46] But a few weeks later, the Supreme Court ordered the death sentences to be suspended.[47]

By now it was early October. Things had gradually returned to normal in Casale Monferrato, although no representative of the Republic had taken seriously the Casale partisans' ultimatum of fifteen days to carry out the executions of the six Fascists. Their fate was only to be decided over the course of years, following the usual sequence of events for condemned collaborators: death sentences commuted to life imprisonment, life reduced to thirty years, then to twenty, then a further reduction.[48] The collaborators of Casale would ultimately find refuge—just as Edilio Cagni did—at the "port of shadows" of Perugia, but not until the mid-1950s, when the goriest memories of Nazi-Fascist violence had lost some of their sting.[49] By then few Italians would recall the events of September 1947 in Casale: the strike that came too late to breathe new life into the Northern wind, too late to counter the damp and sticky wind of pardon.

The winners defeated

In the long run, the memory of the Resistance would win out. The decisive turn came in July 1960, after a new generation of young anti-Fascists joined ranks with the older partisans, following huge popular protests against the neo-Fascist–backed government of Fernando Tambroni.[50] The values of the Resistance would thenceforth be set down as the values of the Republic, the only danger being that they would become commandments engraved in stone rather than beliefs to stir consciences. As the years went by, even the most rousing of Resistance stories had a way of becoming rhetorical, monumental. That rhetoric, though, served in some way to compensate for the grief for the fallen, and for the disappointment that the dreams of the Resistance had been betrayed. Even medals helped. The Rossi family would earn four of them: posthumously, a gold medal for Italo and a silver for Oreste; and for courage, a silver medal for Francesco and a bronze for Bruno.

But the years before that turn were utterly different. In the long decade from 1948 to 1960, many Italians thought that having fought for the Resistance was a mark of discredit. The risky bet that Communist secretary Palmiro Togliatti had made in agreeing to promote the amnesty—that he would win ex-Fascists to the Communist ranks rather than leave them to the Christian Democrats—had bitter consequences for the Resistance movement. By giving collaborationists of Salò and partisans of the mountains an equal judicial status, the amnesty led moderate public opinion to view the two sides in the civil war as equal factions, albeit with different values. It was in this context that, around 1950, plans started being made to provide war pensions (not to mention ordinary pension contributions) for Salò militiamen, hitherto excluded from government contributions for the years 1943–45.[51]

It was in this context, too, that partisans began to be put on trial, beginning after the April 1948 election, when the political parties of the Resistance were swept from power once and for all by the massive victory of the Christian Democrats. In most cases, partisans tried for crimes committed during the Resistance or the Liberation were acquitted, or benefitted from the Togliatti amnesty, or received sentences that were considerably reduced by mitigating circumstances. Still, after 1948 partisans were more likely to appear in courtrooms as the accused than as the accusers, and sometimes their reputations as freedom fighters were tarnished.[52] A striking example was that of Primo Levi's close friend Silvio Ortona, the indomitable partisan leader from Biella. A Communist Party deputy in Rome after the war, in 1949 he was accused of having ordered the massacre of dozens of Fascists at the Vercelli psychiatric hospital in May 1945.[53] The case, highly polarized politically, was never brought to trial.

To avoid prison, those Communists most compromised in the episodes of rough justice that followed the Liberation expatriated to former Czechoslovakia. Dozens of them remained in Prague for years, sometimes for decades, the winners defeated. But there were others who also felt themselves defeated and decided to leave Italy even though arrest warrants were never issued for them. Alimiro, the partisan Mario Pelizzari, was one of these. When in April 1954 the distinguished jurist Piero Calamandrei came to Ivrea to celebrate the memory of the audacious sabotage of the railway bridge over the Dora River, Pelizzari, the man who had carried out that mission, was not on hand. He had been living for some years in Belo Horizonte, Brazil, working as either a truck driver or a surveyor.[54] And that is where he still was in 1955, when Calamandrei's speech was published in *Men and Cities of the Resistance* and Alimiro became a national hero.

Just after the Liberation, Pelizzari had been named police chief of Ivrea. After a few months he had returned to work at the Olivetti factory, now as head of personnel. Even a company as eccentric as Olivetti, however, could not permit itself a chief of personnel as eccentric as Pelizzari. During his first negotiations with the union Pelizzari made an incautious promise to the workers, was quickly removed from the post, and given a new job as sales representative in Como. Nor did things go better for him inside the hierarchy of the National Association of Italian Partisans. The association did not give desirable positions in its central Rome office to those who denounced partisan profiteers, as Pelizzari had done at its 1946 congress in Florence. When his difficulties expanded to include family problems, he decided to put an ocean between his past and his future.[55]

Today, viewing the "Casa De Alimiro" in Belo Horizonte on the Web, improvising with my sketchy knowledge of Portuguese, I can't help but think that a man like Alimiro deserves a historian all his own. The Casa De Alimiro is a center for orphan children, a place Pelizzari worked to build throughout his years in Brazil. Not long before he died in 1977, he donated the home to a lay charitable institution. The Web site of the Casa sports photos of happy-looking children at work in their classrooms or sitting at lunch tables. The restless Resistance veteran Alimiro must certainly have been proud to see such an institution come to life.

Gold

No one has written better about the gold rush that overwhelmed Italians just after the Liberation than Italian author Piero Chiara. It seems that all of Italy dreamed of finding one of those lost treasures the disorder of war had left behind: in hiding places near borders, in cellars, in gardens, in the waters of a lake or the undergrowth of a wood. Treasures hidden away by Jews in flight, soldiers abandoning their posts, Germans on the run, unreliable partisans: the Synagogue Gold, the Fourth Army Gold, the Wehrmacht Gold, the Dongo Gold.

Chiara's tale "After the War" is the story of two traffickers from Lombardy who set out for the northeast of Italy in October 1945, looking to make money. Stopping in a tavern along the way, they meet a sergeant from their own parts. He's "a cheerful type, half bandit, half soldier, with the stripes of the Legnano Brigade sewn on his sleeve, although he looked in every way like a soldier of fortune, armed and clothed with the remains of two or three armies." He tells the two travelers about some metal in the countryside—a lot of metal—and indeed, under a carpeting of leaves near a creek, they find "a glittering swath of aluminum-colored bricks." The travelers buy one of these bars, paying the price for lead. They take it back to Milan in the hopes it is tin. When they saw into it, they find, instead, gold. Getting hold of a truck "that costs a fortune," they race back toward the tavern. The sergeant has disappeared. The traffickers manage to retrace their steps to that spot by the creek, where the wet ground "bears the marks, still fresh, of those ingots." They are tempted to ask around but decide it is wiser to remain silent, because "that gold might have an ugly story behind it and to act interested in it was surely dangerous." The truck returns to Milan with nothing more than large yellow plastic sheets, which might be good for making improvised raincoats at the stadium.[56]

Fanned by hard times, but also by the "good humor" of the postwar years,[57] the gold rush was but a latter-day version of the old dream of El Dorado. Yet as it happened, the very Val d'Ayas contained one of the richest veins of gold ever discovered in the Alps, a vein that had been excavated since the late nineteenth century. That mine where Emilio Bachi hid on the night of the December 13 raid[58] had supplied dozens of kilos of gold over the years, first extracted by a Swiss company, then by an English concession holder, and then by the Rivetti firm of Biella.[59] The rock face of the Val d'Ayas really did have gold nuggets in the quartz. For half a century the people of the valley had been spending some of their free time armed with shovels and buckets and sieves, digging in the gravel along the Evançon creek above where it met the great Dora River.[60]

It was Primo Levi's encounter in the Aosta jail with the gold smuggler—the one who told him that the Dora was made of gold and that when it froze you could extract it—that gave the title "Gold" to his chapter about the Resistance in *The Periodic Table*. That smuggler might have been real or invented, but the postwar gold fever was real enough. Indeed, it struck not only impoverished and battered Italy but even prosperous, neutral Switzerland. From the spring of 1945 until the early 1950s, the Swiss police blotter records dozens of rumors about various treasures supposedly secreted in plausible and not so plausible hideaways inside the Confederation. German gold, twenty-seven crates of it, at the home of a certain Wertlaufer in Geneva;[61] "valuables" taken from "prisoners at the camp of Auschwitz" and exchanged for Swiss francs at the Zurich branch of the Reichsbank;[62] silver plate stolen from the queen of Holland and now hidden away in a castle near Basel.[63] And so on it went.

Plenty of treasure truly existed: as the outcome of the European war grew more certain in autumn 1944, the transfer of war spoils and general capital flight toward Switzerland had expanded. In September the Swiss Banking Association had sent special instructions to all banks in the Confederation: they were not to cooperate in transferring money to anonymous accounts or in depositing gold of suspect provenance, and they were to be especially cautious regarding the Third Reich and the Italian Social Republic.[64] Those orders were soon stiffened considerably. Now banks were not to open any new accounts in the names of individuals or companies based in belligerent or occupied countries; nor were they to accept deposits that notably increased the value of existing accounts above the maximum that those accounts had been worth in 1943.[65]

These stern measures would not prevent a scandal from arising half a century later about the "Nazi gold" tucked away in Switzerland during World War II. Less attention, however, has been paid to the Italian

Fascist gold. In the winter of 1944–45, American diplomatic services in Bern had warned Swiss authorities that "Mussolinian gerarchs" (the ruling elite) were transferring capital from Salò to Switzerland, capital that one day "neo-Fascists" might use not only for private gain but to organize subversive plots against a future democratic Italy.[66] In this light, a 1956 document sent to the Vaud cantonal police by the federal police in Bern brings us back to one of the protagonists of our story.

Thanks to an informer in Rome, the Bern police told their colleagues in Lausanne, they had learned that "a certain Edilio Cagni," born in Genoa, an ex-officer of the Alpine troops, had knowledge of "around 300 kilos of gold" secretly withdrawn from the Milan office of the Banca d'Italia and transferred to Switzerland. According to this Cagni, the gold bars had been buried "around the foundations of a villa" under construction on the banks of Lake Geneva between Geneva and Lausanne, more precisely between the towns of Allaman and Aubonne. The villa belonged to a certain "Monsieur Petraquin" and would be easy to identify, because it was located about two hundred meters from a police station and about a hundred meters from a railway crossing on the Geneva–Lausanne line.

The Bern police also specified that the information received might not be reliable, because Cagni faced "criminal charges for fraud." Nevertheless, the Vaud police were invited to make a "discreet inquiry."[67]

Monsieur Petraquin

In the summer of 1956, Inspector Georges Allamand was close to retirement. The "discreet inquiry" he was assigned by the commander of the Vaud cantonal police was among the very last he undertook in his career. And it was not one of his most difficult. Allamand filed a report in just three days' time, a report also sent to the federal police in Bern.[68]

As had been anticipated, it was easy to identify the land where the villa was meant to stand, between the Allaman police station and the road for Aubonne that crossed the rail line. However, it seemed that no

villa had been built in that space anytime between 1943 and the end of
the war. The only villa dating from that period stood elsewhere, where
the road for Grands Bois began. Inspector Allamand had not thought it
useful to bother the resident of this other villa, in part because he did
not want to be indiscreet about why he was asking questions. He thought
it would be better if the informant were questioned again "so that he
can be as precise as possible about the exact place where the gold was
hidden and above all in what circumstances." When exactly, on whose
initiative, with whose assistance? If new information were to come to
light, Inspector Allamand was ready to continue the investigation. As
for Monsieur Petraquin, the report made no mention of him.[69]

In the federal archives of Bern the matter ends there. It was only in
the year 2000 that the question came up again, in the Swiss news weekly
L'Hebdo, under the title "Treasure Hunt: Who's Sleeping on Mussolini's
Gold?" The journalist, who had seen the relevant documents in the federal archives, described the "feeble" investigation undertaken by Allamand and posed some questions. Had Edilio Cagni been questioned
further? Supposing there was substance to the story, had the Italian
police told the Swiss exactly where the stash was located? Had the Swiss
authorities perhaps taken it? Or had Cagni himself stepped in: "had he,
or one of his boys, come to get the gold bars back?"[70] The story was
picked up by just one Italian paper, the Genoa edition of La Repubblica,
which played up Cagni's Genoese roots but otherwise merely recapitu-
lated the details from L'Hebdo.[71]

We, however, know far more than the Bern or Lausanne police in
1956, and more than the Swiss and Italian reporters in the year 2000.
Cagni was not just a nobody from Genoa, nor was he just any resident
in Rome with a criminal record. We know Cagni's past, and have learned
not to underestimate the man.

At Cagni's first trial in Aosta, after all, Captain Balestrieri had testified that Cagni once helped the partisans search for some gold bars connected to Paolo Zerbino, the stalwart Fascist whose career had put him
in the top ranks of the collaborationist government: prefect of Turin,

then high commissioner for the Province of Rome, then high commissioner for Piedmont, and finally, two months before the Liberation, interior minister of Salò. It was not a lucky promotion for Zerbino: in the convoy of the Salò command trying to flee Italy on April 28, 1945, he was arrested along with Mussolini by the partisans at Dongo and shot on the banks of Lake Como. In the well-known, terrible photos of the bodies of Il Duce and his companions strung up by the heels in Milan to public derision, Zerbino's corpse is farthest to the left, hanging next to that of Mussolini.[72]

During Zerbino's time in the Salò High Commission for Piedmont, his right-hand man had been Cesare Augusto Carnazzi, whose right-hand man was Edilio Cagni. It was during the period when all three were part of the High Commission that emissaries from Salò stepped up their contacts with the Swiss police, exploring the possibility that Switzerland might grant asylum, if not to Mussolini and other high-ranking Fascists, then at least to their families.[73] And although it was Foreign Ministry functionaries, not those from the Interior Ministry, who were engaged in those negotiations, it is nevertheless possible that sometime between the autumn of 1944 and the spring of 1945 someone acting on Zerbino's behalf may have tried to arrange for Salò currency or gold reserves to be secretly exported to Switzerland. And therefore it is possible that Cagni may have known about it, either because he was directly involved or because he had secondhand knowledge of the conversations.

It is also possible that Cagni learned something later, after the Liberation, when he persuaded the Americans of the OSS and the Italians of the Cremona Division to let him out of jail to help search for hidden Salò gold. Notably, when Cagni was persuading the naive Albertina Porciani to help him locate Baroness von Hodenberg, he told her he was reorganizing the Fascist Party and counting on "a treasure of the Social Republic's Interior Minister that had been deposited with a lawyer in Zurich or Geneva." To get it back, Cagni told her, one would need among other things his own signature, because he had been Zerbino's "secretary . . . under the name of Redi."[74]

Of course, it may be that all these details—Cagni's secretarial service to Zerbino, the three hundred kilos of gold withdrawn from the Milan office of the Banca d'Italia, the deposit of those gold bars with a lawyer in Zurich or Geneva, the hiding of them in a villa under construction on Lake Geneva—were just the products of Cagni's lively imagination. The fact that Porciani had believed him about the Salò treasure could certainly be explained by the gold frenzy of the time. But we could also decide to treat his story as did the Swiss federal police, regarding it as a matter worthy of investigation. And rather than resign ourselves to accepting Inspector Allamand's nonfindings of 1956, we might want to put a bit more energy into our inquiry than did a Swiss policeman just about to retire.

When I first sat down in the Swiss federal archives and read that a certain "Monsieur Petraquin" was supposed to be the owner of the villa near Lausanne where the gold of Salò was allegedly hidden, I asked myself (as any halfway decent police detective in a Francophone country would) how else the name *Petraquin* might be spelled in French. The Swiss counterintelligence agent in Rome may have heard Cagni say "Petraquin," but the presumed owner of the villa might be instead Monsieur Pétraquain, or Monsieur Pétraquein. Or perhaps the trouble lay in Cagni's Italianized pronunciation, and the man's surname was more like Peitraquin or Peytrequin?

Searching with Google again and again, one day in January 2011 I came across Jean Peitrequin, whose name meant nothing to me. Born in Lausanne in 1902, a degree in civil engineering from the Lausanne Polytechnic, well known in the canton of Vaud for his long career in the Radical Party, holder of various government posts at the canton level. He was also a writer who had published in the *Revue de Lausanne* in the 1930s and written plays and detective stories in the 1940s. As I glanced through the online catalog for French Swiss libraries, though, an entry made me start in my chair: a detective novel published in Lausanne in 1945 under the name of Ariste Vertuchet, which, the catalog informed me, was a pseudonym of Jean Peitrequin. It was called *Villa for Rent*.

Monsieur Petraquin and the villa on the lake! It was perfect. That detective story of 1945 could only be a novel written in code; it must surely hold, encrypted, the secret of the Salò gold. I still recall the impatience with which, just twenty-four hours after learning of the existence of Jean Peitrequin, I boarded a train for Freiburg, where a seller of vintage books had a copy of *Villa for Rent* listed for sale. I paid a few francs for the novel and devoured it on the return train. The stylized drawing of a villa on the cover was promising. It took me a good half of the train trip to see that the book was leading nowhere, the other half to come to terms with my mistake. What had I ever thought I would find out? What was the novel supposed to tell me—the exact address where I would find three hundred kilos of gold? And if Jean Peitrequin had really been involved with it, would he have been foolish enough to broadcast the fact left and right in a two-bit novel?

A couple of days passed before I could digest the disappointment. And then some more time went by before I guessed that the possible significance here lay not in Peitrequin the dilettante writer but Peitrequin the civil engineer and politician, for the latter two roles had been his principal activities in life. He'd been elected to the Lausanne municipal government with the Radical Party in 1937 and was director of public works from then until 1945. In 1946–49 he headed the city department of social welfare, and in 1950–57 led the general administration (which in effect made him the city's mayor). In short, Jean Peitrequin had been a leading man in local politics for twenty years. In 1956, when Inspector Allamand failed to identify him as the "Monsieur Petraquin" mentioned by Cagni, he was Lausanne's highest public official.

I find the Peitrequin connection intriguing for two other reasons. First, the Radical Party in Lausanne during the second half of the 1930s was decidedly philo-Fascist.[75] These were the circles that in 1937 decided to confer on Benito Mussolini an honorary degree in social and political science from the University of Lausanne.[76] Secondly, Peitrequin was commissioner of public works for Lausanne in the years 1943–45, and in that role Cagni might have heard him mentioned as someone connected to the lost gold bars.

I do not, let me be clear, by any means wish to suggest that the well-known radical Peitrequin was so enamored of the Fascist cause as to collaborate with the Salò regime by hiding a treasure in the foundations of a villa on the lake, or in any other building project he may have authorized around Lausanne. A couple of coincidences do not in any way add up to proof. Indeed, I have no real idea what happened. But I do have a suspicion that Inspector Allamand, when he chose not to pursue the part of his inquiry connected to Monsieur Petraquin, was much more keen to receive his pension than to ascertain the truth.

Demons

The inquiries of the Swiss police also bring up a more immediate question, of the kind we have become accustomed to when it comes to Cagni. How was it he could move freely around Rome in 1956 when he had been sentenced to thirty years in prison by the Special Court of Perugia in 1947?

It is much the same question as we had regarding Cagni's apparent freedom as "Italic Dreamer" in the fall of 1946, after the Special Court of Aosta had sentenced him to death that May. But this time, there is no need for conjecture or competing hypotheses. The answer is a matter of public record.

In 1948 the Court of Cassation had heard Cagni's second appeal and annulled his thirty-year sentence, finding that the Perugia court had not properly taken into account "the guilty man's character" when deciding on the severity of the punishment. Cagni had to be tried again, this time in the Court of Assizes of Viterbo.[77] In 1949 Cagni was therefore transferred to the Viterbo penitentiary, and in October of that year he appeared in court, once again charged with collaborationism. The only witness to appear in the Viterbo court was Don Federico Bosticco, the priest from Asti who had already testified in Cagni's favor in the Aosta trial of 1946. Ferdinando Trombin, the Quixote of Casale, was also on the list of witnesses, but after his appearance at the Perugia court he seems to have decided to stay at home.

At the turn of the 1950s, when this third trial took place, the political atmosphere had never been less forgiving of the partisans, more willing to give credit to collaborators. When Cagni appeared before the three magistrates and four lay jurors of the Viterbo Court of Assizes, he had no reason to minimize the role he had played in the Valle d'Aosta in December 1943, and he even seemed to boast that he had helped to maintain public order. "The prefect at the time assigned me the job of combatting banditry, given that the partisan movement had not yet come into being," he said. And thus he had gone to the Val d'Ayas, where he found more than a hundred criminals, and was able to "dissolve the band which was engaged in serious offenses," he testified. Regarding his activities in the Canavese, he told the court that "once again, operating as an observer for the prefecture, I also took part in some raids." His nonchalant reference to raids—*rastrellamenti*—eloquently suggests how much that word had by then lost its sting of terror.[78]

Cagni's third trial lasted less than a single day. The court was convened at 4 p.m., and the jury pronounced a sentence that evening. Cagni was given twenty years in prison, with two-thirds of that term cancelled due to the joint effects of the Togliatti amnesty and a further clemency measure of 1948. His remaining punishment was to be "six years and seven months of detention."[79] In fact, Cagni would remain in jail for only a few more months. In June 1950 he was granted clemency and released, with only the requirement that he go to Rome. There the former collaborator established his residence and celebrated his thirty-third birthday as a free man.

And what then? I've devoted so much effort to the figure of Edilio Cagni that I can hardly be expected not to want to know what became of him. What did Cagni do in the second act of his life? Leaving aside wild speculations—that he got his hands on the Salò gold, for instance—where did he end up? Did he marry? Have children? Did he remain in Italy, and if so in what guise, working on what and for whom? Or did he perhaps go far away, as far away as possible from those nowhere places of his adventures in crime—the prefecture and the police command, the courts and the jails? Did he turn over a new leaf, as they say? Take an office job, sit down to Sunday lunch, a paycheck at the end of the month? Or stay the same as always: shape-shifting, impenetrable, unreadable, changing only his avatar, no longer Lieutenant Redi or the Italic Dreamer?

I mulled over those questions at length. And often, I admit, they became genuine obsessions. I typed "Edilio Cagni" into Google a thousand times, working and reworking key words in every possible combination. I hunted for Cagni in cyberspace under his real name and his false ones, pursued the obvious and the less obvious: the Italian telephone directory; the list, revealed in 1990, of NATO-backed clandestine anti-Communist operatives in Italy; databases of Italian immigrants to New York. The very failure of my research only made my demons torment me more. If after 1956 Cagni had been able to disappear, I said to myself, to sink into the depths of the second half of the twentieth century without leaving a trace, was that not proof that his criminal adventures hadn't ended when he reached forty, that he'd kept on going somewhere, somehow? How could I finish telling the story without revealing what had become of Cagni?

Abandoning Google, I continued searching in a more professional way. From records I learned that Cagni's middle name was Renato. I learned, more significantly, that in December 1952 he had married a woman from Sicily whose name I shall not record here, and that his marriage had not been a success: the two were divorced in December 1973, in effect just about as soon as Italian divorce law permitted. He was therefore still alive in the 1970s, not too surprising for a man born in 1917. He was in his middle to late fifties when I was a boy and my mother read me the letters of condemned partisans; when my teacher assigned me my first Primo Levi book; when Levi himself was composing his portrait of the "complete spy" in the chapter titled "Gold" of *The Periodic Table*.

I might have kept pursuing that research, and perhaps learned more. I might have learned Cagni's date of death, assuming he is not still alive and nearing a hundred. I might even have learned whether he had any offspring: the children, innocent by definition, of a hunter of human prey. But at a certain point obsession gave way to lucidity, and I decided to stop and search no more. It was what seemed right. Right in a historical sense, in that any second act in Cagni's life pertained to another story, not that of the early Resistance. And right in what I'd like to think of as a literary sense, for this way each reader can imagine what became of Edilio Cagni, and supply a denouement of choice.

9

—

And Calls On Him to Explain

Lieutenant Oppezzo

I KNEW BEFORE I WENT TO THE TOWN OF CERRINA MONFERRATO that its main square is named after Fulvio Oppezzo. Is there anything we don't know, thanks to Google? I had bought an old postcard on eBay showing the Piazza Lieutenant Fulvio Opezzo (with a single *p*, but what did it matter). That sepia postcard, though it was neither postmarked nor sent, still has much to say. In the background you can see the apse of the parish church, a triangle of the bell tower, and the back side of the oratory. The piazza is not much more than a broad patch of dirt, with a cart drawn by a donkey and two farmer women with scarf-covered heads standing beside a bale of hay next to a barber pole. It's a postcard of modest artistic pretensions, but decidedly neorealist in style, clearly dating from around 1948 or 1950.

Before I went I also learned from Google that the Cerrina elementary and middle schools, too, are named after "Opezzo." Again the one *p*, and no matter. What does matter from the point of view of this story is how large Oppezzo's name has been written on his birthplace, his home until he went up to the mountains and died at eighteen. At least in Cerrina Monferrato, with its 1,500 inhabitants, forty kilometers from Turin and twenty from Casale, a place I'd never visited before, the name of Fulvio Oppezzo meant something to someone. I had to go there, for history must be covered on foot as well as read. I had to go there to see, to ask, to listen. Fulvio's memory as a fallen partisan was inscribed on his territory. My job was to reconstruct how that memory had been shaped.

An old friend of mine put me in touch with Corrado Calvo, a native of Cerrina Monferrato. Calvo is a business executive with little time to devote to history, but he was polite, and quick to get my point when I phoned him. Both his parents had taught in the school named "Fulvio Opezzo," and he himself had studied there. Fulvio's name was well known to the children of Cerrina. Calvo told me that a photograph of Fulvio adorns the entrance to the Cerrina middle school: "a portrait of Oppezzo in military uniform," he said.

Calvo also spoke of the young man's mother, Idalia Oppezzo. In the early postwar years, according to Calvo's parents, she became a sort of professional mother of the fallen, knocking on every door in hopes of getting the memory of her only child inscribed somewhere. Calvo further told me that it had sometimes been rumored that Oppezzo had died in "strange" circumstances, but the matter had never gone beyond rumors. And he suggested I do some research in Cerrina at the parish church. Chiara Cane, a reporter for the local paper, would be my best introduction, he said.[1]

I arranged to meet Cane in front of the Cerrina middle school one October afternoon in 2011. Lessons were over and the school was deserted except for the janitor, who kindly took down for us the portrait of Oppezzo posted at the entrance. We carried it into a nearby room, and I took my own photograph of it there. After all this time during which I'd been interested in Oppezzo, I now finally saw what he looked like: an adolescent, less shaven than beardless, proudly wearing a brand-new

Royal Army uniform with the rank of second lieutenant. Apparently Idalia Oppezzo had given the school a copy of a photograph taken at the military academy of Milan in the summer of 1943, when Oppezzo had earned his stripes. In childish script at the bottom of the picture were the words "Fulvio to his dearest mother."

Outside, the rain was coming down, and Cane and I huddled under an umbrella to walk up to Via dei Bastioni on the heights (called the *muraglia*, the great wall) where the Oppezzo family house stood. It was a dilapidated two-story structure, though once evidently a dwelling of note suitable for Fulvio's grandfather Marcello Oppezzo, Fascist *podestà* of Cerrina in the 1930s. The rain kept falling as she and I went to the town hall to see the monument to the war dead, with its nineteen names from the Great War and four from World War II—and no trace of Fulvio Oppezzo. Cane had also arranged a meeting for me with the town "elders" at the parish church, for which I was grateful. It was an intense and memorable afternoon. Drying off inside the church, I met three people who still remembered Fulvio well: Angelo Brignoglio, Maria Cerruti, and Renato Porta. All of them had known him as children, and as young adults after the war they had been there as he made his transition from the *podestà*'s grandson to Resistance hero.

"Our cowshed was under Via dei Bastioni, and everyone who lived up there would come down in the evening, men on one side of the road and women on the other," recalled Maria Cerruti. Fulvio also enjoyed coming down to take part in those gatherings, even though he was "from a good family" and his mother put on airs—so much so that the farmers in town, more in mockery than with respect, called her *Madame* Oppezzo. Once, although "his parents didn't want him to," Fulvio went to work in the field with four or five villagers right behind the thresher, despite the "terrible noise and dust." He helped out with the harvest, "and he ate with them."

Certainly, his background meant he was privileged. He had skis, for instance, and during the winter holiday he used to ski on the meadow near the school with two city girls. "I do remember him with those skis.

We used to stare at him—we'd never seen skis before." Fulvio even had a bicycle with gears! It had been built by Salvino Porta, a bicycle-maker and the father of Renato, who was telling me the story. "He wanted a bike with a big frame, so we had to modify it . . . because Fulvio himself was tall, handsome . . . We were good friends."

These good senior citizens, for all the sprightliness of their conversation and clarity of their minds, could not be expected to know the details of Fulvio's background and education. However, the parish documentation collected by Don Giuseppe Ferrando, the parish priest, came to my aid. Just as Corrado Calvo said, it was a marvelous source for local history. The Oppezzo family arrived in Cerrina in 1935, when Marcello was named *podestà*.[2] Fulvio then began his studies at the Collegio Trevisio in Casale, where he boarded for five years. In the summer of 1940, as Mussolini led Italy into World War II, he entered the military academy of Milan. It was a natural choice for the fifteen-year-old son of Ugo Oppezzo, who had been decorated for bravery in World War I[3] and twenty years later was an officer leading a battalion in the Battle of Ethiopia.[4]

After the ceremony in the summer of 1943 in which he was awarded his stripes, Fulvio scarcely had time to put on his uniform before September 8 arrived, and with it the German occupation. The Royal Army scattered; the uniforms were folded up and put away. Fulvio went home to Cerrina but did not stay long: for a few weeks, at most three months. As we know, around December 5 he left Cerrina with his nineteen-year-old friend Giuseppe Villata and the twenty-three-year-old Eligio Costelli of Casale. Armed and disguised with scarves wrapped around their faces, the young men went off to the Val d'Ayas to join the Casale band. Of the three, only Villata would be alive when the Liberation came. Costelli was executed in June 1944 in a reprisal following a partisan attack.[5] And Oppezzo, as we know, died in Frumy on December 9, 1943.

"They used to say here that Fulvio was one of the very first partisans," Maria Cerruti told me. How did they learn of his death, I asked, and what did people say about it? Renato Porta's reply was laconic. "The news of Fulvio's death arrived. But there weren't a lot of comments. It was war, he had died." Angelo Brignoglio's memory of that day, though, had the kind of magic that oral history sometimes provides, when a single image can somehow capture an entire time and place. "A street musician was passing by, up there, on the *muraglia*. And they told him, 'don't play by that door, and don't ask for money, because they just had the news that their boy is dead.'"

Idalia Oppezzo had to wait a long time to get back her son's remains. In October 1945, the Turinese engineer Vincenzo Grasso, president of the association of political prisoners, completed his investigation of "Fulvio (surname unknown)," who had fallen alongside Luciano Zabaldano "after being wounded, more precisely wounded by a machine gun."[6] Once the identification was made, the town of Saint-Vincent allowed the body to be transferred to his hometown, and Idalia Oppezzo was able to receive the comfort of some of her fellow townspeople. Nearly two years after he was shot by his partisan companions and buried in the snow of Frumy, Fulvio Oppezzo finally lay beside his grandfather in the family tomb.[7]

The school in the hills

In a scene from Cesare Pavese's *The Moon and the Bonfires*, two dead men are found some years after the war on an upland plain, not far from Cerrina. "Two Fascist Republican spies, their heads smashed, shoes missing . . . They had to be men of Salò because the partisans died down below, shot in the squares and hanged from balconies, or were sent to Germany." The bodies are brought down to the old hospital in a cart, and a lot of people go to look, but no one is able to identify them ("after three years what was left to identify?"). Still, the townspeople are quite certain about the circumstances of their deaths: those two must have been assassinated by the Reds, "because, they said in low voices in the square, it's the Reds who shoot people in the back of the head without a trial." And on Sunday, speaking on the church steps, the parish priest delivers some "big thoughts." Too much blood has been shed; there is too much hatred going around. Fatherland, family, and religion are still under threat. "We, too, must repent, purify ourselves, make reparation," the priest says. Those two poor fellows, "barbarously slaughtered, done away with, God knows, without the comfort of the sacraments," must be given a Christian burial. The townspeople must "atone, pray for them, raise a barricade of hearts."[8]

Pavese's scene is fictional, but this might as well be the story of Fulvio Oppezzo and Luciano Zabaldano. They, too, were not shot in a main square or hanged from a town balcony, but struck down on the spot, without a trial, and like the spies of Salò buried without a coffin. In Zabaldano's case, the partisans of Turin moved quickly after the Liberation to include him in the ranks of Resistance martyrs. For Oppezzo, matters were different: the partisans of Cerrina stayed aloof, and only his neighbors went to the funeral. Idalia Oppezzo, if she thought about it, might well have wondered whether Fulvio had been shot by the Reds. And the parish priest of the time, who never failed to thunder against the Communists in his sermons,[9] most likely considered Fulvio's death a threat to God and country.

If Cesare Pavese didn't know Fulvio Oppezzo, he did know whereof he spoke. Pavese had taken refuge near Cerrina after the eighth of September and got a teaching job under a false name at the Collegio Treviso in Casale, around the same time Fulvio (a former student at the Collegio) left for the hills. That he had not dared to take sides tormented Pavese; it was "an ugly thing to be in history's clutches."[10] But for that very reason he was able to see the civil war from a broader perspective than those who did take sides, and with a sensibility lacking, for example, in some of his postwar colleagues at the influential Einaudi publishing house, who'd had the courage to choose and had chosen the Resistance.[11] Pavese knew that the youth of Monferrato who joined the partisans after the armistice were a tiny minority. He knew that the consciences of the majority had been roused very late, sometimes at the last minute, as with those students at the Collegio

Trevisio who took up arms only on Liberation day. And the local farmers, he knew, much as they may have detested the Germans and the Salò regime, had not joined the rebels but remained spectators of the tragedy.

Pavese's earlier novel *The House on the Hill*[12] was as far away as could be from a celebration of the war of liberation as a magnificent, progressive struggle.[13] A monument not to the rhetoric of the Resistance but to Resistance anti-rhetoric, it ended with words about "the unknown dead"—the Salò dead, witnesses to the futility of all bloodshed. The Salò dead might as well be any of them, Pavese suggested: there was no difference. "Every war is a civil war: every man who falls resembles another who lives, and calls on him to explain."

In Cerrina, though, it would be a while yet before someone tried to explain what happened to Fulvio Oppezzo, whose death resembled less that of a partisan than of a man of Salò. In 1949, when Don Ferrando became parish priest of Cerrina, he asked no questions about Oppezzo, preferring to honor the *mater dolorosa* Idalia in her mourning for a fallen son. In church bulletins, Don Ferrando's representation of that war was ever soothing: a battle without sides, without reds and blacks. Reading the bulletins he wrote in the early 1950s, one understands how in provincial Italy of those times it was possible to nurture an image of the freedom fighters at once adamantine and hackneyed, partisans portrayed as if on holy cards. The very word *partisan* was shunned, as was the term *Resistance*.

"Fulvio, that is, Italy": thus the parish bulletin of Cerrina for September 1952 announced some good news from Milan. "In June a committee in Milan decreed that a new street in the Porta Genova district be dedicated to the memory of Lt. Fulvio Oppezzo. We are honored that the sons of this land of ours are so remembered . . . During those most difficult days of the nation he saw and chose his place without hesitation: for Italy! The war of liberation, first in the Val Cerrina, then in Valle d'Aosta. He met death on 12/12/1943, in the flower of his youth and prospects, with the courage of his generous spirit. The telegram to the family read: 'Lt. Fulvio Oppezzo died heroically for the liberation of Italy.'"

Perhaps Fulvio's family did indeed receive such a telegram. Or rather perhaps his mother Idalia did, for at the time of Fulvio's death his father was a prisoner of war in Africa, and he did not return to Cerrina or to his wife after the war. Idalia Oppezzo had some connections with the military elite, particularly with the commander of the military academy of Milan, who possibly wanted to raise Fulvio to the level of national martyr by naming a street after him in the city. In the process, Second Lieutenant Oppezzo was also incidentally promoted to lieutenant.

No Milan street was ever named for Fulvio. In 1950, though, Don Ferrando announced the "solemn benediction and inauguration of the new schools" dedicated to Oppezzo, "the Cerrina youth who fell in the liberation."[14] Enlarged in the following decades, these classrooms are still used today by the students of Cerrina; every morning middle schoolers file noisily past Fulvio's portrait. But his canonization began in the years when his death was still fresh, still painful. To judge by the essays written by Cerrina schoolchildren in the 1950s, his memory back then had already been collected, sanitized, and made edifying, his life shaped by parents and teachers into that of a saint.

Thus in the school year 1952–53, a third-grade girl wrote: "Our school is named after the martyr for Liberty Fulvio Opezzo, who died in war. In the school entryway there is a photograph of him and we often put fresh flowers there. We try to be always worthy of the sacrifice of our Fallen."[15] In October 1953, another third grader described how "the mamma of Fulvio Opezzo, the heroic partisan to whom the school building is dedicated, came to our school. She is a tall, fair-haired lady with a sweet and maternal smile . . . She spoke to us as a mother, urging us to be grateful to those who are concerned about our welfare and that of the Nation. She had a good word for everyone, from the Head of the Government to our priest, the benefactors of our school, and our teachers. Then she gave out sweets and bid us a kind farewell. We thanked her for her gracious visit and promised to think of her often along with her beloved Fulvio."[16]

Idalia Oppezzo did not just give out sweets in her efforts to keep

Fulvio's memory alive; she dedicated a motorbike race to her son. In July 1954, the parish news recorded a celebration of the patron saints of Cerrina, a fair with livestock and goods for sale, the showing of a French film musical, a bocce tournament, a tamburello match between two local teams—and the "Lt. Fulvio Opezzo Cup motorcycle gymkhana."[17] The following year, the parish news reported the rich list of prizes for the event: eleven large fine ceramic flower vases, forty smaller flower vases, six medals, three bottles of cordials, four bottles of vermouth, and eight gasoline vouchers.[18]

In April 1955, according to the parish news, the people of Cerrina "gathered in the bosom of their great Church packed with adults and youth" to celebrate the tenth anniversary of the Liberation. The priest pronounced "a few emotional words" calling for gratitude to those who had suffered during the war, and prayers for those who had lost their lives. "Homage was paid to the partisan Second Lt. Fulvio Opezzo, and to Attilio Cerretti and Mario Villata, captured in raids and deceased in Germany." All the dead were solemnly celebrated, especially one of them. "The mother of Second Lt. Opezzo, present at the ceremony, expressed her deepest thanks for the condolences and sympathy for her beloved Fulvio."[19]

Sassi

Had Fulvio Oppezzo and Luciano Zabaldano not been shot on December 9, 1943, at Frumy, they would almost certainly have survived the Val d'Ayas raid of December 13, in which only Giuseppe Carrera died. And had they escaped that day, as many others from the Arcesaz band did, they might well have joined the Rossi brothers once again when they regrouped in the spring of 1944. As part of the Matteotti Brigades they would then have fought in a mature Resistance, first in the upper Canavese and then in lower Monferrato. Had they survived those battles unharmed, as well as the enemy raids and reprisals, they would have enjoyed the intoxicating days of the Liberation. When the partisans of the Italo Rossi division split their forces to liberate two different cities, Oppezzo and Zabaldano might have ended up going in different directions: Fulvio with Commander Rossi toward Cerrina and Casale; Luciano following Commander Cappa toward Turin and his home quarter, Sassi.

Sassi, located across the Po River from most of Turin, is a virtual island within the city. It owes its name, Sassi—"stones"—to the stones collected at the foot of the hill in the early eighteenth century, when the foundations for the basilica were being excavated. And it owes its strong identity to its firm detachment from Turin; until 1928 there was not even a bridge across the river to connect them, and Sassi could only be reached by boat. Even today, Sassi maintains a kind of independence. Or so it seems to me, an outsider myself in Turin although I have taught in the city for more than ten years. Perhaps it was because of this shared outsiderness that Sassi charmed me immediately the first time I was there not just as a passerby but on the trail of Luciano Zabaldano.

The document I'd seen at the Institute for Resistance History in Turin, a request for death benefits for Zabaldano's parents, gave their address in the quarter.[20] I didn't have much confidence that this would lead me very far. Seventy years had gone by; what could I expect to find? But I hadn't counted on how insular Sassi is, and how rooted its inhabitants are in the neighborhood. The phone directory told me the Zabaldano family was still there, and after that everything happened quickly. I called Andrea Zabaldano in October 2011 and learned that yes, Luciano Zabaldano had been his uncle, and had died in the Resistance. And certainly, he'd be happy to meet me. There was also his brother Davide, who was more interested in history and who for some time had been trying to learn more about that uncle he'd never known, the partisan. We made plans to get together in early November in the bar-cafeteria owned by the family and run by Davide himself, meeting around 6 p.m. when customers were few and we'd be left alone.

I printed out a map of the quarter just in case, but I knew the problem would not be finding the bar. The problem would be figuring out what to say to Luciano's nephews. I knew what I hoped to learn from them: what family stories they had heard at home about that partisan who had died at seventeen in the mountains of Valle d'Aosta. But what would I say? At that point in my research I had not yet found the documentation that would allow me to reconstruct in detail the events at Amay and Frumy on December 8 and 9, 1943. Still, it was already clear to me that Zabaldano and Oppezzo were the victims of their fellow partisans, not of the Germans or of Salò militias. And it was clear I could not walk into that bar in Sassi, shake the hands of two men I'd never met before, and say: oh, by the way, please don't be upset, but that uncle you've always thought of as a young anti-Fascist hero was eliminated by his fellow band members because he was out of control. He and another guy were stealing left and right and threatening their comrades, threats like: "If you don't let us be we'll shoot you, and if you try to stop us we'll run away and denounce you."

I couldn't say it and I didn't. I let Andrea and Davide speak, and right away I sensed that we understood one another, that there was common ground. They were nearly my age; they could have been my younger brothers. Our children were the same age, and so were our parents, those who were still alive. We were from different cities, different ways of life, yet after a few minutes of conversation at our bar table I felt I'd always known them. Perhaps their mother too—that smiling, discreet woman who brought us coffee with amaretti—had read the letters of the condemned of the Resistance to her children? Or perhaps she had merely shown them the photo of Uncle Luciano in his sailor's uniform, the one in the black frame on the plaque at the Sassi cemetery, five hundred meters from the bar.

Davide opened an orange folder on the table before us, the results of his research. There were photocopied pages of two or three histories of the Resistance in Valle d'Aosta, and a few letters he'd written, many years ago, to those in charge of libraries here and there. And then there were photocopies from Primo Levi's *The Periodic Table*. Davide took out the page that contained the ten lines about the "ugly secret." The lines were marked in pencil, and now he was showing them to me. He asked me if I'd read them carefully. "Conscience had compelled us to carry out a sentence, and we had carried it out, but we had come away devastated, empty, wanting everything to finish and to be finished ourselves." Davide told me that those lines had made him think, because they clearly referred to a death sentence issued not to enemies but to companions. He had begun to look into the matter, asking for documents from librarians and archivists. He had calculated the dates and discovered that the episode related by Levi corresponded with the date of death on the marker at Sassi cemetery. Perhaps *The Periodic Table* referred to Uncle Luciano's death sentence. "From that moment," he told me, "I did not have the courage to go on." He turned to his brother, Andrea. "I decided not to say anything to you either."

I didn't know—and I don't know—whether Davide has ever read Pavese's *The House on the Hill*, but as I listened to him that evening, as he read those pages from Primo Levi and reflected on the dates—the ninth, the tenth, the thirteenth of December 1943—I knew he understood. *Every man who falls resembles another who lives, and calls on him to explain.* If Davide decided to continue his research it would not be to shine up Luciano Zabaldano's name in the roster of Resistance heroes, nor to blame some other partisan, nor to unmask the murderers. To call on someone to explain is not the same as to call someone to account. A year later, in a room at the back of the bar, Davide told me as much. It didn't matter to him to have the family verities confirmed, or to maintain the martyr's halo around his partisan uncle's head. Nor did he want to solve any mysteries about what had gone on at the Col de Joux, or to uncover any Resistance scandals. His purpose, like my own, was not to chip away and undermine the Pyramids of Giza. "I just want to understand what happened, and why."

Since we first met, Davide and I have exchanged notes on what we've learned about Luciano's life and death. I've sent him, over time, copies of the documents I've uncovered. Davide, in turn, has shared with me what he has discovered in questioning some of the "elders" of Sassi, whom he has found partly by chance and partly by searching. Some came by the bar, others he went looking for, knocking on doors and ringing bells in that island in the city. Between the two of us we didn't come up with much. But what we did learn, added to what Davide and Andrea already knew from the family, allowed us to create if not a portrait then at least a sketch of Luciano Zabaldano.

The fourth of eight children, Luciano was born in Monforte d'Alba to a family with no particular political inclinations. His father had worked for a private Italian transport business before settling in Turin to work for the city rail company. A rebellious kid, Luciano had not been cut out for school, and twice failed the third grade. By age twelve he was working as a delivery boy for a shop in town. People in Sassi knew him as a good kid and a strong one: they called him Due, "Two," because he was as strong as two boys together. Between one minor job and another he reached the age of sixteen and volunteered for the Navy. Luciana Quarà of Sassi, then a young girl, had been Luciano's "war godmother"—a kind of soldier's pen pal—during his first year of service.[21] Davide and I went to see her in September 2012. "Your uncle was in Liguria, and he always wrote back regularly." What did they write about? "Not much. I was twelve and didn't have much to say." Had the letters survived? She had no idea what had become of them.

How that rebellious boy from Sassi, maybe partly domesticated by his year as an electrician in the Navy,[22] became a political rebel in Valle d'Aosta after September 8 is what I'd most like to know, and what Davide and I were unable to find out. Like just about every other Italian in the services when that day came, he swiftly jettisoned his uniform. In one of the family stories, Luciano, on the train coming into Turin after the armistice, heard a rumor that the police were checking passengers at the Porta Nuova station, and jumped off the train twenty minutes before reaching it, fearful of being arrested as a deserter. The family also recalled a certain Signor Cioppettini who had a ground-floor shop at the same address where the Zabaldanos lived. According to Davide's aunt Albina and aunt Marina, it was this Cioppettini who encouraged Luciano to leave Sassi for the mountains not long after September 8.

Fausto Cioppettini does not loom large in the history of Turinese anti-Fascism. If indeed he was the inspiration for Luciano's partisan vocation, it would confirm how casual were the motives that led some of the early rebels to take to the hills, how rarely the choice was well considered rather than the offhand result of a combination of circumstances.[23] Still, Cioppettini did oppose the Nazi-Fascists during the twenty months of occupation, working as an informer for a group of urban rebels.[24] He didn't do much, but perhaps that was because he was fifty-five years old in 1943. He had been an inventor, with a few patents to his name; he had been in trouble with the law. In his application for partisan status, Cioppettini called himself a "chemist." And in fact, the Zabaldano aunts do recall him in his workshop immersing photographic film in huge vats—probably leaching out the silver salts.

Why Luciano Zabaldano joined the Casale band at Arcesaz in particular, rather than any of the other rebel groups that were then coming together in Piedmont and Valle d'Aosta, remains unknown. I found no solid information on this. The surname Cioppettini is rare in Piedmont, but there was a family of that name not far from Cerrina Monferrato. Could a Fausto Cioppettini family connection have led Luciano to join up with Fulvio Oppezzo and the other young men on December 5, 1943?[25] I do not know, nor do I know anything else about Luciano apart from the circumstances that led to his death. I told Davide, the nephew born too late to know this uncle who had died so young, about those circumstances. I wanted him to know about the snowy dawn and the Soviet method.

Davide accepted that knowledge. But he was understandably concerned about Luciano's surviving sisters, Albina, Marina, and Bruna. They'd made it to eighty, in one case almost ninety, believing their brother had been shot in the Nazi-Fascist raid of December 1943, the first partisan to fall in Valle d'Aosta. Was it right, was it fair that they should learn a different truth seventy years later? "Aunt Bina may be ninety but she reads two books a week!" Davide told me. "She worked as a clerk at the Einaudi publishing house, and she has never stopped reading since." We did not want to have Aunt Bina discover the story in the very first history book ever to mention partisan Zabaldano. And yet, Davide and I reflected, did this new truth about the deaths of Zabaldano and Oppezzo really alter the ultimate truth about their sacrifices? We thought it didn't. They were and are the first two men to have died in the Resistance in Valle d'Aosta.

Back in early May 1945, when for more than twenty months—ever since a postcard of October 1943—the Zabaldano family had received no word from Luciano, it was his older sister Albina who sought to find out what had happened to him. Along with their father she went to Saint-Vincent a number of times and made contact with partisans there. Finally someone mentioned Frumy, where a kid was buried next to a tree not far from another kid buried next to another tree. The trees had markers on them with the noms de guerre "Furio" and "Mare." A message was sent asking the family to come and identify the body. Albina was unable to face this, and so her older brother Enrico and her father, Carlo, went. They walked up to Frumy, where the body of Luciano had been unearthed. They recognized the sweater of rough wool he was wearing. Albina had knitted it.

The funeral was held in Sassi in October 1945. It was not a ceremony for Luciano alone. That day Sassi also mourned two brothers from the Garibaldi Brigade, Eugenio and Giuseppe Marzano. The younger, nineteen, had died in battle in November 1944; the other, twenty-one, had been killed in Valle d'Aosta in March 1945.[26] A single funeral announcement with the names and photos of the three partisans was posted. "From their flesh torn by enemy lead, a cry bursts forth. They are and they will always be alive and among us; their sacrifice will be an example and a spur to our future deeds."[27] "When I go to the cemetery, I always go to see your uncle," Signora Quarà told Davide, she who had been Luciano's youthful correspondent.

One year, Davide went up to Amay for an annual celebration that honors the memory of the Resistance around Saint-Vincent. "The ceremony was simple and honest, without any silly rhetoric or clumsy attempts to exploit the occasion, as often happens on the April 25 anniversary at Sassi," he wrote to me. He had been politely received by the partisans' association at Aosta. "They helped me to break the ice with some veterans of the Col De Joux, although not much came of it." Davide spoke with Yves Francisco, the nephew of the managers of the Hotel Ristoro, and with the daughter of a commander in the Aosta Resistance, among others. He tried to explain. He asked for explanations.

Epitaphs

The final page of *If This Is a Man* has a burial scene. Or, rather, the semblance of a burial. It is January 27, 1945, the tenth day of "The Story of Ten Days": the day the camp is liberated, when the Russians arrive at Auschwitz. It has begun, however, with yet another snowy dawn, something Levi and his fellow prisoners would prefer to have been spared. "Dawn. On the floor the shameful wreck of skin and bones, the Sòmogyi thing." Sòmogyi, a Hungarian chemist, had been desperately ill with typhus; his delirious cries had filled the infectious diseases hut at Monowitz for days. He'd died the previous night. "The Russians arrived while Charles and I were carrying Sòmogyi a little ways outside. He was very light. We overturned the stretcher onto the gray snow. Charles took off his cap. I regretted not having a cap."[28] This too was one of the ways Primo Levi and his friend Charles became men again, by restoring, within the limits of the concentration camp, something like a funeral rite.

Whether Levi took part in burying the bodies of Oppezzo and Zabaldano after they were shot, I do not know. Did he climb up the Col de Joux from the Hotel Ristoro on December 9, 1943, and help to dig the two graves at Frumy? I think he may have because we know that the two women in the Amay group, Luciana Nissim and Vanda Maestro, were made to leave the place where the youngsters were executed,[29] which suggests the men were probably present. I think he may have because the numbers of the band were so few—in Levi's count eleven in all, including the women—that all the men would have been needed to shovel the snow and dig up the frozen earth where the bodies of "Furio" and "Mare" were to be laid without coffins. But there is also another reason that leads me to think Levi participated in the burials at Frumy—an indirect, suggestive reason, far from any kind of historical proof. It is his poem called "Epitaph," written in 1952.

For anyone who knows the story of the early partisan-bandits, "Epitaph" is not difficult to interpret. Nor is it difficult to imagine where Levi drew his inspiration, for in the early 1950s Fernanda Pivano's translation of Edgar Lee Masters's *Spoon River Anthology* sat on the bookshelves of many Italians. The speaker in "Epitaph" is deceased; he lies beneath the soil of the Col de Joux. He is a partisan who has been condemned to death by his comrades for some serious wrong. He could be Fulvio Oppezzo, or he could be Luciano Zabaldano.

Oh you who stand and look, oh walker in the hills,
One of the many in this no more barren snow,
Hear me; and slow your pace for an instant
Here where my comrades dry-eyed buried me,
Where every June the sweet field grass, fed by me,
Grows thicker and greener than anywhere around.
I, Micca the partisan, lie here. Brought down by my comrades
For no small wrong, not many years ago,
Nor many years did I have when I met the night.

Walker, I ask not you or anyone for clemency,
Nor prayers, nor tears, nor any kind of mark.
One thing I ask: May this peace of mine endure
So that heat follows chill follows heat forever,
And no new blood trickles through the clods
To find me with its baleful warmth
And bring these stony bones to life again.[30]

As in many of Primo Levi's poems, this one is full of allusions. He belonged to a generation that knew Giosuè Carducci's verses by heart, and his opening line was surely modeled on Carducci's address to his brother who died a suicide ("O thou who 'neath the flower-clad Tuscan hill . . ."). As for the second stanza, it may remind us (beyond Levi's typical classical tone) of one of the most celebrated arias in Verdi's *La Traviata*: *Non lagrima o fiore avrà la mia fossa / Non croce col nome che copre quest'ossa!* "No tears, no flowers, upon my grave shall rest / No cross, no name, shall sit upon my bones."

The year 1952, when Levi wrote this poem, was a season of epitaphs, of memorial literature. In *Men and Cities of the Resistance*, Piero Calamandrei (who had read Primo Levi's earliest postwar writings) wrote elegies both real and imaginary. These were the years in which the editors of *Letters of Italian Partisans Condemned to Death* proposed that the biographical sketches of the letter writers be printed centered on the page and in capital letters, as if on a tombstone. ("The next thing we know they'll be draped in mourning!" Italo Calvino remarked sarcastically.[31]) They were the years when even a Resistance agnostic like Beppe Fenoglio, writing to Calvino to have a letter by a friend included in a second edition of that volume, called it "a sacred book."

Primo Levi tended toward a marbled language himself, in prose and especially in his poetry. In *The Periodic Table*, he called his Italian "good for memorial plaques."[32] But in "Epitaph," that language, transformed by *Spoon River*, gave voice to a special type of the partisan condemned to death: one condemned by his own comrades. Although Levi does not forswear the sentence of December 9, 1943—he speaks of "no small wrong"—he nevertheless feels the need to adopt the point of view of one (either one) of the dead young men. A writer for whom the pronouns count, Levi is making a clear choice here. If it does not mean that he identifies with them, it means that he acknowledges them. Every man who falls resembles another who lives, and calls on him to explain.

As early as June 1945, the partisans of Saint-Vincent had collected their dead in a cemetery halfway between Amay and the Frumy pasture.[33] In the years just after the war, the veterans of the local bands met every September 7 to mark the raids that had devastated Saint-Vincent in September 1944. In 1950, *La Stampa* wrote of the "unique" partisan cemetery at the Col de Joux and of the efforts of Edoardo Page, a commander of the Aosta Resistance, to preserve it.[34] The following year Page began working to build a chapel at the site.[35] This little church, built with local stone, bears a simple plaque: "To the Fallen for Liberty, September 9, 1943–April 25, 1945."

In theory, those dates would include the only two partisans who died there in 1943: Fulvio Oppezzo and Luciano Zabaldano. And in fact the existence of that chapel led a priest of Cerrina Monferrato, Ermenegildo Gonella, to seek answers about what had happened at Frumy that day in December 1943. Don Gonella knew the area well because he had directed a mountain camp for the diocese of Casale in 1947–49.[36] He wanted the memory of Oppezzo to be inscribed not only in Cerrina but in the place he had died.

"I took him up to Saint-Vincent at least three times," Renato Porta told me of Don Gonella. Porta had worked as a bus driver in the 1950s, up and down the hills of Monferrato. He had also gone up and down the hills of Saint-Vincent (by then paved all the way to the Col de Joux) with the priest, who asked everyone the same questions: Commander Page, the ex-partisans, the farmers of Amay. "His fixation was Fulvio Oppezzo, to know what happened to him. To know why his name wasn't inscribed on the plaque at Amay. He had asked to see the mayor; the people there said they didn't know anything," Porta told me. "To my mind Don Gonella was somewhat obsessed about the matter. He really wanted to know." Finally, "the mayor of Saint-Vincent promised Oppezzo's name would be put on the plaque."

Forty years later, a new plaque did get installed in front of the partisan chapel of Amay. But neither Oppezzo or Zabaldano were listed on it. Unveiled in September 1995 on behalf of the region of Valle d'Aosta,[37] the plaque read: "Arrested by the Nazi-Fascists on December 13, 1943, with their partisan companions, Primo Levi, Vanda Maestro, and Luciana Nissim, because they were Jewish, experienced the horrors of Auschwitz. Below, under the title *If This Is a Man*, is the poem that Levi had used to preface the book. 'You who live safe / In your warm houses . . .'"[38]

In 1995, Luciana Nissim was the only one still alive of those three young Jews who had hoped to escape the Final Solution at the Hotel Ristoro in Amay. Feeling unwell, she was not present when the plaque was unveiled. But Primo's sister, Anna Maria Levi, who did attend, sent her a note and a photograph. "My dear," she wrote, "look; they paid tribute to the defeated."[39]

More than four decades before, something like an elegy, an epitaph, for Vanda Maestro had been provided by one of her companions in the partisan cause and in the horrors of Auschwitz. It came from Primo Levi, who at Fossoli had said and done "many things" not deemed worthy of recording, who during the voyage to the bottom had said and heard said "things that living people do not say," who when he said farewell to Maestro had said farewell "to life."[40] In the early 1950s, for a volume in memory of Piedmontese women who had died in the Resistance, Levi had written a brief biography of Maestro, unsigned but uncontestably his, that was also a tribute to the defeated.[41]

He wrote of how difficult it had been for her—and perhaps for him—to go up into the mountains. "Having seen her, on those trails already covered with snow, one cannot forget that small, kind face of hers, marked by physical strain and also by a deeper tension. For her, and for the best in their situation and in those times, the choice had not been simple, or joyous, or problem-free." Vanda had "feared death, and more than death, she feared pain, suffering. The strength she showed in those days developed little by little, it grew out of a determination made good minute by minute," Primo Levi went on. Here too, perhaps, he was speaking of himself.[42]

10

───

If Not Then, When?

IN 1981, THE SAME YEAR THAT HE WROTE THE POEM "PARTIGIA," Primo Levi also wrote his one and only novel, *If Not Now, When?* Published in 1982, it was, according to the cover of the Einaudi edition, an "epic" about the Jews of Eastern Europe. That was also how the critics perceived the book: Levi revisiting, as a free man, the lands he had been forced to travel through after he left Auschwitz, and reflecting on that Ashkenazi humanity he had previously only been able to meet in the Lager. The novel told a story of Jewish partisan brigades who join with the Red Army and fight to free Eastern Europe from German occupation, and some commentators pointed to the connection between that theme and the Israeli-Palestinian conflict. In that reading, it was a work in code commenting on Israel's role in the Middle East wars.

Few, if any, saw *If Not Now, When?* as a comment on the Italian Resistance. Here, however, anyone who has followed the story of the roughneck partisans in Valle d'Aosta, whether Jews from Turin or gentiles from Casale, will not fail to see the connection. It is so direct that one cannot but wish to simply quote page upon page from the novel. Its themes and characters reprise the narrative we have been following up to now: the threatened Jew; his reluctance to join the Resistance; the early partisans, half fighters, half bandits; the risk of anarchy and the Soviet method; the obligation to do wrong and the obligation to endure it; the hunger for justice and the thirst for vengeance; the criminals of war and their scapegoats. It is all there, although one must resist the temptation to try to match the individual partisans from Levi's circle with the characters of the novel—the watchmaker Mendel as Levi, the commander Gedaleh as Guido Bachi, and so on. Levi himself warned against such an interpretation in an essay he published when the novel appeared,[1] noting that all the characters in it "are a way of saying *I*."[2]

"He had to choose, and the choice was hard; on the one hand there was his thousand-year-old weariness, his fear, his horror of the weapons he had buried and then brought along after all, on the other side there was not much. There was the little coiled spring that *Pravda* perhaps would call his 'sense of honor and duty,' but that would perhaps be more appropriately described as a 'dumb need for decency.'"[3] Right from the start the novel evokes memory. *If Not Now, When?* seems to beg to be called *If Not Then, When?* It has all the marks of a writer who has battled narrative reticence for "thirty-five years of apprenticeship, of disguised or acknowledged autobiography"[4] that has blocked any real depiction of his experience as a partisan. From the beginning, when Levi writes of Eastern Jews, he is writing about himself. He's writing about his passive forebears, the inert and noble gases. About his own lack of courage, or at least of physical courage. About how he found himself in the Resistance almost without intending to, without any political baggage, with only one sort of moral baggage: a notion of dignity.

In the entire first part of the novel—until Mendel's small and uncertain band of Jews begins to cooperate with a large band of assorted Russians—the action takes place on the Belorussian plain, but it might as well be Valle d'Aosta and the bands of Amay and Arcesaz. These are "the terrible months of the beginning of the partisan war, when everything, food, weapons, shelter, plans for action, strategy, the courage to fight and to live were the fruit of a few men's desperate initiative";[5] the cardinal adjective *desperate* maps exactly onto what Levi wrote in the final chapter of *If This Is a Man* in 1946–47, where he spoke of the "desperate and murky" beginnings of the Italian Resistance. When Levi compares the early bands to "drops of mercury" ("they come together, they break apart, they join up again") he speaks as the chemist he is.[6] But when he writes of the rebels of the steppes as "stragglers or deserters or partisans or bandits, depending on one's point of view,"[7] he seems to be writing the history of the Casale band in their wild journeys between Monferrato and Val d'Ayas.

It would be foolish to interpret a book as lively and compelling as *If Not Now, When?* as a roman à clef about three months of the early Italian Resistance. With all the freedom fiction permits, the novel explores matters that would increasingly occupy Primo Levi after 1981, until they became part of that brilliant and powerful work of nonfiction *The Drowned and the Saved*: matters such as various grades of oppression, how a crime is remembered, the legitimacy of revenge.[8] Nevertheless, when read at a more immediate level, the novel offers, to anyone familiar with the story of the early Resistance, situations and episodes that could well have come from Primo Levi's time in Valle d'Aosta. In his essay about the novel, Levi said the story was a swarm of remembered details, "a mosaic of incidents, snapshots from times forgotten sent upstairs to the attic of memory."[9]

When the Eastern European partisans in Levi's novel must face the problem of controlling indiscipline in their ranks, the situation mirrors Levi's own experience in the Italian Resistance. "To live outside the law didn't mean not having any law"; fighting the German enemy meant having to repress the enemy within, they learn.[10] The episode in which the Belorussian kid Fedya is killed is even more immediately related to the story of the hothead partisans of Amay. Mendel's band of Jews have at last connected with a group of serious fighters with ties to the Red Army. Fedya, who is turning seventeen, is given leave to go home to Turov to celebrate.

The young man has all the energy, the grace, and the negligence of his young age. "He darted on his skis, silent and sure as a lynx in the darkness." At his birthday celebration Fedya begins to drink wine. He goes on a three-day bender, then returns to the band and admits he has drunk, and talked, maybe far too much. A venial sin in peacetime is a mortal sin in wartime, in the resistance. "Ulybin had Fedya locked up in the woodshed. He sent Zachar to take him food and tea but at dawn they all saw Zachar going to the woodshed barefoot, and they all heard the pistol shot. Sissl and Line had the job of undressing the boy's body to recover the clothes and the boots; Pavel and Leonid were assigned to digging the grave in the ground soaked with water of the thaw. Why Pavel and Leonid particularly?"[11]

There's no need to read further to be reminded of Fulvio and Luciano, who had talked and boasted so much on their final night, and of the following dawn, when Berto sent the two outside the hut—a hundred meters, a hundred and fifty, and then a blast of machine gun fire. Which members of the Amay band dug those graves beside the two trees with their markers? Was Levi among them? I believe we ought to read certain passages of *If Not Now, When?* as the unspoken continuation of the ten lines about the "ugly secret" in *The Periodic Table*, as a further reflection on the state of moral alienation in which the most thoughtful of the partisans of Amay found themselves after conscience compelled them to execute two comrades.[12]

Is guilt felt in retrospect justified?[13] Primo Levi's most tormenting question to himself in *The Drowned and the Saved* emerges from his "suspicion that each man is his brother's Cain, that each of us (but this time I say 'us' in a much vaster, and indeed universal, sense) has usurped his neighbor's place and lived in his stead."[14] The same suspicion troubles Mendel in *If Not Now, When?*, Mendel who was never a Jewish deportee but a Jewish partisan. "Maybe this is really how it is, maybe each of us is Cain to some Abel, and slays him in the field without knowing it, through the things he does to him, the things he says to him, and the things he should say to him and doesn't."[15] Perhaps Primo Levi, independent of whatever role he may have had in condemning the two young men, felt retrospective guilt thinking of what he did or did not do, did or did not say, that might have saved their lives.

It's instructive to compare a page of *If Not Now, When?* with "The Survivor," a poem of Levi's from 1984. Once again, the thoughts of the survivor of Auschwitz are remarkably like those of the partisan in Belorussia. Guilt, retrospective guilt, grips each one as they are visited by the ghosts of the drowned. Levi, addressing those ghosts, says it is unjust to blame him for having supplanted them in life; Mendel the partisan rejects any weighty notion of "us" and takes responsibility only for what he has personally done. In "The Survivor" Levi writes:

> *Stand back, leave me alone, submerged people,*
> *Go away. I haven't dispossessed anyone,*
> *Haven't usurped anyone's bread.*
> *No one died in my place. No one.*
> *Go back into your mist.*
> *It's not my fault if I live and breathe,*
> *Eat, drink, sleep, and put on clothes.*[16]

While in *If Not Now, When?* Mendel says: "If I've sinned I bear the burden of my sins, but only those, and I have more than enough. I don't bear the sins of anybody else. I wasn't the one who sent out the squad to be bombed. I didn't shoot Fedya while he was asleep. If we have to go into the desert, we'll go, but without bearing on our heads the sins we haven't committed."[17]

It is not until a later part of the novel, when Mendel's little band leaves the Russians to join a group of "ragged and bold" Jews, veteran partisans led by Gedaleh, that Levi's story changes tone, and the penitential air gives way to an epic manner. Gedaleh and his men and women are the strongest, most astute, most fortunate survivors of what were once the communities of Polesia, Volynia, and Belorussia. They have survived the tragic days during which the disproportionate force of the murderers against the victims made Operation Barbarossa the apocalypse of Eastern Jewry. They have survived the sacking of their villages, the flamethrowers of the Einsatzkommandos, the mass graves of Kovno and Riga. "They were tired, poor, and dirty, but not defeated; children of merchants, tailors, rabbis, and cantors; they had armed themselves with weapons taken from the Germans; they had earned the right to wear those tattered uniforms, without chevrons, and they had tasted several times the bitter food of killing."[18] Gedaleh's men and women inhabit a world turned upside down, in which the victims punish the executioners.

In other words, Gedaleh's Jews are (adjusting the proportions) the Jewish partisans who escaped both the first, terrible blows of the Final Solution and the desperate, murky beginnings of a resistance that then still had only a lowercase *r*. They are those friends to whom Primo Levi, Luciana Nissim, and Vanda Maestro addressed a postcard printed with the Fascist slogan VINCEREMO ("we will win") thrown from the train for Auschwitz—and lo and behold they really did win, they made a Resistance with a capital *R*. For them and only for them (not for the drowned of the Lager, or for the saved) could the tale of some Jewish partisans become epic. "In the frozen steppe, in the snow and the mud, they had found a new freedom unknown to their fathers and grandfathers . . . They were cheerful and savage, like animals let out of their cages, like slaves rising up in revenge. And they had tasted revenge, although the price was high: on various occasions, in acts of sabotage, bombings, assassinations, rear-guard conflicts . . . They were cheerful because there was no tomorrow and they didn't care, and because they had seen the supermen thrashing about in the icy water like frogs, and that was a prize no one could ever take from them."[19]

Notes

Translator's note: For ease of reference, the citations below refer to the English editions of Primo Levi's works available when the translation was completed. In some cases, I have adjusted the translation of passages quoted in this text in order to improve the precision, the tone, or the style, or because Luzzatto's analysis focuses on a particular phrase that has several possible translations in English and I wanted to give the one most suited to the context.

Key to Abbreviations

AAPT	Personal papers of Aldo Piacenza, Turin
ACDEC	Archive of the foundation Centro di documentazione ebraica contemporanea, Milan
ACPL	Archive of the Centro internazionale di studi Primo Levi, Turin
AFBT	Personal papers of the Bachi family
AFS	Archives féderales suisses, Bern, Switzerland
AFZT	Personal papers of the Zabaldano family, Turin
AISRAL	Archive of the Istituto per la Storia della Resistenza e della società contemporanea in provincia di Alessandria, Alessandria
AISRT	Archive of the Istituto storico della Resistenza in Toscana, Florence
AISRVdA	Archive of the Istituto storico della Resistenza e della società contemporanea in Valle d'Aosta, Aosta
AISTORETO	Archive of the Istituto piemontese per la Storia della Resistenza e della società contemporanea, Turin
ARAVdA	Archive of the Regione autonoma Valle d'Aosta, Aosta
ASAt	State Archives, Asti

ASMi   State Archives, Milan
ASTo   State Archives, Turin
ATA   State Archives, Aosta
NARA   National Archives and Records Administration, Washington
WLA   Wiener Library Archives, London

Prologue

1   P. Malvezzi and G. Pirelli, eds. *Lettere di condannati a morte della Resistenza italiana (8 September 1943–25 April 1945)* (Turin: Einaudi, 1952).

2   See M. Franzinelli, *Ultime lettere di condannati a morte e di deportati della Resistenza, 1943–1945* (Milan: Mondadori, 2005).

3   See G. Pansa, *Il sangue dei vinti* (Milan: Sperling & Kupfer, 2003).

4   See S. Luzzatto, *La crisi dell'antifascismo* (Turin: Einaudi, 2004).

5   P. Levi, *The Periodic Table*, trans. Raymond Rosenthal (New York: Schocken, 1984), 130.

6   P. Levi, *Survival in Auschwitz*, trans. Stuart Woolf (New York: Summit, 1986), 13. This book is almost universally known as *If This Is a Man* and is referred to thus throughout the text rather than by the title of the U.S. edition.

7   In 1973, in a note to the Italian scholastic edition of *If This Is a Man*, Levi wrote: "The phrase is obviously ironic; here 'justice' is that inhuman, wartime sort that admits no indulgence." P. Levi, *Se questo è un uomo*, edited and with notes by A. Cavaglion (Turin: Einaudi, 2012), 162.

8   P. Levi, *The Periodic Table*, 132.

9   P Levi, *If This Is a Man*, 114. Here, citation from *Inferno*, trans. Allen Mandelbaum, Canto XXVI, 139–41.

10 S. Luzzatto, *Il Terrore ricordato. Memoria e tradizione dell'esperienza rivoluzionaria* (1988) (Turin: Einaudi, 2000), 192–93.

11 This book was already at the printers by the time I was able to consult the (fairly modest) study by F. Sessi, *Il lungo viaggio di Primo Levi. La scelta della resistenza, il tradimento, l'arresto. Una storia taciuta* (Venice: Marsilio, 2013).

12 See S. Luzzatto, *Il risorgimento degli ebrei*, in S. Luzzatto and G. Pedullà, eds., *Atlante della letteratura italiana*, vol. 3, *Dal Romanticismo a oggi*, ed. D. Scarpa (Turin: Einaudi, 2012), 188–95.

13 Beginning with the fundamental work on the nature of the Resistance and the definition of the conflict by C. Pavone, *A Civil War: A History of the Italian Resistance*, trans. P. Levy (London: Verso, 2013).

14 Levi, *The Periodic Table*, 130–1.

15 P. Levi, "Partigia" (1981), in the collection *Ad ora incerta* (1984). Trans. F. Randall. Many of Levi's poems are available in English in *Primo Levi: Collected Poems*, trans. R. Feldman and B. Swann (London: Faber, 1988). Levi dated the poem July 23, 1981. It was published in *La Stampa* on August 18, 1981.

16 Ibid.

17 See P. Levi, *Conversazioni e interviste, 1963–1987*, ed. M. Belpoliti (Turin: Einaudi, 1997); S. Woolf, "Primo Levi's Sense of History," in *Journal of Modern Italian Studies* 3, no. 3 (autumn 1998), 273–92; F. Carasso, *Primo Levi. La scelta della chiarezza* (1997) (Turin: Einaudi, 2009), 161ff.

18 Levi, "Partigia."

19 P. Levi, *The Reawakening* (New York: Summit, 1986), 218. This book is almost universally known as *The Truce*, and is referred to thus throughout the text rather than by the title of the U.S. edition.

1. Inventing the Resistance

1 M. Pelizzari, *Le memorie di Alimiro* (1945), ed. G. Maggia, (Ivrea: Enrico editori, 1979), 23–24.

2 Ibid. See G. Maggia, Introduzione, 11–12.

3 See G. Maggia, *"La Olivetti nella Resistenza,"* in *Quaderni del Centro di documentazione sull'antifascismo e la Resistenza nel Canavese*, no. 1 (April 1973), 176–77.

4 E. Artom, *Diari di un partigiano ebreo (January 1940–February 1944)*, ed. G. Schwarz (Turin: Bollati Boringhieri, 2008), 52 (September 3, 1943).

5 See P. Levi, "Il faraone con la svastica" (1983), in Levi, *Opere*, ed. M. Belpoliti (Turin: Einaudi, 1997), 2:1190.

6 See S. Presa, *Le fasi della Resistenza in valle d'Aosta* (Aosta: Le Château, 2009), 42–43.

7 See T. Aymone, "Un frammento autobiografico," in Aymone, *Scritti inediti*, ed. G. Mottura, "Materiali di discussione," Dipartimento di Economia politica, Università degli studi di Modena e Reggio Emilia, 2005, 19–20.

8 See Ch. Passerin d'Entrèves, *La tempëta dessu noutre montagne. Épisodes de la Résistance en Vallée d'Aoste* (Aosta: Institute for Resistance History of the Valle d'Aosta, 1975), 16–17 (diary, September 18, 1943).

9 See I. Thomson, *Primo Levi* (2002) (London: Vintage, 2003), 132–33.

10 See ACDEC, Fondo Vicissitudini dei singoli, fasc. "Finzi, cugini," "Diario dei cugini Finzi che nel September 1943 tentarono invano di rifugiarsi in Svizzera," 6.

11 See A. Villa, *Ebrei in fuga. Chiesa e leggi razziali nel Basso Piemonte (1938–1945)* (Brescia: Morcelliana, 2004), 266–67.

12 See R. Broggini, *La frontiera della speranza. Gli ebrei dall'Italia verso la Svizzera* (Milan: Mondadori, 1998); A. Cavaglion, "Juifs étrangers dans l'arc alpin occidental" (1939–1945), in J.-W. Dereymez, ed., *Le refuge et le piège: les Juifs dans les Alpes (1938–1945)* (Paris: L'Harmattan, 2008), 179–98.

13 See Governo italiano, Commissione per la ricostruzione delle vicende che hanno caratterizzato in Italia le attività di acquisizione dei beni dei cittadini ebrei da parte di organismi pubblici e privati, Rapporto generale, Presidenza del Consiglio dei ministri, Rome 2001, 244ff.

14 See ACDEC, Fondo Vicissitudini dei singoli, "Diario dei cugini Finzi," 6ff.

15 ACPL, Fondo Marco Pennacini, interview with Primo Levi (1973), typed transcript prepared by G. Giannone, M. Luzzatti, and D. Muraca, 8.

16 See Thomson, *Primo Levi*, based on correspondence with Anna Maria Levi, 136.

17 In the words of G. Pedullà, "Una lieve colomba," in Pedullà, ed., *Racconti della Resistenza* (Turin: Einaudi, 2005), x.

18 C. Mortari, "Le mucche dell'abate Pierret," *La Stampa*, June 26, 1932.

19 See G. Bocca, *Partigiani della montagna. Vita delle divisioni "Giustizia e Libertà" del Cuneese* (1945) (Milan: Feltrinelli, 2005).

20   See Thomson, *Primo Levi*, 125.

21   From A. Chiappano, *Luciana Nissim Momigliano: una vita* (Florence: Giuntina, 2010), 61–62.

22   Interview with M. Pezzetti (July 17, 1995) in A. Chiappano, "La figura di Luciana Nissim e le deportazioni femminili. Necessità di una storiografia di genere?," in L. Nissim Momigliano, *Ricordi della casa dei morti e altri scritti*, ed. A. Chiappano, (Florence: Giuntina, 2008), 126.

23   From an interview with Eugenio Gentili Tedeschi, USC Shoah Foundation Institute (Milan: March 10, 1998), viewable online. See also E. Gentili Tedeschi, *I giochi della paura. Immagini di una microstoria: libri segreti, cronache, resistenza tra Milan e Valle d'Aosta, 1942–1944* (Aosta: Le Château, 1999).

24   See AFBT, Emilio Bachi papers, "Il filo della memoria," typed transcription, p. 28.

25   See G. Cecini, *I soldati ebrei di Mussolini. I militari israeliti nel periodo fascista* (Milan: Mursia, 2008), 92ff.

26   See P. Spriano, *Storia di Turin operaia e socialista. Da De Amicis a Gramsci* (Turin: Einaudi, 1972), 289ff.

27   See AFBT, papers of Emilio Bachi, "Il filo della memoria," p. 34.

28   See S. Bachi, *Vengo domani, zia* (Turin: Genesi, 2001), photographic album.

29   Ibid.

30   Ibid., from the same diary, July 27, 1938, p. 157.

31   See Thomson, *Primo Levi*, 80–81.

32   P. Levi, *The Periodic Table*, trans. Raymond Rosenthal (New York: Schocken, 1984), 37.

33   Bachi, *Vengo domani*, 158.

34   From the bulletin of the Aosta Curia di Aosta, September 1943, remarks of Chanoux cited in Presa, *Le fasi della Resistenza*, 48.

35   Cited in T. Omezzoli, *Prefetti e fascismo nella provincia d'Aosta, 1926–1945* (Aosta: Le Château, 1999), 257.

36   See E. Collotti, *Il fascismo e gli ebrei: Le leggi razziali in Italia* (Rome-Bari: Laterza, 2003), 128–29; M. Sarfatti, *La Shoah in Italia. La persecuzione degli ebrei sotto il fascismo* (Turin: Einaudi, 2005), 98–102.

37   See K. Elsberg, *Come sfuggimmo alla Gestapo e alle SS. Racconto autobiografico* (1945), ed. K. Voigt (Aosta: Le Château, 1999), 67–72.

38   See G. Arian Levi, "Gli ebrei jugoslavi internati nella provincia di Aosta (1941–1945)," in *Questioni di storia della valle d'Aosta contemporanea*, no. 3 (1990): 9.

39   See ibid., citations pp. 9 and 26.

40   ARAVdA, Prefettura Gabinetto, cat. 29/5, "Movimento turistico," sottofasc. "Rifugi alpini questioni varie" (Aosta, 31 July XX). In Italy's Fascist calendar, Mussolini's 1922 March on Rome marked the start of year I; the year XX thus ran from October 28, 1941, to October 27, 1942.

41   ARAVdA, Prefettura Gabinetto, non classificati, 1943–46, *Curriculum vitae* of dott. Cesare Augusto Carnazzi (no date, but autumn 1943).

42   A. Levi, *Gli ebrei jugoslavi*, 31.

43   ARAVdA, Prefettura Gabinetto, cat. 14/1, sottofasc. "Personale, impiegati, funzionari di razza ebraica" (Ivrea, 10 November 1943); Archive comunale di Saint-

Vincent, "Atti di matrimonio," anno 1943 (Paolo Momigliano Levi kindly supplied this document).

44 See M. Nozza, *Hotel Meina. La prima strage di ebrei in Italia* (Milan: Mondadori, 1993).

45 See L. Ventura, "Ebrei con il duce." *"La nostra bandiera" (1934–1938)* (Turin: Zamorani, 2002), 21ff.

46 See A. Stille, *Benevolence and Betrayal: Five Italian Jewish Families Under Fascism* (New York: Summit Books, 1991), 85–89.

47 The Stefani press agency released the news at 11 p.m. on November 30 and it was picked up in radio reports the following day: see M. Sarfatti, *Gli ebrei nell'Italia fascista. Vicende, identità, persecuzione* (Turin: Einaudi, 2000), 248n.

48 See Chiappano, *Luciana Nissim Momigliano*, 62; Ph. Mesnard, *Primo Levi. Le passage d'un témoin* (Paris: Fayard, 2011), 67, 117.

49 See L. Klinkhammer, *L'occupazione tedesca in Italia, 1943–1944* (Turin: Bollati Boringhieri, 1993), 277ff.

50 See Sarfatti, *Gli ebrei*, 232–33.

51 For an exemplary case see M. Piazza, *Cronaca di una restituzione. Sergio Piazza (1916–1944)* (Aosta: Le Château, 2011).

52 See M. Ottolenghi, *Per un pezzo di patria. La mia vita negli anni del fascismo e delle leggi razziali* (Turin: Blu edizioni, 2009), 27, 52.

53 See G. De Luna, "Dall'antifascismo alla Resistenza," in A. Cavaglion, ed., *La moralità armata. Studi su Emanuele Artom (1915–1944)* (Milan: FrancoAngeli, 1993), 59–71.

54 Ibid., 75 (December 1, 1943).

55 Ibid., 100 (December 18, 1943).

56 Ibid., 102–3 (December 20, 1943).

57 The milieu can be seen in photographs in A. Chiappano, ed., *A noi fu dato in sorte questo tempo* (Florence: Giuntina, 2010).

58 See L. Binel, *Cronaca di un valdostano* (1981), ed. E. Riccarand (Sarre: Tipografia Testolin, 2002), 31; G. De Luna, *Storia del Partito d'Azione, 1942–1947* (1982) (Rome: Editori Riuniti, 1997), 85ff.

59 See AISRVdA, Fondi vari, estratto dal giornale *L'Opinione* del 20 May 1945 (on letterhead of the town of Saint-Vincent).

60 On Reynaud's ties with Bachi, see AFBT, papers of Emilio Bachi, "Il filo della memoria," p. 47.

61 WLA, Ian Thomson Papers, 1406/2/6, correspondence with Guido Bachi (copy of document, dated Turin: 29 October 1946).

62 See B. Guidetti Serra (with Santina Mobiglia), *Bianca la rossa* (Turin: Einaudi, 2009).

63 See Thomson, *Primo Levi*, 137.

64 Letter of June 19, 1992, in Thomson, *Primo Levi*, 137.

65 See T. Snyder, *Bloodlands: Europe Between Hitler and Stalin* (New York: Basic Books, 2010), 204.

66 See ATA, Corte straordinaria d'assise, 15/1946, interrogation of Aldo Piacenza (Aosta, 11 January 1944); WLA, Ian Thomson Papers, 1406/2/6, correspondence with Guido Bachi (doc., 29 October 1946).

67 See Cecini, *I soldati ebrei*, 88–89.
68 AISTORETO, database of partisans in Piedmont.
69 See A. Cavaglion, *La scuola ebraica a Turin (1938–1943)* (Turin-Florence: Pluri-verso, 1993), 17ff.
70 AFBT, papers of Emilio Bachi, "Il filo della memoria," pp. 32–33.
71 Quoted in G. Poli and G. Calcagno, *Echi di una voce perduta. Incontri, inter-viste e conversazioni con Primo Levi* (Milan: Mursia, 1992), 68 (1975: interview with G. De Rienzo).
72 See P. Levi, *The Drowned and the Saved*, trans. Raymond Rosenthal (New York: Summit, 1988), 23.
73 Quoted C. Angier, *The Double Bond: Primo Levi, A Biography* (New York: Far-rar, Straus and Giroux, 2002), 246.
74 Quoted in G. Poli and G. Calcagno, *Echi di una voce perduta. Incontri, inter-viste e conversazioni con Primo Levi*, 242 (from a conversation with Massimo Mila, broadcast by Raitre, November 29, 1983).
75 WLA, Ian Thomson Papers, 1406/2/6, correspondence with Guido Bachi (doc., 29 October 1946).
76 Ibid., "Opinione personale sulla banda autonoma 'Ayas'" (no date, but October 1946).
77 ATA, Corte straordinaria d'assise, 15/1946, interrogation of Edilio Cagni (Aosta, 17 January 1946).
78 Some two hundred people lived in Graines during World War II, fed by the abundant grain harvests that gave the place its name. See T. Bo and G. Rossi, *Di villaggio in villaggio, di ricordo in ricordo*, vol. 2 (Châtillon: Edizioni Cervino, 2009), 20–21.
79 ATA, Corte straordinaria d'assise, 15/1946, rapporto del prefetto Carnazzi al Tri-bunale speciale per la difesa dello Stato e alla Direzione generale della Pub-blica Sicurezza (Aosta, 7 March 1944).
80 See AISTORETO, database of partisans in Piedmont.
81 Previously, in September 1943, the Rossi brothers had forged a secret connection with some anti-Fascist industrialists of Casale, including the Communist printer Carlo Eugenio Carretto, who had been trying to bring together an early alliance of anti-Fascist forces, as well as with several former Royal Army officers. See F. Meni, *Quando i tetti erano bianchi. Casale e il Basso Monferrato dal Fascismo alla Resistenza* (Alessandria: Edizioni dell'Orso, 2000), 126ff.
82 See S. Peli, *La Resistenza in Italia. Storia e critica* (Turin: Einaudi, 2004), 20ff.
83 See S. Favretto, *Resistenza e nuova coscienza civile. Fatti e protagonisti nel Mon-ferrato casalese* (Alessandria: Edizioni Falsopiano, 2009), 21.
84 AISRAL, Fondo Pansa, fasc. 24, "Guardia nazionale repubblicana in provincia di Alessandria" (lettera del Comando 11a legione Milizia al Comando del Presi-dio militare germanico, Casale Monferrato, 12 September 1943).
85 See ARAVdA, Prefettura Gabinetto, cat. 14/7, "Ministero della Guerra, 1943–45," sottofasc. "Ribelli," telegram from chief of province to *podestà* (Aosta, 11 December 1943).
86 AISRAL, Fondo Pivano, busta 4, fasc. 5, "Ufficio politico investigativo Guardia nazionale repubblicana," telegrams from commander of the eleventh legion (30 November, 7 December, 13 December 1943).

87 AISRAL, Fondo Pivano, busta 4, fasc. 5, letter from chief of province to the Questura and Militia (Alessandria, 13 December 1943).

88 AISRAL, Fondo Pivano, busta 4, fasc. 5, letter from Seniore Morandi to Command of the eleventh Militia legion (Borgo S. Martino, 30 November 1943).

89 AISRAL, Fondo Pivano, busta 4, fasc. 5, interrogation of Federico Barbesino (Casale Monferrato, 28 December 1943).

90 See D. Marchesini, *L'Italia a quattro ruote. Storia dell'utilitaria* (Bologna: il Mulino, 2012), 76–77.

91 See Meni, *Quando i tetti erano bianchi*, 92–93.

92 AISRAL, Fondo Pivano, busta 4, fasc. 5, doc. (interrogation of 28 December 1943).

93 Ibid.

94 See V. Ochetto, *Adriano Olivetti* (Milan: Mondadori, 1985), 120–21.

95 AISRAL, Fondo Pivano, busta 4, fasc. 5, doc. (interrogation of 28 December 1943).

96 AISTORETO, Fondo Conti, mat./ac. 13, Report of "Italo Rossi" division commander to "brigate Matteotti" command in Turin (undated, around November 1944).

97 See G. Pansa, *Il bambino che guardava le donne* (Milan: Sperling & Kupfer, 1999), 158ff. Although this is a novel, Pansa re-creates the destruction of the Casale Jewish community on the basis of the most thorough research yet done.

98 See G. Pansa, *Guerra partigiana tra Genova e il Po. La Resistenza in provincia di Alessandria* (1967) (Rome-Bari: Laterza, 1988), 63.

99 See the memoir of a Jewish boy who took temporary refuge in Casale and was able to flee in time: E. Pacifici, *Non ti voltare. Autobiografia di un ebreo* (Florence: Giuntina, 1993), 43ff.

100 See C. Manganelli and B. Mantelli, *Antifascisti, partigiani, ebrei. I deportati alessandrini nei campi di sterminio nazisti* (Milan: FrancoAngeli, 1991), 69–71; L. Picciotto, *Il libro della memoria. Gli Ebrei deportati dall'Italia (1943–1945)* (Milan: Mursia, 1991).

101 See Favretto, *Resistenza e nuova coscienza*, 132.

102 See A. Villa, *Ebrei in fuga. Chiesa e leggi razziali nel Basso Piemonte (1938–1945)* (Brescia: Morcelliana, 2004), 181.

103 On dating the first draft to 1946, see G. Tesio, *Piemonte letterario dell'Otto-Novecento. Da Giovanni Faldella a Primo Levi* (Rome: Bulzoni, 1991), 169. But A. Cavaglion maintains there is no proof of any draft before that of 1973. *Notizie su Argon. Gli antenati di Primo Levi da Francesco Petrarca a Cesare Lombroso* (Turin: Instar libri, 2006), 8.

104 See Cavaglion, ibid., 12.

105 Levi, *The Periodic Table*, 4.

106 On Swiss limitations to granting asylum, see S. Calvo, *A un passo dalla salvezza. La politica svizzera di respingimento degli ebrei durante le persecuzioni, 1933–1945* (Turin: Zamorani, 2010).

107 See Omezzoli, *Prefetti e fascismo*, 252–67; L. Ganapini, *La repubblica delle camicie nere* (Milan: Garzanti, 1999), 275ff.

108 ARAVdA, Prefettura Gabinetto, cat. 14/7 doc. (telegram of 11 December 1943).

109 See ARAVdA, Prefettura Gabinetto, cat. 14/7, "Ministero della Guerra," sotto-fasc. "Presentazione alle armi classi di leva," notes and drafts of prefect Carnazzi (27 November 1943).

110 Quoted in Klinkhammer, *L'occupazione tedesca*, 280.

111 See ARAVdA, Prefettura Gabinetto, cat. 14/1, "Ministeri. Presidenza consiglio ministri. Ebrei," sottofasc. "Variazioni stato civile ed anagrafico degli ebrei e misti" (various documents, November–December 1943).

112 See R. Levi, *Ricordi politici di un ingegnere* (Milan: Vangelista, 1981), 52–64.

113 See Momigliano Levi, *La quotidianità negata. Da Issime ad Auschwitz: il caso della famiglia di Remo Jona* (Aosta: Le Château, 2001), 20–21.

114 See ibid., 48–50.

2. Part Partisan, Part Bandit

1 P. Levi, *Survival in Auschwitz*, trans. Stuart Woolf (New York: Summit, 1986), 112. The term "Lilliputian" is that of Alberto Cavaglion in a comment to P. Levi, *Se questo è un uomo* (Turin: Einaudi, 2012), 217.

2 It's unclear whether Frenkl can even be considered a "figure"—a *figura* in the sense that Erich Auerbach used the notion in writing about Dante's *Divine Comedy*, something between symbol and allegory, prefiguration and fulfillment. See E. Auerbach, "Figura," in *Scenes from the Drama of European Literature*, trans. Ralph Manheim (Minneapolis: University of Minnesota Press, 1984), 11–71.

3 P. Levi, *The Periodic Table*, trans. Raymond Rosenthal (New York: Schocken, 1984), 133.

4 On this point see T. Judt (with T. Snyder), *Thinking the Twentieth Century* (London: Penguin, 2012), 194.

5 See S. Peli, *La Resistenza difficile* (Milan: FrancoAngeli, 1999), 53–54.

6 See ATA, Corte straordinaria d'assise, 15/1946, interrogation of Edilio Cagni (Aosta, 17 January 1946).

7 Levi, *The Periodic Table*, 133.

8 Quoted in I. Thomson, *Primo Levi* (2002) (London: Vintage, 2003), 144 (letter from Guido Bachi to the author, 14 June 1992).

9 See ATA, Corte straordinaria d'assise, 15/1946, verbali di denuncia della Questura (Aosta, 21 June and 28 July 1945); Ufficio del Pubblico Ministero, citazione in giudizio (Aosta, 13 March 1946).

10 See ATA, ibid.

11 See Thomson, *Primo Levi*, 144 (letter from Guido Bachi, 14 June 1992).

12 See L. Allegra, *Gli aguzzini di Mimo. Storie di ordinario collaborazionismo (1943–45)* (Turin: Zamorani, 2010), 63ff.

13 ATA, Corte straordinaria d'assise, 15/1946, statement of Renato Corrado (Aosta, 8 August 1945).

14 ATA, fondo, statement of Lino Binel (Aosta, 8 March 1946).

15 See E. Riccarand, *Profilo di un uomo libero*, in L. Binel, *Cronaca di un valdostano* (1981) (Sarre: Tipografia Testolin, 2002), vii–viii.

16 Mussolini's fall had come in Verrès several weeks before the official date of July 25, 1943. In May, "unidentified" patrons of a restaurant on Via Roma had "turned a painting depicting Il Duce to the wall on which it was hanging" and had "written on the back side in pencil the phrase 'Viva Stalin.'" The carabinieri had made inquiries but the matter had not been resolved. It had proved impossible to identify those responsible, whether local pranksters or genuine Valle d'Aosta Commu-

nists. ARAVdA, Prefettura Gabinetto, cat. 6, "Ordine pubblico," anno 1943, dispaccio del tenente comandante la tenenza dei Carabinieri di Castel Verres (4 May 1943).

17   Reconstruction based on ATA, Corte straordinaria d'assise, 15/1946: words quoted from, respectively, "Deposition of s.ten. Cerri Carlo," "Deposition of tenente Renato Redi," and "Relazione del s.t. tenente Meoli Mario" (all undated, December 1943).

18   ATA, fondo, doc. (statement of Redi).

19   ATA, fondo, doc. (statement of Cerri).

20   AISRAL, Fondo Upi, Casellario B, busta 13, fasc. 42, "Informazioni su antifascisti, ammoniti, confinati," under "Barbesino, Giuseppe" (various documents, 1935).

21   See Peli, La Resistenza difficile, 16ff.

22   ATA, Corte straordinaria d'assise, 15/1946, doc. (statement of Redi).

23   See WLA, Ian Thomson Papers, 1406/2/6, correspondence with Guido Bachi (copy of document, dated Turin: 29 October 1946).

24   ATA, Corte straordinaria d'assise, 15/1946, doc. (statement of Redi).

25   See ATA, fondo, rapporto del prefetto Carnazzi al Tribunale speciale per la difesa dello stato e alla Direzione generale della Pubblica Sicurezza (Aosta, 7 March 1944).

26   See T. Bo and G. Rossi, Di villaggio in villaggio, di ricordo in ricordo, vol. 2 (Châtillon: Edizioni Cervino, 2009), 21.

27   See T. Bo and G. Rossi, Di villaggio in villaggio, di ricordo in ricordo, vol. 1 (Châtillon: Edizioni Cervino, 2008), 13.

28   Quoted in Omezzoli, I processi in Corte straordinaria, 207.

29   AISRVdA, Fondi vari, H. Passerin d'Entrèves, "Diario di un patriota valdostano," p. 5.

30   See G. Bocca, Le mie montagne. Gli anni della neve e del fuoco (Milan: Feltrinelli, 2006), 36–37.

31   Quoted in G. Pansa, Guerra partigiana tra Genova e il Po. La Resistenza in provincia di Alessandria (1967) (Rome-Bari: Laterza, 1998), 30n.

32   See AISRAL, Fondo Pivano, busta 4, fasc. 5, "Ufficio politico investigativo Guardia nazionale repubblicana," interrogations of brothers Angelo and Luigi Allara (Casale Monferrato, 21 and 22 December 1943).

33   AISRAL, fondo, interrogation of Giovanni Conti (Casale Monferrato, 22 December 1943).

34   See Peli, La Resistenza difficile, 109–10.

35   AISRAL, Fondo Pivano, busta 4, fasc., interrogation of Federico Barbesino (Casale Monferrato, 28 December 1943); ibid., Legione territoriale dei Carabinieri di Alessandria, rapporto giudiziario su Cantele Giovanni e altri (Casale Monferrato, 10 January 1944).

36   Ibid.

37   R. Battaglia, Un uomo, un partigiano (1945) (Bologna: il Mulino, 2004), 127–30; and of course Battaglia, Storia della Resistenza italiana (8 September 1943– 25 April 1945) (Turin: Einaudi, 1953).

38   See F. Meni, Quando i tetti erano bianchi. Casale e il Basso Monferrato dal Fascismo alla Resistenza (Alessandria: Edizioni dell'Orso, 2000), 92–93.

39 AISRAL, Fondo Pivano, busta 4, fasc., doc. (rapporto dei Carabinieri, 10 January 1944).

40 See "Notiziario italiano," in *La Stampa*, April 10, 1934.

41 See AISRAL, Fondo Upi, Casellario A, busta 5, fasc. 22, under "Oppezzo, Ugo" (various documents, 1935); parish archive, Cerrina Monferrato, "Liber Chronicus" compiled by Don Giuseppe Samarotto, 29 April 1937 (I thank Chiara Cane for bringing this to my attention).

42 See Chapter 9, "And Calls On Him to Explain."

43 Quoted in S. Favretto, *Il liceo classico di Casale Monferrato dal 1940 al 1945. Fatti e documenti inediti*, in "Quaderno di storia contemporanea," no. 38 (2005), 179–81.

44 Quoted in S. Favretto, *Resistenza e nuova coscienza civile. Fatti e protagonisti del Monferrato casalese* (Alessandria: Edizioni Falsopiano, 2009), 248–49.

45 Quoted in G. Pansa, *"Nascita della RSI in una città di provincia: Casale Monferrato"*, in *Il Movimento di Liberazione in Italia*, no. 84 (1966), 51–52.

46 ARAVdA, Prefettura Gabinetto, non classificati, 1943–46, Promemoria per il ministero delle Corporazioni (Aosta, 12 December 1943).

47 ARAVdA, Prefettura Gabinetto, cat. 6, "Ordine pubblico," segnalazione al prefetto del commissario reggente il Partito fascista repubblicano, Guido Molinar (Aosta, 7 December 1943).

48 See ATA, Corte straordinaria d'assise, 15/1946, interrogation of Aldo Piacenza (Aosta, 11 January 1946).

49 ARAVdA, Prefettura Gabinetto, cat. 6, "Ordine pubblico," rapporto del Seniore Luigi Del Favero (Aosta, 9 December 1943).

50 WLA, Ian Thomson Papers, 1406/2/6, correspondence with Guido Bachi, "Opinione personale sulla banda autonoma 'Ayas'" (undated, but October 1946).

51 See ATA, Corte straordinaria d'assise, 15/1946, interrogation of Piacenza, doc. (11 January 1944).

52 AISTORETO, D/Ur, fasc. 1, "Divisione Italo Rossi," various (undated, but 1946–47).

53 AISRAL, Fondo Pivano, busta 4, fasc. cit, doc. (rapporto dei Carabinieri, 10 January 1944).

54 "Notiziario italiano" in *La Stampa*, February 21, 1944.

55 "Notiziario italiano," ibid., February 29, 1944.

56 Levi, *The Periodic Table*, 132.

57 Levi, *Survival in Auschwitz*, 11.

58 See P. Levi, *Al visitatore*, in P. Levi, *Opere*, a cura di M. Belpoliti (Turin: Einaudi, 1997), 2:1335–36.

59 Quoted in C. Angier, *The Double Bond: Primo Levi, A Biography* (New York: Farrar, Straus and Giroux, 2002), 252.

60 See R. Botta, *Il senso del rigore. Il codice morale della giustizia partigiana*, in M. Legnani and F. Vendramini, eds., *Guerra di liberazione, guerra civile* (Milan: FrancoAngeli, 1990), 141–61; C. Pavone, *A Civil War: A History of the Italian Resistance*, trans. P. Levy (London: Verso, 2013).

61 See B. Fenoglio, "Old Blister," in *The Twenty-Three Days of the City of Alba*, trans. John Shepley (South Royalton, Vt.: Steerforth, 2002), 57–69; S. Tutino, "Morti male," in Tutino, *La ragazza scalza. Racconti della Resistenza* (Turin: Einaudi, 1975), 79–83.

62 Fenoglio, "Old Blister."
63 E. Artom, *Diari di un partigiano ebreo (January 1940–February 1944)*, ed. G. Schwarz (Turin: Bollati Boringhieri, 2008), 87 (December 9, 1943).
64 ATA, Corte straordinaria d'assise, 15/1946, interrogation of Piacenza, doc. (11 January 1944).
65 See Pavone, *A Civil War*; Peli, *La Resistenza difficile*, 110ff.
66 See AISTORETO, database of partisans in Piedmont.
67 ATA, Corte straordinaria d'assise, 15/1946, doc. (interrogation of 11 January 1944).
68 Ibid.
69 Quoted in A. Chiappano, *Luciana Nissim Momigliano: una vita* (Florence: Giuntina, 2010), 64–65.
70 AFBT, papers of Emilio Bachi, "Il filo della memoria," typed transcript, p. 38.
71 ACPL, Fondo Marco Pennacini, interview of Primo Levi (1973), typed transcript prepared by G. Giannone, M. Luzzatti, and D. Muraca, p. 8.
72 G. Arbib and G. Secchi, *Italiani insieme agli altri. Ebrei nella Resistenza in Piemonte* (Turin: Zamorani, 2010), 197 (interview with Primo Levi, June 8, 1981).
73 AISRAL, Fondo Formazioni partigiane, fasc. 13, "Divisione Matteotti," various (undated, 1945).
74 See P. Urati, *Piero Piero. Autobiografia di un protagonista della guerra partigiana, 1943–1945*, ed. R. Tappero (Aosta: Le Château, 2005), 24–25, 196.
75 See R. S. C. Gordon, *Primo Levi's Ordinary Virtues: From Testimony to Ethics* (Oxford: Oxford University Press, 2001).
76 See Arbib and Secchi, *Italiani insieme agli altri*, 197 (interview June 8, 1981).
77 I. Calvino, *The Path to the Spiders' Nests*, trans. Archibald Colquhoun, revised Martin McLaughlin (London: Penguin, 2009), 159.

3. A Snowy Dawn

1 P. Levi, *Survival in Auschwitz*, trans. Stuart Woolf (New York: Summit, 1986), 1, 13.
2 See ATA, Corte straordinaria d'assise, 15/1946, interrogation of Aldo Piacenza (Aosta, 11 January 1946); WLA, Ian Thomson Papers, 1406/2/6, correspondence with Guido Bachi (copy of a document dated Turin, 29 October 1946).
3 ATA, fondo, "Relazione del s.t. Meoli Mario" (undated, December 1943).
4 AISTORETO, database of partisans in Piedmont.
5 ATA, Corte straordinaria d'assise, 15/1946, "Relazione del s.t. Meoli."
6 ATA, fondo, "Deposition of s.ten. Cerri Carlo."
7 ATA, fondo, "Deposition of tenente Renato Redi," and "Deposition of s.ten Cerri."
8 P. Levi, *The Periodic Table*, trans. R. Rosenthal (New York: Schocken, 1984), 131.
9 AISRVdA, Fondi vari, "Pro memoria per l'eccellenza Dolfin–Segretario particolare del Duce," dal Capo della Provincia di Aosta (Aosta, 11 January 1944).
10 ATA, Corte straordinaria d'assise, 15/1946, interrogation of Edilio Cagni (Aosta, 17 January 1946).
11 ASMi, Corte straordinaria d'assise, 1947, cart. 65/18, deposition of Giovanni Vinzio, 20 July 1945.
12 ATA, Corte straordinaria d'assise, 15/1946, rapporto giudiziario della tenenza dei Carabinieri di Castel Verrès (Castel Verrès, 23 January 1944).

13 Levi, *The Periodic Table*, 131.

14 Interview of Luciana Nissim by the USC Shoah Foundation Institute (Milan: 3 July 1998), in A. Chiappano, *Luciana Nissim Momigliano: una vita* (Florence: Giuntina, 2010), 127–28.

15 See AFBT, papers of Guido Bachi, "Ricordi" (1977), typed transcript, p. 59.

16 Levi, *The Periodic Table*, 131.

17 AFBT, papers of Guido Bachi, "Diario dal carcere di Aosta, 1943–1945," typed transcript, p. 76 (13 December 1944).

18 Levi, *The Periodic Table*, 131.

19 See ATA, Corte straordinaria d'assise, 15/1946, rapporto del prefetto Carnazzi al Tribunale speciale per la difesa dello stato e alla Direzione generale della Pubblica Sicurezza (Aosta, 7 March 1944).

20 Levi, *Survival in Auschwitz*, 17.

21 Nissim interview in Chiappano, *Luciana Nissim Momigliano*, 128; AFBT, "Diario," Guido Bachi, p. 76 of typescript.

22 On this subject, see C. Greppi, *L'ultimo treno. Racconti del viaggio verso il lager* (Rome: Donzelli, 2012).

23 Levi, *The Periodic Table*, 131. The words "and a timed fuse" were omitted from the English translation.

24 P. Levi, "Fine del Marinese," in *Il Ponte*, August–September 1949, 1170–73. About the point of view of the voice narrating the story, see the thoughtful comment of Gabriele Pedullà, in Pedullà, ed., *Racconti della Resistenza* (Turin: Einaudi, 2005), 193–94.

25 Ibid.

26 AISRT, Archive Piero Calamandrei, Carteggio, letter from Primo Levi to Piero Calamandrei (Turin: 14 March 1948).

27 See S. Luzzatto, Introduzione, to P. Calamandrei, *Uomini e città della Resistenza* (1955) (Rome-Bari: Laterza, 2006).

28 R. Loy, *Ahi, Paloma* (Turin: Einaudi, 2000), 58.

29 Ibid., 58–60.

30 See A. Gobetti, *Diario partigian* (Turin: Einaudi, 1956), 81ff.; and B. Guidetti Serra (with Santina Mobiglia), *Bianca la rossa* (Turin: Einaudi, 2009), 52–53.

31 ACDEC, Fondo Vicissitudini dei singoli, fasc. "Luzzati, Vittorio," "L'odissea di un Ebreo" (May 1945), pp. 2–3 of typescript.

32 Ibid., pp. 3–4 of typescript.

33 See M. Belpoliti, "Due deposizioni giurate di Primo Levi," in M. Belpoliti and A. Cortellessa, *Da una tregua all'altra* (Milan: Chiarelettere, 2010), 13; see also G. Arbib and G. Secchi, *Italiani insieme agli altri. Ebrei nella Resistenza in Piemonte, 1943–1945* (Turin: Zamorani, 2011), 197 (interview with Primo Levi of 8 June 1981, where "Cesare Vita" should be spelled "Vitta").

34 See "Gazzetta Ufficiale del Regno d'Italia," October 19, 1939, p. 4914.

35 See G. Coriasco, *Storia operaia della Riv* (Milan: FrancoAngeli, 1986).

36 See L. Picciotto, *Il libro della memoria. Gli Ebrei deportati dall'Italia (1943–1945)* (Milan: Mursia, 1991), 645.

37 See AISTORETO, database of partisans in Piedmont.

38 AFBT, papers of Emilio Bachi, "Il filo della memoria," typed transcript, p. 38.

39 Ibid., p. 39.

40 See T. Omezzoli, *Tra fascismo e Resistenza. Aosta al tempo della Repubblica sociale italiana, 1943–1945* (Aosta: Le Château, 2012).

41 AISRAL, Fondo Pivano, busta 4, fasc. 5, informativa della Guardia nazionale repubblicana, Comando 11a legione (Casale Monferrato, 16 December 1943).

42 ARAVdA, Prefettura Gabinetto, unclassified, 1943–46, passes authorized by prefect (Aosta, 21 December 1943).

43 AISRAL, Fondo Pivano, busta 4, fasc., interrogation of Federico Barbesino (Casale Monferrato, 28 December 1943).

44 AISRAL, Fondo Pivano, busta 4, fasc. interrogation of Carlo Eugenio Carretto (Aosta, 7 January 1944).

45 ATA, Corte straordinaria d'assise, 15/1946, interrogation of Giuseppe Barbesino (Aosta, 18 January 1944).

46 AISRVdA, Fondi vari, "Pro memoria per l'eccellenza Dolfin."

47 Levi, *The Periodic Table*, 132–34.

48 See P. Levi, *Il pugno di Renzo*, in Levi, *L'altrui mestiere* (1985), in Levi, *Opere*, 2:702; A. Cavaglion, *Primo Levi, il 1938, il fascismo e la storia d'Italia*, in "Belfagor," November 30, 2008, 719–23.

49 Levi, *Survival in Auschwitz*. See also the reflections of R. S. C. Gordon, *"Sfacciata fortuna." La Shoah e il caso* (Turin: Einaudi, 2010), 59–63.

50 Levi, *The Periodic Table*, 132.

51 ATA, Corte straordinaria d'assise, 15/1946, interrogation of Piacenza, doc. (11 January 1944).

52 ATA, fondo, rapporto del prefetto Carnazzi, doc. (7 March 1944).

53 See I. Tibaldi, *Primo Levi e i suoi "compagni di viaggio": ricostruzione del trasporto da Fossoli ad Auschwitz*, in P. Momigliano Levi and R. Gorris, eds., *Primo Levi testimone e scrittore di storia* (Florence: Giuntina, 1999), 149–232.

54 See A. Della Torre, *Messaggio speciale* (1968) (Bologna: Zanichelli, 1972), 13ff.

55 See A. Poma and G. Perona, *La Resistenza nel Biellese* (Parma: Guanda, 1972), 129.

56 See R. Mira, *Tregue d'armi. Strategie e pratiche della guerra in Italia fra nazisti, fascisti e partigiani* (Rome: Carocci, 2011).

57 See Della Torre, *Messaggio speciale*, 17.

58 Ibid.

4. Passing the Torch

1 P. Levi, *Survival in Auschwitz*, trans. Stuart Woolf (New York: Summit, 1986), 20. "Treacherously" (*a tradimento*) is omitted in the English.

2 Ibid., 123–30.

3 Ibid., 16.

4 Quoted in A. Chiappano, *Luciana Nissim Momigliano: una vita* (Florence: Giuntina, 2010), 129 (interview by the Centro documentazione ebraica contemporanea, Milan: 17 July 1995).

5 The letter is quoted in full in L. Nissim Momigliano, *Ricordi della casa dei morti e altri scritti*, ed. A. Chiappano (Florence: Giuntina, 2008), 87.

6 The Levi family has the original postcard. For a reproduction made by Levi himself, see Ph. Mesnard, *Primo Levi. Una vita per immagini* (Venice: Marsilio, 2008), 38.

7   AFBT, papers of Emilio Bachi, "Il filo della memoria," typed transcript, p. 40.

8   G. Bassani, *Pagine di un diario ritrovato,* in Bassani, *Opere,* ed. R. Cotroneo (Milan: Mondadori, 1998), 974 (2 February 1944).

9   See AFBT, papers of Emilio Bachi, "Il filo della memoria," 41–42; ibid., various (1944–45).

10   See R. Nicco, *La Resistenza in Valle d'Aosta* (Aosta: Musumeci editore, 1990).

11   F. Camon, *Conversazione con Primo Levi* (1982–86) (Parma: Guanda, 2006), 16.

12   See L. Klinkhammer, *L'occupazione tedesca in Italia, 1943–1945* (Turin: Bollati Boringhieri, 1993), 282–85.

13   See ibid., 264n.

14   "La Provincia Alpina," February 9, 1944.

15   See T. Giannetti, *Nasce il battaglione "Moschettieri delle Alpi,"* in *La Stampa,* March 4, 1944.

16   ASMi, Corte straordinaria d'assise, 1947, cart. 65/18, rapporto del prefetto Carnazzi a Renato Ricci, comandante generale della Guardia nazionale repubblicana (Aosta, 25 March 1944).

17   ASMi, fondo, rapporto del tenente colonnello De Filippi al Comando generale della Guardia nazionale repubblicana (Aosta, 19 March 1944).

18   ATA, Corte straordinaria d'assise, 15/1946, "Rapporto del ten. Cagni Edilio sui rastrellamenti eseguiti nel Canavese," undated (March 1944).

19   See G. Dolino, *Partigiani in val di Lanzo* (Milan: FrancoAngeli, 1989), 22–28.

20   See G. Pansa, *Storia e documenti del primo Comitato Militare del C.L.N. regionale piemontese* (Turin: Istituto per la storia della Resistenza in Piemonte, 1964).

21   V. Fusi, *Fiori rossi al Martinetto. Il processo di Turin: April 1944* (1968) (Milan: Mursia, 1972), 102.

22   See Pansa, *Storia e documenti,* 10–12.

23   Fusi, *Fiori rossi al Martinetto,* 123.

24   See ATA, Corte straordinaria d'assise, 15/1946, interrogation of Edilio Cagni (8 March 1946). See also Fusi, *Fiori rossi al Martinetto,* 123, 131.

25   Ibid., 124.

26   D. Gay Rochat, *La Resistenza nelle valli valdesi, 1943–1945* (1968) (Turin: Claudiana, 2006), 84–85.

27   See note by the editor, Guri Schwarz, in E. Artom, *Diari di un partigiano ebreo (January 1940–February 1944)* (Turin: Bollati Boringhieri, 2008), 150–51.

28   See S. Peli, *La Resistenza in Italia. Storia e critica* (Turin: Einaudi, 1993), 60; S. Peli, *La Resistenza difficile* (Milan: FrancoAngeli, 1999), 104ff.

29   AISTORETO, D/Ur, fasc. 1, "Divisione Italo Rossi," various (undated, 1946–47).

30   AISRVdA, Fondo Manganoni, "Breve cenno sulla lotta di liberazione ad Arnaz," relazione firmata "Riccardino" (31 January 1946).

31   Ch. Passerin d'Entrèves, *La tempëta dessu noutre montagne. Épisodes de la Résistance en Vallée d'Aoste* (Aosta: Institut historique de la Résistance en Vallée d'Aoste, 1975), 43–44.

32   Fenoglio, "The Twenty-Three Days of the City of Alba," in *The Twenty-Three Days of the City of Alba,* trans. John Shepley (South Royalton, Vt.: Steerforth, 2002), 1.

33 See Nicco, *La Resistenza in Valle d'Aosta*, 68–71; S. Presa, *Le fasi della Resistenza in valle d'Aosta, 1943–1945* (Aosta: Le Château, 2009), 86–87.

34 See T. Omezzoli, *I processi in Corte d'assise straordinaria di Aosta, 1945–1947* (Aosta: Le Château, 2011), 257–58.

35 ARAVdA, Prefettura Gabinetto, cat. 14/7, "Ministero della Guerra, 1943–45," segnalazione della Milizia forestale al capo della provincia (Aosta, 13 May 1944).

36 See A. Gyppaz, "Vicende della 178a Brigata 'Matteotti' nella rievocazione di Giuseppe Thuegaz," in *Questioni di storia della Valle d'Aosta contemporanea*, no. 1, 1981, 58.

37 See ARAVdA, Prefettura Gabinetto, cat. 14/7, "Ministero della Guerra," various (Aosta, April and June 1944).

38 See S. Goyet, *Émile Chanoux. L'uomo dietro al mito* (Aosta: Le Château, 2008).

39 See P. di Martino, *"Lassù i rumori del mondo non arrivano." Cronaca dell'arresto e della morte di Émile Chanoux, May 1944* (Aosta: Le Château, 2000), 52–56.

40 L. Binel, *Cronaca di un valdostano* (1981), ed. E. Riccarand (Sarre: Tipografia Testolin, 2002), 39.

41 See di Martino, *"Lassù i rumori del mondo,"* 59–71.

42 See Nicco, *La Resistenza in Valle d'Aosta*, 85–88.

43 See Presa, *Le fasi della Resistenza*, 97–110.

44 AISRVdA, Fondi vari, H. Passerin d'Entreves, "Diario di un patriota valdostano," 8.

45 See Nicco, *La Resistenza in Valle d'Aosta*, 139.

46 See P. Levi, *The Periodic Table*, trans. R. Rosenthal (New York: Schocken, 1984), 132.

47 Gyppaz, *Vicende della 178a Brigata*, 60.

48 See Presa, *Le fasi della Resistenza*, 114–33.

49 As of September 1944: see G. Ciardullo, *1943–1945. Cronologia della lotta di liberazione in valle d'Aosta* (Aosta, 1986), 134.

50 M. Pelizzari, *Le memorie di Alimiro* (1945), ed. G. Maggia (Ivrea: Enrico editori, 1979), 59.

51 Ibid.

52 On Second Lieutenant Bianchi's career in 1944, see ARAVdA, Prefettura Gabinetto, cat. 14/7, f. 070 (24 August 1944) and f. 071 (28 September 1944).

53 ATA, Corte straordinaria d'assise, 15/1946, interrogation of Edilio Cagni (Aosta, 17 January 1946).

54 See L. Meneghello, *Bau-sète!* (1988) (Milan: Bompiani, 1996), 39–40.

55 See Presa, *Le fasi della Resistenza*, 206ff.

56 P. Calamandrei, *Uomini e città della Resistenza* (1955), ed. S. Luzzatto (Rome-Bari: Laterza, 2006), 251–52. In his account Calamandrei anticipates the day of the sabotage by 24 hours.

57 They included the architect Eugenio Gentili Tedeschi, one of Primo Levi's set of Turinese Jews and the distinguished historian Federico Chabod. See E. Gentili Tedeschi, *I giochi della paura. Immagini di una microstoria: libri segreti, cronache, resistenza tra Milan e Valle d'Aosta, 1942–1944* (Aosta: Le Château, 1999); ACDEC, Fondo Vicissitudini dei singoli, fasc. "Gentili Tedeschi in Verona, Gabriella," "Sei anni di paura, 1939–1945," pp. 11–21 of the typescript.

Also Nicco, *La Resistenza in Valle d'Aosta*, 246–48; S. Soave, *Federico Chabod politico* (Bologna: il Mulino, 1989), 64–65.

58 Notes from my conversation with Yves Francisco, Verrès, December 16, 2010.

59 ASMi, Corte straordinaria d'assise, 1947, cart. 65/18, denuncia di Guido Bachi contro Cesare Augusto Carnazzi (Turin, 31 July 1945).

60 See AFBT, papers of Emilio Bachi, "Il filo della memoria," p. 46; papers of Guido Bachi, "Ricordi" (1977), typed transcript, pp. 60–62.

61 See A. Poma and G. Perona, *La Resistenza nel Bielles* (Parma: Guanda, 1972).

62 AISRAL, Fondo Formazioni partigiane, fasc. 13, "Divisione Matteotti," various (undated, 1945).

63 See S. Favretto, *Resistenza e nuova coscienza civile. Fatti and protagonisti del Monferrato casalese* (Alessandria: Edizioni Falsopiano, 2009), 179; F. Meni, *Quando i tetti erano bianchi. Casale e il Basso Monferrato dal Fascismo alla Resistenza* (Alessandria: Edizioni dell'Orso, 2000), 187ff.

5. Justice and Revenge

1 G. Pansa, "I miei 25 April e quelli dei bigotti rossi" in *Il Riformista*, April 24, 2009.

2 G. Pansa, *Il revisionista* (Milan: Rizzoli, 2009), 35.

3 See S. Luzzatto, *La crisi dell'antifascismo* (Turin: Einaudi, 2004).

4 See works of G. Pansa, *Ma l'amore no* (Milan: Sperling & Kupfer, 1994); *Il bambino che guardava le donne* (Milan: Sperling & Kupfer, 1999); *I figli dell'Aquila* (Milan: Sperling & Kupfer, 2002); *Sconosciuto 1945* (Milan: Sperling & Kupfer, 2005); *La Grande Bugia* (Milan: Sperling & Kupfer, 2006).

5 G. Pansa, *Il sangue dei vinti* (Milan: Sperling & Kupfer, 2003).

6 G. Oddone, *Nuovi aspetti sull'esperienza di Cesare Pavese al Collegio Trevisio di Casale. Memorie del P. Luigi Frumento, rettore del Trevisio*, Genova Nervi, Collegio Emiliani, Web site (Padre Frumento errs in writing "Forieri" rather than "Fornero").

7 Pansa, *Il sangue dei vinti*, 9.

8 *La Stampa*, July 26, 1966.

9 See *Gazzetta Ufficiale del Regno d'Italia*, April 15, 1931, p. 1658.

10 See ibid., July 18, 1935, p. 3632.

11 See S. Favretto, *Resistenza e nuova coscienza civile. Fatti e protagonisti del Monferrato casalese* (Alessandria: Edizioni Falsopiano, 2009), 95–98.

12 See Pansa, *La Grande Bugia*, 219–32.

13 See F. Meni, *Quando i tetti erano bianchi. Casale e il Basso Monferrato dal Fascismo alla Resistenza* (Alessandria: Edizioni dell'Orso, 2000), 170–74.

14 Quoted in Pansa, *La Grande Bugia*, 229.

15 See G. Crainz, *Il conflitto e la memoria. "Guerra civile" e "Triangolo della morte,"* in *Meridiana* 13 (1992): 17–55; G. Crainz, "Il dolore e la collera: quella lontana Italia del 1945," in *Meridiana* 22–23 (1995): 249–73; G. Crainz, *L'ombra della guerra. Il 1945, l'Italia* (Rome: Donzelli, 2007).

16 See T. Omezzoli, *I processi in Corte straordinaria di Assise di Aosta, 1945–1947* (Aosta: Le Château, 2011), 115–16.

17 T. Aymone, *Un frammento autobiografico*, in T. Aymone, *Scritti inediti*, ed.

G. Mottura, "Materiali di discussione," Dipartimento di Economia politica, Università degli studi di Modena e Reggio Emilia, 2005, p. 30.

18   See M. Dondi, *La lunga liberazione. Giustizia e violenza nel dopoguerra italiano* (Rome: Editori Riuniti, 2004), 97; Pansa, *Il sangue dei vinti*, 78ff.

19   See Omezzoli, *I processi in Corte straordinaria*, 229–30.

20   See R. Rues, "Le 'radiose' giornate dell'Ossola. I militi della R.S.I. assassinati nella regione dell'Ossola e Verbano dopo il 25 April 1945," in *Storia del XX secolo*, no. 32 (January 1998), accessible online.

21   P. Chiara, "I fratelli Mascherpa" from *Il capostazione di Casalino e altri racconti* (1986), in P. Chiara, *Racconti*, ed. M. Novelli (Milan: Mondadori, 2007), 1429–30.

22   The first quote (from 1960) comes from M. Belpoliti, *Due deposizioni giurate di Primo Levi*, in M. Belpoliti and A. Cortellessa, *Da una tregua all'altra* (Milan: Chiarelettere, 2010), 14; the second from P. Levi, *The Periodic Table*, trans. Raymond Rosenthal (New York: Schocken, 1984), 132.

23   See G. Schwarz, *Tu mi devi seppellir. Riti funebri e culto nazionale alle origini della Repubblica* (Turin: Utet Libreria, 2010).

24   *La Nuova Stampa*, December 9, 1945.

25   B. Fenoglio, *Una questione privata* (1963), in B. Fenoglio, *Tutti i romanzi*, ed. G. Pedullà (Turin: Einaudi, 2012), 1071–72.

26   On this legendary partisan commander see the sharply drawn portrait by G. Bocca, *Il provinciale. Settant'anni di vita partigiana* (Milan: Mondadori, 1991), 67–68; as well as his own memoirs, "P." Rocca, *Un esercito di straccioni al servizio della libertà* (Canelli: Edizioni Art pro Arte, 1984).

27   See M. Renosio, *Colline partigiane. Resistenza e comunità contadina nell'Astigiano* (Milan: FrancoAngeli, 1994), 266; H. Woller, *I conti col fascismo. L'epurazione in Italia, 1943–1948* (Bologna: il Mulino, 1997), 407–8.

28   Quoted in A. Bravo, *La repubblica partigiana dell'Alto Monferrato* (Turin: Giappichelli, 1964), 233.

29   See context in M. Ruzzi, "Presenza ed attività delle forze della RSI in provincia di Asti" in *Asti contemporanea*, no. 6 (2000): 63–102.

30   ASAt, Prefettura Gabinetto, mazzo 40, "Ordine pubblico," lettera riservata dal Commissario straordinario per il Piemonte ai prefetti delle province (Turin, 28 January 1945).

31   ASAt, Prefettura Gabinetto, fondo, lettera del capo della provincia al ministro dell'Interno (Asti, 9 March 1945).

32   ASAt, Prefettura Gabinetto, fondo, telegram from chief of province to *podestà* and commissioners of towns Villanova d'Asti, Valfenera, Villafranca, San Paolo Solbrito, Dusino San Michele, Ferrere, and Montavia (Asti, 16 March 1945).

33   ASAt, ibid., telegram, chief of province to the same (Asti, 15 April 1945).

34   ACDEC, Fondo Vicissitudini dei singoli, fascicolo "Levi, Primo," transcript of letter signed "Perrone Lorenzo" and dated 25 June 1944, 20 August 1944, 1 November 1944.

35   Ibid., typed transcript of handwritten letter.

36   "Quelle che oggi non sono con noi" in *La nuova realtà. Organo del movimento femminile Giustizia e Libertà*, special edition, Turin, 3 May 1945: in *Donne*

piemontesi nella lotta di liberazione. 99 partigiane cadute, 185 deportate, 38 cadute civili (Turin: Tipografia Impronta, 1953), 88.

37 See A. Chiappano, *Luciana Nissim Momigliano: una vita* (Florence: Giuntina, 2010), 108–32.

38 P. Levi, *The Reawakening*, trans. Stuart Woolf (New York: Summit, 1986), 200.

39 See ibid., 362–63.

40 See Chiappano, *Luciana Nissim Momigliano*, 144–49.

41 See ACDEC, Fondo Vicissitudini dei singoli, fasc. "Vitta, Cesare"; sul colonnello Vitale, vedi G. Schwarz, *Ritrovare se stessi. Gli ebrei nell'Italia postfascista* (Rome-Bari: Laterza, 2004), 158ff.

42 See D. Blatman, *The Death Marches: The Final Phase of Nazi Genocide* (Cambridge: Harvard University Press, 2011).

43 See L. Picciotto Fargion, "Gli ebrei di Turin deportati: notizie statistiche (1938–1945)" in F. Levi, ed., *L'ebreo in oggetto. L'applicazione della normativa antiebraica a Turin: 1938–1943* (Turin: Zamorani, 1991), 159–90.

44 See C. Angier, *The Double Bond: Primo Levi, A Biography* (London: Viking, 2002), 359–60.

45 See A. Segre, *Il coraggio silenzioso. Leonardo De Benedetti, medico, sopravvissuto ad Auschwitz* (Turin: Zamorani, 2008), 31–41.

46 See Angier, *The Double Bond*; I. Thomson, *Primo Levi* (2002) (London: Vintage, 2003); M. Anissimov, *Primo Levi ou la tragédie d'un optimiste* (Paris: JC Lattès, 1996), 403ff.; Ph. Mesnard, *Primo Levi. Le passage d'un témoin* (Paris: Fayard, 2011), 112ff.

47 ACDEC, Fondo Vicissitudini.

48 ASMi, Corte straordinaria d'assise, 1947, cart. 65/18, interrogation of Cesare Augusto Carnazzi (Asti, 23 September 1945).

49 ASMi, Corte straordinaria d'assise, 1947, cart. 65/19, statement of Vittorio Labbro at the Pretura di Chivasso (9 June 1945).

50 ASMi, fondo, statement of Germano Bianchin, fireman of Aosta (Aosta, 15 June 1945); statement of Giuseppe Borghesio, fireman, Aosta (Aosta, 20 June 1945).

51 ASMi, fondo, letter from Guido Bachi to Procura di Asti (Turin, 31 July 1945).

52 Decreto legislativo luogotenenziale, 22 April 1945, Istituzione di Corti straordinarie di Assise per i reati di collaborazione con i tedeschi, in *Gazzetta Ufficiale del Regno d'Italia*, supplemento ordinario del n. 49 del 4 April 1945, p. 3.

53 See Omezzoli, *I processi in Corte straordinaria*, 54–56.

54 See Woller, *I conti col fascismo*, 411ff.

55 ASMi, fondo, letter from Roberto Peccei (Aurelio Peccei's father) to Procura di Asti (Mongreno, 21 May 1945). On Peccei's detention (and his torture), see L. Allegra, *Gli aguzzini di Mimo. Storie di ordinario collaborazionismo (1943–45)* (Turin: Zamorani, 2010), 177–82; V. Castronovo, *Fiat. 1899–1999: un secolo di storia italiana* (Milan: Rizzoli, 1999), 674.

56 ASMi, fondo, statement of Renato Corrado at Procura di Aosta (Aosta, 18 July 1945).

57 ASMi, fondo.

58 ASMi, f. 13, fondo (deposition of Rosi, statement of Corrado).

59 ASMi, fondo.

60 Ibid.

61   See G. Oliva, *La Resistenza alle porte di Turin* (Milan: FrancoAngeli, 1989).

62   ASMi, Corte straordinaria d'assise, 1947, cart. 65/18, f. 24, second hearing, doc. (Asti, 20 October 1945).

63   ASMi, fondo, lettera da Ivrea, 4 October 1945.

64   See Woller, *I conti col fascismo*, 422.

65   See ibid., 415–16.

66   ASMi, Corte straordinaria d'assise, 1947, cart. 65/18, sentenza nella causa contro Cesare Augusto Carnazzi (Asti, 20 October 1945).

67   Decreto legislativo luogotenenziale, in *Gazzetta ufficiale del Regno d'Italia*, p. 2.

68   ASMi, sentenza nella causa contro Cesare Augusto Carnazzi.

69   ASMi, fondo, "Dichiarazione di ricorso per Cassazione" (Asti, 20 October 1945).

70   Ibid.

71   Ibid.

72   ASMi, fondo, "Dichiarazione" di Salomone Gerber e altri (Milan, 7 August 1945).

73   R. Hilberg, *Perpetrators, Victims, Bystanders: The Jewish Catastrophe 1933–1945* (New York: Aaron Asher Books, 1992).

74   See S. Friedländer, *Nazi Germany and the Jews, 1933–1945* (New York: Harper Collins, 2009).

75   See S. Cavati, *Ebrei a Bergamo: 1938–1945*, thesis, Università degli Studi di Milan: 2004–2005, pp. 40–41.

76   The distinction between curtailing rights and deadly persecution is made by M. Sarfatti, *Gli ebrei nell'Italia fascista. Vicende, identità, persecuzione* (Turin: Einaudi, 2000).

77   See I. Colombi, "Memoria di gente ebrea a Gandino," in *Civitas. Periodico di informazione del comune di Gandino*, March 2006, pp. 6–7; B. Enriotti, A. Ferranti and I. Paolucci, "Gandino: tutto il paese salvò gli ebrei dai lager nazisti negli anni cupi dell'occupazione tedesca," in *Triangolo rosso* 24, nos. 3–4 (October 2006): 6–13.

78   ASMi, Corte straordinaria d'assise, 1947, cart. 65/18, second hearing, doc. (Asti, 20 October 1945).

79   In an interview done by the USC Shoah Foundation Institute (Milan, 14 April 1998) and accessible online, Oscar Gerber said he had never fought in a partisan formation but had assisted the band operating in Val Seriana under partisan commander Giuseppe Lanfranchi ("Bepi"), serving as their interpreter.

80   See I. Gutman, B. Rivlin, and L. Picciotto, eds, *I giusti d'Italia. I non ebrei che salvarono gli ebrei, 1943–1945* (Milan: Mondadori, 2006), 178–80.

6. Body of Proof

1   ASAt, Fondo Questura, "Fascisti repubblicani," mazzo 7, fasc. 22, "Cagni, Edilio": telegram from Questore of Turin (Turin, 5 June 1945).

2   ASAt, ibid., telegram from Questore of Aosta (Aosta, 11 June 1945).

3   ATA, Corte straordinaria d'assise, 15/1946, statement of accusations (Turin, 6 June 1945).

4   ASAt, Fondo Questura, "Fascisti repubblicani," mazzo 7, fasc. 22, "Cagni, Edilio": various (Turin and Asti, 11–21 June 1945).

5   ATA, fondo, questura di Turin: interrogation of Edilio Cagni (25 June 1945).
6   ATA, fondo, carceri giudiziarie di Turin (13 July 1945).
7   ATA, fondo, denuncia di Guido Bachi presso l'Ufficio politico della questura di
     Turin (13 July 1945).
8   ATA, Corte straordinaria d'assise, 15/1946, various (April and November 1945).
9   See S. Soave, *Federico Chabod politico* (Bologna: il Mulino, 1989), 127ff.
10   See T. Omezzoli, *I processi in Corte straordinaria d'assise di Aosta, 1945–1947*
     (Aosta: Le Château, 2011).
11   ATA, Corte straordinaria d'assise, 15/1946, rinvio a giudizio di Cagni Edilio e
     altri (Aosta, 13 March 1946).
12   ATA, fondo, "Verbale di vane ricerche" (Aosta, 7 January 1946).
13   Ibid.
14   ATA, fondo, interrogation of Edilio Cagni (Aosta, 17 and 19 January 1946).
15   ATA, fondo, statement by Maria Carrera presso il Comando del corpo speciale
     di Polizia ausiliaria (Casale Monferrato, 16 July 1945).
16   ATA, fondo, letter from Alessandro Del Rosso to the Turin royal prosecutor
     (Casale Monferrato, 29 January 1946).
17   ATA, fondo, letter to the president, Corte straordinaria d'assise (Turin, 6 April
     1946).
18   See Soave, *Federico Chabod*, 139–40.
19   See ibid., 157–58.
20   ATA, Corte straordinaria d'assise, 15/1946, letter from Guido Bachi to Aosta royal
     prosecutor (Turin, 23 April 1946).
21   Ibid.
22   L. Nissim and P. Lewinska, *Donne contro il mostro* (Turin: Ramella, 1946).
23   See I. Thomson, *Primo Levi* (2002) (London: Vintage, 2003), 429–40.
24   P. Levi, Prefazione to A. Bravo and D. Jalla, *La vita offesa. Storia e memoria dei
     Lager nazisti nei racconti di duecento sopravvissuti* (Milan: FrancoAngeli,
     1996), 9.
25   Primo Levi, interviewed by Enrico Lombardi, in a broadcast of the Radio
     svizzera italiana, "Il frangitempo," June 3, 1985 (transcript ed. M. Belpoliti on
     Web journal *doppiozero*).
26   See A. Chiappano, "Nota al testo," in L. Nissim Momigliano, *Ricordi della casa
     dei morti e altri scritti* (Florence: Giuntina, 2008), 25–26.
27   See A. Chiappano, *Luciana Nissim Momigliano: una vita* (Florence: Giuntina,
     2010), 161.
28   See M. Fadini, "Su un avantesto di 'Se questo è un uomo' (con una nuova
     edizione del 'Rapporto' sul Lager di Monowitz del 1946)," in *Filologia italiana*, 5
     (2008): 209–40.
29   P. Levi, *Survival in Auschwitz*, trans. Stuart Woolf (New York: Summit, 1986), 9.
30   Ibid., 49.
31   Levi, *Survival in Auschwitz*, 41.
32   Quoted in J. Samuel (with Jean-Marc Dreyfus), *Il m'appelait Pikolo. Un compa-
     gnon de Primo Levi raconte* (Paris: Robert Laffont, 2007), 87.
33   Cited in ibid.
34   See the presentation of *If This Is a Man* written by Primo Levi in *L'Italia che*

scrive, October 1947, when the book was published: in M. Belpoliti, "Note al testo," in P. Levi, *Opere* (Turin: Einaudi, 1997), 1:1384.

35 Levi, *Se questo è un uomo* (Turin: De Silva, 1947 edition), 13, 18, 96.

36 ACDEC, Fondo Vicissitudini dei singoli, fasc. "Levi, Primo," typescript of *Storia di dieci giorni*, p. 14. In the typescript Levi wrote Ardèches instead of Provenchères, later corrected.

37 ATA, Corte straordinaria d'assise, 15/1946, fondo.

38 None of the three articles were signed. On Mussolini's purloined corpse, see S. Luzzatto, trans. F. Randall, *The Body of Il Duce: Mussolini's Corpse and the Fortunes of Italy* (New York: Metropolitan, 2006).

39 See L. Paggi, *Il "popolo dei morti." La repubblica italiana nata dalla guerra (1940–1946)* (Bologna: il Mulino, 2009); G. Schwarz, *Tu mi devi seppellir. Riti funebri e culto nazionale alle origini della Repubblica* (Turin: Utet Libreria, 2010).

40 See M. Franzinelli, *L'amnistia Togliatti. 22 June 1946: colpo di spugna sui crimini fascisti* (Milan: Mondadori, 2006), 37ff.

41 See Omezzoli, *I processi in Corte straordinaria*, 279–85.

42 ATA, Corte straordinaria d'assise, 15/1946, transcript (Aosta, 4 May 1946).

43 See ibid.

44 Ibid.

45 ATA, Corte straordinaria d'assise, 15/1946, transcript.

46 See ibid.

47 Ibid.

48 Ibid.

49 Ibid.

50 Ibid.

51 Ibid.

52 See ATA, Corte straordinaria d'assise, 15/1946, sentenza nella causa penale contro Cagni Edilio e altri (Aosta, 4 May 1946).

53 Ibid.

54 See ATA, fondo, hearing transcript.

55 Ibid. On the role of Don Bosticco, see W. E. Crivellin, *Cattolici, politica e società in Piemonte tra '800 and '900* (Cantalupa: Effata, 2008), 147.

56 ATA. Corte straordinaria d'assise, 15/1946, hearing transcript.

57 Ibid.

58 ATA, Corte straordinaria d'assise, 1946, Sentenza n. 33, causa penale contro Cagni Edilio e altri (Aosta, 4 May 1946).

59 Ibid., 247–48.

60 See ibid., 247.

61 See ibid., 116ff.; H. Woller, *I conti col fascismo. L'epurazione in Italia, 1943–1948* (Bologna: il Mulino, 1997), 419ff.

62 ATA, Corte straordinaria d'assise, 1946, Sentenza n. 33, doc. cit.

63 Ibid.

64 Ibid.

65 See C. Pavone, *Alle origini della Repubblica. Scritti su fascismo, antifascismo e continuità dello Stato* (Turin: Bollati Boringhieri, 1995).

7. Role Play

1   See D. De Masi, *C'è urgente bisogno di carabinieri!* (Modena: Il Fiorino, 2011), 157–60.

2   *La Domenica del Corriere*, September 22, 1918. The cover was drawn by the legendary Achille Beltrame.

3   See B. Tobia, *L'altare della Patria* (Bologna: il Mulino, 1998), 73–74.

4   AISRAL, Fondo Pivano, busta 4, fasc., interrogation of Martino Veduti (Casale Monferrato, 16 December 1943).

5   See A. A. Mola, *Giellisti* (Cuneo: Cassa di risparmio di Cuneo, 1997): vol. 2, *Dalla Resistenza armata all'impegno civile*, 27–29: vol. 3, *Documenti*, 133–35.

6   See ASMi, Corte straordinaria d'assise, 1947, cart. 65/18, "Circa ricerche di criminali di guerra" (Cuneo, 8 May 1945).

7   ASMi, fondo, informativa del Comando compagnia della Polizia ausiliaria alla procura del Regno di Asti (Casale M., 24 July 1945).

8   ASMi, fondo, court transcript, first hearing (Asti, 19 October 1945).

9   WLA, Ian Thomson Papers, correspondence with Guido Bachi (copy of a document dated Turin, 29 October 1946); ibid., "Opinione personale sulla banda autonoma 'Ayas'" (undated, October 1946).

10 See M. Mondini and G. Schwarz, *Dalla guerra alla pace. Retoriche e pratiche della smobilitazione nell'Italia del Novecento* (Sommacampagna: Cierre edizioni, 2007), 131–41.

11 See ibid., 142.

12 See AISTORETO, database of partisans in Piedmont. Veduti referred to the Arcesaz group as the "Verrès Band."

13 AISTORETO, Corpo volontari della Libertà, Formazioni Giustizia e Libertà, VII Divisione GL "Pietro Ferreira."

14 Ibid.

15 WLA, fondo, "Opinione personale."

16 Così nel decreto luogotenenziale n. 518 del 21 August 1945: see Mondini and Schwarz, *Dalla guerra alla pace*, 141.

17 AISTORETO, database of partisans in Piedmont; WLA, Ian Thomson Papers, 1406/1/2, "Cuttings and copy documents re Primo Levi's military career," various (1938–1953).

18 On Fenoglio's efforts to persuade Alba to honor the memory of Dario Scaglione ("Tarzan"), see P. Negri Scaglione, *Questioni private. Vita incompiuta di Beppe Fenoglio* (Turin: Einaudi, 2007), 140–41.

19 See A. M. Banti, *La nazione del Risorgimento. Parentela, santità e onore alle origini dell'Italia unita* (Turin: Einaudi, 2000); M. D'Amelia, *La mamma* (Bologna: il Mulino, 2005).

20 Corpo Volontari della Libertà, *La vita per l'Italia: brigata G. C. Puecher*, Milan, Stab. Tip. Stefano Pinelli, undated (1945), pp. 21ff.

21 See D. Gagliani, "Funerali di sovversivi" in *Rivista di storia contemporanea*, no. 1 (1984), 119–41; M. Filippa, *La morte contesa. Cremazione e riti funebri nell'Italia fascista* (Turin: Paravia Scriptorium, 2001).

22 See S. Favretto, *Resistenza e nuova coscienza civile. Fatti e protagonisti del Monferrato casalese* (Alessandria: Edizioni Falsopiano, 2009), 36–37.

23 On this matter, see G. Schwarz, *Tu mi devi seppellir. Riti funebri e culto nazionale alle origini della Repubblica* (Turin: Utet Libreria, 2010).

24 M. Rigoni Stern, "Un ragazzo delle nostre contrade" (1973), in G. Pedullà, ed., *Racconti della Resistenza* (Turin: Einaudi, 2005), 225–38 (citations from 237–38).

25 AISTORETO, D/Ur. fasc. 1, "Divisione Italo Rossi," various (undated, 1946–47).

26 AISRVdA, Fondi vari, letter from the president of the Associazione politici superstiti campi di concentramento to the Giunta consultiva regionale per il Piemonte del Comitato di liberazione nazionale (Turin, 1 September 1945).

27 AISRVdA, Fondi vari, letter from town governmrnt of Saint-Vincent to the Giunta consultiva regionale per il Piemonte del Comitato di liberazione nazionale (15 October 1945).

28 AISTORETO, database of partisans in Piedmont, "Zabaldano, Luciano" and "Opezzo [sic], Fulvio."

29 AFZT, "Attestato" del Comitato regionale dell'Associazione partigiani "Matteotti" del Piemonte, undated.

30 See ASTo, Distretto militare di Turin: "Fogli caratteristici," fondo Dichiarazione integrativa per l'equiparazione delle qualifiche gerarchiche partigiane (Turin, 22 April 1948).

31 AISTORETO, Pratiche caduti per la lotta di liberazione, busta 7.

32 Levi, *Survival in Auschwitz*, 171. (Translator's note: S. Woolf translates *torbido e disperato* as "turbid and desperate," but "the murky and desperate beginnings" is closer to the Italian, bearing in mind that *disperato* conveys "despairing" more than it does "frantic, wild.")

33 See unsigned articles: "A morte: Serloreti e Fagnola," in *La Nuova Stampa*, May 22, 1946; "Si inizia questa mattina a Napoli il processo contro il cap. Schmidt delle SS," ibid., March 31, 1950. On the international implications of the Schmidt trial, see F. Focardi, *Criminali di guerra in libertà. Un accordo segreto tra Italia e Germania federale, 1949–55* (Rome: Carocci, 2008).

34 See F. Cassata, *"La Difesa della Razza." Politica, ideologia e immagine del razzismo fascista* (Turin: Einaudi, 2008), 151, 191n.

35 While defending Cagni, D'Amico was also working on behalf of Giuseppe Viola, a killer at large following the Matteotti murder: see M. Canali, *Il delitto Matteotti. Affarismo e politica nel primo governo Mussolini* (Bologna: il Mulino, 1997), 599–601; G. Mayda, *Il pugnale di Mussolini. Storia di Amerigo Dùmini, sicario di Matteotti* (Bologna: il Mulino, 2004), 337–39.

36 ATA Corte straordinaria d'assise, 15/1946, letter from Ubaldo Prosperetti to the president of the Committee for free legal representation of the Perugia Appeals Court (Perugia, 4 March, 1947).

37 ATA, fondo, istanza dell'avvocato Tancredi Gatti al presidente della Suprema Corte di Cassazione (Roma, 2 May 1946).

38 Ibid.

39 See M. Franzinelli, *L'amnistia Togliatti. 22 June 1946: colpo di spugna sui crimini fascisti* (Milan: Mondadori, 2006), pp. 66ff. (for the full text of the decree see ibid., pp. 313–16).

40 See L. Lajolo, *I ribelli di Santa Libera. Storia di un'insurrezione partigiana, August 1946* (Turin: Edizioni Gruppo Abele, 1995), 97–98.

41 See ibid., 80–81.

42 See M. Renosio, *Tra mito sovietico e riformismo. Identità, storia e organizzazione dei comunisti astigiani, 1921–1975* (Turin: Edizioni Gruppo Abele, 1999), 282.

43 See Lajolo, *I ribelli*, 14–15.

44 See Lajolo, *I ribelli*, 115ff.; Franzinelli, *L'amnistia Togliatti*, 102–6.

45 See unsigned article "L'episodio Piero-Piero a Florence" in *La Nuova Stampa*, September 12, 1946.

46 See A. M. Imbriani, *Vento del Sud. Moderati, reazionari, qualunquisti (1943–1948)* (Bologna: il Mulino, 1996); G. Parlato, *Fascisti senza Mussolini. Le origini del neofascismo in Italia, 1943–1948* (Bologna: il Mulino, 2006).

47 See G. Tosi, "L'oro di Dongo" (Padova, 1957), in G. Tosi, ed., *La bilancia e il labirinto. Istruttorie e processi esemplari* (Padua: Il Poligrafo, 2003), 47ff.

48 See S. Luzzatto, trans. F. Randall, *The Body of Il Duce: Mussolini's Corpse and the Fortunes of Italy* (New York: Metropolitan, 2006).

49 See the communique from the PCI secretary, "Al col. Valerio, Walter Audisio, deve essere data la più alta onorificenza militare" in *l'Unità*, national edition, March 22, 1947.

50 "La coda del mostro," in *l'Unità*, Piedmont edition, February 14, 1947.

51 Ibid., February 15, 1947.

52 Ibid., M. Liprandi, "Con il segnale nella sinistra aspettavano in Piazza S. Carlo," February 16, 1947.

53 Ibid., "Dopo aver visto il cifrario vado alla riunione con Scorza," February 19, 1947.

54 Ibid., "Calvo, occhietti grigi, Scorza parla così," February 20, 1947.

55 Ibid., "Dice Scorza: appoggiamoci alla monarchia e torneremo insieme al potere," February 22, 1947.

56 Ibid., "Perché fu uccisa Brunilde Tanzi e perché Zorzoli fabbrica mitra," February 25, 1947.

57 See ibid., "La sensazionale cattura del criminale Novena incolpato di 195 omicidi," Piedmont edition, June 23, 1945.

58 G. Pansa, *Il revisionista* (Milan: Rizzoli, 2009), 138.

59 ATA, Corte d'assise straordinaria, 15/1946, istanza degli avvocati Domenico D'Amico e Camillo Corsanego al presidente della Corte Suprema di Cassazione (Rome), 12 November 1946.

60 Ibid.

61 ATA, fondo, estratto di sentenza della Suprema Corte di Cassazione (Roma, 13 November 1946); ibid., sentenza sul ricorso interposto da Cagni Edilio (Roma, 20 December 1946).

62 See D. Gurrey, *Across the Lines: Account of Axis Intelligence and Sabotage Operations in Italy, 1943–45* (Tunbridge Wells: Parapress, 1994).

63 See R. Cairoli, *Dalla parte del nemico. Ausiliarie, delatrici e spie nella Repubblica sociale italiana (1943–1945)* (Milan-Udine: Mimesis Edizioni, 2013).

64 NARA, Reg. 226, Entry 174, boxes 4, 11, 13, various (1943–44). I thank Roberta Cairoli for her generosity in letting me know about this and all the other documents deposited in the National Archives in Washington.

65 See NARA, Reg. 226, Entry 174, box 160, reports by Lt. Charles Siracusa to OSS headquarters in Rome (Turin, 30 October 1945; 16 November 1945; 19 November 1945).

66 NARA, Reg. 226, fondo, report by Lieutenant Charles Siracusa to OSS head-quarters in Rome (Turin, 6 December 1945).

67 NARA, Reg. 226, fondo, interrogation of Albertina Porciani (Turin, 2 December 1945).

68 NARA, Reg 226, fondo, report by Lieutenant Siracusa (19 November 1945).

69 See T. Mangold, *Cold Warrior: James Jesus Angleton, the CIA's Master Spy Hunter* (London: Simon & Schuster, 1991).

70 See Parlato, *Fascisti senza Mussolini*, 83–95.

71 See N. Tranfaglia, *Come nasce la Repubblica. La mafia, il Vaticano e il neofas-cismo nei documenti americani e italiani, 1943–1947* (Milan: Bompiani, 2004), 64ff.

72 NARA, Reg. 226, Entry 174, box 160, report by Lieutenant Charles Siracusa to OSS headquarters in Rome (Turin: 19 November 1945; 23 November 1945).

73 NARA, Reg. 226, fondo, ibid.

74 I'll limit myself to T. Judt, *Postwar: A History of Europe Since 1945* (New York: Penguin, 2005); F. Romero, *Storia della guerra fredda. L'ultimo conflitto per l'Europa* (Turin: Einaudi, 2009).

75 See E. Caretto and B. Marolo, *Made in USA. Le origini americane della Repub-blica italiana* (Milan: Rizzoli, 1996), 200–201.

76 See C. Guerriero, *La Volante rossa* (Rome: Datanews, 1996), 29.

77 See Parlato, *Fascisti senza Mussolini*, 274.

8. The Wind of Pardon

1 ATA, Corte straordinaria d'assise, 15/1946, Sezione speciale della Corte d'assise di Perugia, transcript (Perugia, 17 March 1947).

2 Ibid., various (March 1947).

3 Ibid., transcript, doc. cit.

4 Ibid., letter from Maria Carrera to Perugia general prosecutor (Casale Monfer-rato, 12 March 1947).

5 Ibid., transcript.

6 Ibid.

7 See ibid.

8 See ibid.

9 See P. Levi, *Survival in Auschwitz*, trans. Stuart Woolf (New York: Summit, 1986), 171.

10 See A. Chiappano, *Luciana Nissim Momigliano: una vita* (Florence: Giuntina, 2010), 175ff.

11 See C. Angier, *The Double Bond: Primo Levi, A Biography* (London: Viking, 2002); M. Quirico, *L'Unione culturale di Turin. Antifascismo, utopie e avanguardie nella città-laboratorio (1945–2000)* (Rome: Donzelli, 2010), 23ff. The publishing house De Silva was directed by the distinguished anti-Fascist intellectual Franco Antonicelli.

12 He began publishing chapters of the book in *L'amico del popolo*, a Vercelli Com-munist weekly edited by his old friend Silvio Ortona (who had recently married Primo's cousin Ada Della Torre). P. Levi, "Il viaggio" in *L'amico del popolo*, March 29, 1947.

13 Quoted in A. Segre, *Un coraggio silenzioso. Leonardo De Benedetti, medico, sopravvissuto ad Auschwitz* (Turin: Zamorani, 2008), 48–49.

14 See I. Thomson, *Primo Levi* (2002) (London: Vintage, 2003), 247.

15 See J. T. Gross, *Fear: Anti-Semitism in Poland after Auschwitz, an Essay in Historical Interpretation* (Princeton: Princeton University Press, 2006).

16 See M. Battini, *Peccati di memoria. La mancata Norimberga italiana* (Rome-Bari: Laterza, 2003), 73–115.

17 See J. Staron, *Fosse Ardeatine e Marzabotto. Storia e memoria di due stragi tedesche* (2002), Ital. translation (Bologna: il Mulino, 2007), 137–58.

18 See ASMi, Corte straordinaria d'assise, 1947, Sentenza n. 74 (Milan: 22 May 1947); ASMi, appunto della Cancelleria, 28 June 1947; ASAt, Fondo Questura, "Fascisti repubblicani," mazzo 41, fasc. 5, "Carnazzi, Cesare Augusto," various June 1947–May 1949.

19 See T. Kezich and A. Levantesi, *Una dinastia italiana. L'arcipelago Cecchi D'Amico tra arte, letteratura, giornalismo e politica* (Milan: Garzanti, 2010).

20 ATA, Corte straordinaria d'assise, 15/1946, "Motivi di ricorso per Cagni Edilio" (Perugia, 6 June 1947).

21 ATA, fondo, "Motivi aggiunti" (Rome, 31 July 1947).

22 C. Galante Garrone, "Guerra di liberazione (dalle galere)" in *Il Ponte*, Nov.–Dec. 1947, reprinted in Isnenghi, ed., *Dalla Resistenza alla desistenza. l'Italia del "Ponte" (1945–1947)* (Rome-Bari: Laterza, 2007), 402.

23 Ibid., 394.

24 Ibid., 400, 413.

25 They were Carlo Fornero, Lorenzo Barbano, Mario Iannuzzi, Carlo Ubertazzi, Giovanni Zola, and Luciano Martinotti: see L. Allegra, *Gli aguzzini di Mimo. Storie di ordinario collaborazionismo (1943–45)* (Turin: Zamorani, 2010), 273.

26 See unsigned article "La Cassazione conferma quattro condanne a morte" in *La Nuova Stampa*, December 12, 1946.

27 Unsigned, "Dalle nove a Casale sciopero generale," *Nuova Stampa Sera*, September 1 and 2, 1947.

28 G. Giovannini, signed "Gi. Bo.," "Casale occupata da 1000 partigiani," *La Nuova Stampa*, September 2, 1947.

29 Unsigned, "Sei condanne a morte confermate dalle Assise di Turin," *La Nuova Stampa*, January 15, 1946.

30 "Gi. Bo.," "Casale occupata."

31 Gi. Gi., "Casale sempre occupata," *Nuova Stampa Sera*, September 2–3, 1947.

32 Unsigned, "Solidarietà con Casale dei centri piemontesi," *Nuova Stampa Sera*, September 3–4, 1947.

33 Unsigned, "La risposta del ministro Grassi alla delegazione partigiana," *La Nuova Stampa*, September 4, 1947.

34 Ibid., unsigned, "I negozi riaprono, lo sciopero continua."

35 G. Giovannini, signed "Gi. Bo.," "Lo sciopero di Casale è finito stamane," *Nuova Stampa Sera*, September 4–5, 1947.

36 G. Giovannini, signed "Gi. Bo.," "Diffida al governo dei partigiani piemontesi," *La Nuova Stampa*, September 5, 1947.

37 See AISTORETO, D/Ur, fasc. 1, "Divisione Italo Rossi," various (undated, 1946–47).

38 "Gi. Bo.," "Diffida al governo."

39 See unsigned, "De Nicola respinge la grazia per cinque dei criminali casalesi," *La Nuova Stampa*, September 7, 1947.

40 See unsigned, "Tre dei criminali di Casale attendono nelle carceri di Turin," *Nuova Stampa Sera*, September 8–9, 1947; "In treno con quattro condannati a morte," *La Nuova Stampa*, September 9, 1947.

41 Unsigned, "Per i criminali di Casale ore contate salvo imprevisti" in *l'Unità* (Piedmont edition), September 10, 1947.

42 See unsigned, "È giunto l'ordine di esecuzione dei cinque criminali di Casale," *La Nuova Stampa*, September 10, 1947.

43 See unsigned, "I condannati di Casale giocano l'ultima carta," *Nuova Stampa Sera*, September 10–11, 1947.

44 See unsigned: "Il ricorso: ultima speranza rimasta ai criminali di Casale," *La Nuova Stampa*, September 11, 1947; "L'esecuzione è sospesa," *La Nuova Stampa*, September 12, 1947.

45 Unsigned, "I criminali di Casale sono stati trasferiti," *La Nuova Stampa*, September 16, 1947.

46 Unsigned, "La domanda d'amnistia respinta dalla Corte," *Nuova Stampa Sera*, September 16–17, 1947.

47 See unsigned, "Per i criminali di Casale il P.G. chiede la sospensione dell'esecuzione," *La Nuova Stampa*, October 10, 1947.

48 See Allegra, *Gli aguzzini di Mimo*, 273.

49 See unsigned, "Processati tre collaborazionisti già condannati a morte due volte," *La Nuova Stampa*, November 28, 1957; "Condannati a 24 anni due ufficiali repubblichini," *La Nuova Stampa*, December 7, 1957.

50 See G. De Luna, "I fatti di July 1960," in M. Isnenghi, ed., *I luoghi della memoria. Personaggi e date dell'Italia unita* (Rome-Bari: Laterza, 1997), 359–71.

51 See M. Mondini and G. Schwarz, *Dalla guerra alla pace. Retoriche e pratiche della smobilitazione nell'Italia del Novecento* (Sommacampagna: Cierre edizioni, 2007), 129.

52 See M. Ponzani, *L'offensiva giudiziaria antipartigiana nell'Italia repubblicana (1945–1960)* (Rome: Aracne, 2008).

53 See Atti parlamentari, Camera dei Deputati, Domanda di autorizzazione a procedere in giudizio contro i deputati Moranino e Ortona, annunziata il 14 November 1949, Documenti II, n. 144.

54 See T. Aymone, "Un frammento autobiografico," in T. Aymone, *Scritti inediti*, ed. G. Mottura, "Materiali di discussione," Dipartimento di Economia politica, Università di Modena e Reggio Emilia, 2005, pp. 26–27.

55 See R. Levi, *Ricordi politici di un ingegnere* (Milan: Vangelista, 1981), 59, 83.

56 Comment in *Corriere della Sera*, October 15, 1972, expanded and reprinted as "Il paolotto" in *Le corna del diavolo e altri racconti*, 1977. The story is found in P. Chiara, *Racconti*, ed. M. Novelli (Milan: Mondadori, 2007), 622–32.

57 Ibid., 632.

58 See Chapter 3, "A Snowy Dawn."

59 See P. Castello and G. Cesti, *Miniere della val d'Ayas*, undated (2005).

60 See T. Bo and G. Rossi, *Di villaggio in villaggio, di ricordo in ricordo*, vol. 2 (Châtillon: Edizioni Cervino, 2009), 39, 89.

61 See AFS, serie and 4320, B 1968/195, "Rechsextreme Bewegungen," confidential report (Bern: 5 May 1945).`

62 AFS, fondo, confidential report (Bern, 25 March 1947).

63 See AFS, fondo, confidential report (Bern, 19 December 1947).

64 See AFS, fondo, copy of memo (Basel, 19 September 1944).

65 See AFS, fondo, copy of memo (Basel, 30 September 1944).

66 AFS, fondo, copy of telegram (Bern, 25 January 1945).

67 AFS, fondo, various reports (Bern, 6 May 1956 and 16 May 1956).

68 AFS, fondo, report by Inspector Allamand (Lausanne, 19 July 1956).

69 Ibid.

70 J. Rochat, "Chasse au trésor: qui dort sur l'or de Mussolini?" in L'Hebdo, August 31, 2000.

71 Unsigned, "Un genovese vide il tesoro del Duce," la Repubblica–il Lavoro, September 1, 2000.

72 See S. Luzzatto, trans. F. Randall, The Body of Il Duce: Mussolini's Corpse and the Fortunes of Italy (New York: Metropolitan, 2006).

73 See M. Viganò, "Mussolini, i gerarchi e la 'fuga' in Svizzera," Nuova rivista di storia contemporanea, no. 3 (2001), 47–108.

74 NARA, Reg. 226, fondo, interrogation of Albertina Porciani (Turin: 2 December 1945).

75 See O. Meuwly, La politique vaudoise au 20e siècle. De l'État radical à l'émiettement du pouvoir (Lausanne: Presses polytechniques et universitaires romandes, 2003), 23–59.

76 See C. Cantini, "Benito Mussolini et l'Université de Lausanne" (1987), in C. Cantini, Pour une histoire sociale et antifasciste. Contributions d'un autodidacte (Lausanne: Editions d'en bas, 1999), 158–68; C. Cantini, Le fascisme italien à Lausanne: 1920–1943 (Lausanne: Cedips, 1976).

77 ATA, Corte straordinaria d'assise, 15/1946, Suprema Corte di Cassazione, Sentenza sul ricorso proposto da Cagni Edilio (Rome, 30 November 1948).

78 See ATA, fondo, Sezione speciale della Corte d'assise di Viterbo, transcript (Viterbo, 14 October 1949).

79 Ibid.

9. And Calls On Him to Explain

1 Notes from my telephone conversation with Corrado Calvo, January 21, 2011.

2 See M. Oppezzo, Ugo Oppezzo Idalia Tos: ricordo di babbo Marcello. Cavaglià, 10 October 1921, Biella, A. De Thomatis, undated (1921), and Don G. Samarotto and Don G. Ferrando, Cerrina: cronaca che si fa storia, vol. 1 (Casale Monferrato: Fondazione S. Evasio, 1993), 146–48.

3 See T. Vialardi di Santigliano, Il libro eroico della provincia di Biella (Biella: Istituto del Nastro Azzurro, 2004), 212.

4 See, in the parish archive of Cerrina, the "Liber Chronicus" of Don Giuseppe Samarotto, 29 April 1937 (I thank Chiara Cane for pointing me to this document).

5 See G. Pansa, Guerra partigiana tra Genova e il Po. La Resistenza in provincia di Alessandria (1967) (Rome-Bari: Laterza, 1998), 133–34.

6 See Chapter 7, "Role Play."

7   See AISRVdA, Fondi vari, letter from mayor of Cerrina to mayor of Saint-Vincent (Cerrina Monferrato, 12 October 1945).

8   C. Pavese, *The Moon and the Bonfires*, trans. R. W. Flint (New York: New York Review Books, 2002).

9   See Samarotto and Ferrando, *Cerrina*, 1:196.

10 C. Pavese, *Lettere, 1924–1944*, ed. L. Mondo (Turin: Einaudi, 1966), 740 (letter to Giuseppe Vaudagna, Serralunga di Crea, 18 December, 1944).

11 See L. Mangoni, *Pensare i libri. La casa editrice Einaudi dagli anni trenta agli anni sessanta* (Turin: Bollati Boringhieri, 1999), 229ff.

12 C. Pavese, *The House on the Hill*, trans. W. J. Strachan (London: Mayflower-Dell, 1965).

13 See R. Liucci, *La tentazione della "casa in collina." Il disimpegno degli intellettuali nella guerra civile italiana (1943–1945)* (Milan: Unicopli, 1999), 25ff.

14 Samarotto and Ferrando, *Cerrina*, 1:222.

15 Ibid., 356.

16 Samarotto and Ferrando, *Cerrina*, vol. 2 (1995), 114.

17 Ibid., 175.

18 Ibid., 251.

19 Ibid., 235.

20 AISTORETO, Pratiche caduti per la lotta di liberazione, busta 7.

21 On the figure of the "war godmother" (usually around the same age as the soldier himself) in Italy during World War II, see E. Cortesi, *Reti dentro la guerra. Corrispondenza postale e strategia di sopravvivenxa (1940–1945)* (Rome: Carocci, 2009).

22 See ASTo, Distretto militare di Turin: "Fogli caratteristici," Anagrafe classe 1926, vol. 148, "Zabaldano, Luciano."

23 See M. Calegari, *La sega di Hitler* (Milan: Edizioni Selene, 2004), 113ff.

24 AISTORETO, database of partisans in Piedmont.

25 See Chapter 2, "Part Partisan, Part Bandit."

26 See AISTORETO, database of partisans in Piedmont.

27 AFZT, funeral announcement, undated (mid-October 1945).

28 P. Levi, *Survival in Auschwitz*, trans. S. Woolf (New York: Summit, 1986), 172.

29 See Chapter 2, "Part Partisan, Part Bandit."

30 P. Levi, "Epitaph," is collected in *Primo Levi: Collected Poems*, trans. R. Feldman and B. Swann (London: Faber, 1988). Here translated by F. Randall.

31 See Mangoni, *Pensare i libri*, 684ff.

32 P. Levi, *The Periodic Table* (Turin: Einaudi, 1975), 175.

33 See P. Momigliano Levi, "Premessa," in D. G. Jon and M. Alliod, eds., *Silens loquor. Cippi, lapidi e monumenti a ricordo dei partigiani e dei civili morti nella Resistenza in Valle d'Aosta, 1943–1945* (Aosta: Le Château, 2007), 7.

34 See unsigned "Commemorati al Colle di Joux i Caduti partigiani" in *La Nuova Stampa*, September 8, 1950.

35 See Jon and Alliod, eds., *Silens loquor*, 136.

36 See T. Malpassuto, "Ricordo di don Gonella," in Dun Gunela [Don Gonella], *Puesìj* [*Poesie*], Comune di Villadeati, 2007, 16–17.

37 Sa. B., "Un pezzo di storia in tre cerimonie," in *La Stampa* (Valle d'Aosta edition), September 7, 1995.

38 See Jon and Alliod, *Silens loquor*, 138–40.

39 Quoted in A. Chiappano, *Luciana Nissim Momigliano: una vita* (Florence: Giuntina, 2010), 250.

40 Levi, *Survival in Auschwitz*, 16, 19.

41 See "Testimonianza di un compagno di prigionia," in *Donne piemontesi nella lotta di liberazione. 99 partigiane cadute, 185 deportate, 38 cadute civili* (Turin: Tipografia Impronta, 1953), 87–88. The convincing attribution to Levi was first proposed by G. Falaschi, "'L'offesa insanabile.' L'imprinting del lager su Primo Levi," in the review *allegoria* 13, no. 38 (May–August, 2001): 5–35.

42 "Testimonianza di un compagno," 87.

10. If Not Then, When?

1 P. Levi, "Scrivere un romanzos" in P. Levi, *L'altrui mestiere* (1985), collected in *Opere*, ed. M. Belpoliti (Turin: Einaudi, 1997), 2:775–76 (first published in *La Stampa*, September 19, 1982, with the title "Safari tra i fantasmi").

2 "Un modo di dire io" ("your way of saying 'I'") was Primo Levi's preferred title for his "personal anthology," later called *La ricerca delle radici*: see ASTo, Archive storico casa editrice Einaudi, "Corrispondenza. Autori," fasc. "Levi, Primo," busta 114, unsigned editorial note, undated (1981).

3 P. Levi, *If Not Now, When?*, trans. W. Weaver (New York: Penguin, 1995), 20.

4 Levi, "Scrivere un romanzo," 774.

5 Levi, *If Not Now, When?*, 124.

6 Ibid., 60.

7 Ibid., 38.

8 See D. Scarpa, *Chiaro/oscuro*, in M. Belpoliti, ed., *Primo Levi*, issue of *Riga*, no. 13 (1997): 244–53.

9 Levi, "Scrivere un romanzo," 777.

10 Levi, *If Not Now, When?*, 66.

11 Ibid., 99, 119.

12 On Levi's interest in the "Soviet method" of punishing unreliable partisans, see I. Thomson, *Primo Levi* (2002) (London: Vintage, 2003), 413–14.

13 See P. Levi, *The Drowned and the Saved*, trans. Raymond Rosenthal (New York: Summit, 1988), 81. The translation there reads "Is this belated shame justified or not?" but Levi's words are closer to "Is guilt felt in retrospect justified?"

14 Ibid., 82.

15 Levi, *If Not Now, When?*, 65–66.

16 P. Levi, "The Survivor" (dated February 4, 1984, by the author) in *Primo Levi: Collected Poems*, trans. R. Feldman and B. Swann (London: Faber, 1988). An interpretation of this poem can be found in E. Mattioda, *Levi* (Rome: Salerno, 2011), 180–81.

17 Levi, *If Not Now, When?*, 128.

18 Ibid., 130–31.

19 Ibid., 133.

Acknowledgments

Any piece of historical research, individual and solitary as it may be, is always a group project. And thus I would like to thank all those who assisted in making this book come to life, none of whom are of course in any way responsible for whatever may be arguable in the final product.

In Aosta, Silvana Presa guided me on my first steps into the Resistance in Valle d'Aosta. In Turin, I benefited from the help of the Istituto storico della Resistenza and of the Centro internazionale di studi Primo Levi. In Casale Monferrato, Sergio Favretto and Fabrizio Meni were both speedy and thoughtful in helping me find my way. At the Centro di documentazione ebraica contemporanea in Milan, Liliana Picciotto and her team were unusually solicitous. In London, Ian Thomson guided me in finding sources at the Weiner Library. Special thanks are due to Roberta Cairoli, whose scholarly generosity allowed me to consult papers from the National Archives in Washington. This book also owes much to the actors in this story and their descendants, who opened the doors of their homes, consulted their memories, and shared personal and family documents with me. My thanks to Yves Francisco, Simonetta

Bachi, and Aldo Piacenza; to Corrado Calvi and Chiara Cane, who also made it possible for me to meet Angelo Brignoglio, Maria Cerruti, Teresa Mazzucco, and Renato Porta; and to Andrea and Davide Zabaldano, who after our first meeting agreed to accompany me a ways down the road.

Three colleagues—three friends—read the first draft of this book and discussed it with me at length. They disagreed with certain passages, critiqued the text in detail and as a whole, and offered counsel on both form and substance. My thanks to Walter Barberis, Enrica Bricchetto, and Domenico Scarpa, who were tremendously helpful in making this book better.

Rosaria Carpinelli has been more than a literary agent. In the beginning, she helped me find a tone that I hope my readers will feel is the right one; later, she helped me find the right publisher. At Mondadori, Francesco Anzelmo was quick to recognize the book's defects as well as its merits, and if in the end it is found worthy, much of the credit goes to him.

Finally, as was the case with my two previous books, *The Body of Il Duce* and *Padre Pio*, the American edition of this book has profited from exceptional assistance on the Metropolitan side. Frederika Randall's translation is infused not only with the historical knowledge she has gained as an adopted Italian but with all her literary sensibility. Grigory Tovbis rightly insisted, above all, on what the Anglophone reader needed to know in order to understand the story. And Sara Bershtel once more had faith in me and in what I believe is important to pass on from Italy's twentieth-century history. My heartfelt thanks to all three.

Index

About the Author

SERGIO LUZZATTO is the author of *Padre Pio: Miracles and Politics in a Secular Age,* which won the prestigious Cundill Prize in History, and of *The Body of Il Duce: Mussolini's Corpse and the Fortunes of Italy.* A professor of history at the University of Turin, Luzzatto is a regular contributor to *Il Sole 24 Ore.*